Making a Machine That Sees Like Us

Making a Machine That Sees Like Us

Zygmunt Pizlo, Yunfeng Li,
Tadamasa Sawada,
and
Robert M. Steinman

OXFORD
UNIVERSITY PRESS

OXFORD
UNIVERSITY PRESS

Oxford University Press is a department of the University of Oxford.
It furthers the University's objective of excellence in research, scholarship,
and education by publishing worldwide.

Oxford New York
Auckland Cape Town Dar es Salaam Hong Kong Karachi
Kuala Lumpur Madrid Melbourne Mexico City Nairobi
New Delhi Shanghai Taipei Toronto

With offices in
Argentina Austria Brazil Chile Czech Republic France Greece
Guatemala Hungary Italy Japan Poland Portugal Singapore
South Korea Switzerland Thailand Turkey Ukraine Vietnam

Published in the United States of America by
Oxford University Press
198 Madison Avenue, New York, NY 10016

A copy of this book's Catalog-in-Publication Data is on file with the Library of Congress
ISBN 978-0-19-992254-3

9 8 7 6 5 4 3 2
Printed in the United States of America
on acid-free paper

We dedicate this book to the memory of Azriel Rosenfeld (1931–2004), who contributed greatly to making this book possible. Azriel was one of the most influential researchers in the area of image analysis and computer vision during the second half of the 20th Century. Many consider him to be the "father of computer vision." He was one of the very few computer vision researchers who took the science of human, as well as of machine, vision very seriously. He did not perform psychophysical experiments himself, but he never pursued the development of a new vision algorithm unless he felt that the algorithm had some relevance for biological vision. The book's first author benefited enormously during the years he interacted with Prof. Rosenfeld at the Center for Automation Research at the University of Maryland in College Park. This book's fourth author also benefited from his interactions with Azriel while they both worked at the University of Maryland. We both believe that Azriel would have approved of our approach, and that he would have liked some, maybe even many, of the ideas put forth. We also would like to think that he would have enjoyed the way we told this story.

CONTENTS

Acknowledgments xi

1. How the stage was set when we began 1

1.1 Introduction 1
1.2 What is this book about? 2
1.3 Analytical and operational definitions of shape 6
1.4 Shape constancy as a phenomenon (something you can observe) 15
1.5 Complexity makes shape unique 23
1.6 How would the world look if we are wrong? 28
1.7 What had happened in the real world while we were away 36
1.8 Perception viewed as an inverse problem 39
1.9 How Bayesian inference can be used for modeling perception 43
1.10 What it means to have a model of vision, and why we need to have one? 46
1.11 End of the beginning 49

2. How this all got started 52

2.1 Controversy about shape constancy: 1980–1995 52
2.2 29th European Conference on Visual Perception (ECVP), St. Petersburg, Russia, August 20–25, 2006, where we first proposed our paradigm shift 60
2.3 The role of constraints in recovering the 3D shapes of polyhedral objects from line-drawings 62
2.4 31st European Conference on Visual Perception (ECVP) Utrecht, NL, August 24–28, 2008, where we had our first public confrontation 71
2.5 Monocular 3D shape recovery of both synthetic and real objects 73

3. Symmetry in vision, inside and outside of the laboratory 83

3.1 Why and how approximate computations make visual analyses fast and perfect: The perception of slanted 2D mirror-symmetrical figures 85
3.2 How human beings perceive 2D mirror-symmetry from perspective images 96
3.3 Why 3D mirror-symmetry is more difficult than 2D symmetry 98

3.4 Updating the ideal observer: How human beings perceive 3D mirror-symmetry from perspective images 99
3.5 Important role of generalized cones in 3D shape perception: How human beings perceive 3D translational-symmetry from perspective images 105
3.6 Michael Layton's contribution to symmetry in shape perception 114
3.7 Leeuwenberg's attempt to develop a "structural" explanation of Gestalt phenomena 116

4. Using symmetry is not simple 120

4.1 What is really going on? Examining the relationship between simplicity and likelihood 124
4.2 Clearly, simplicity is better than likelihood—excluding degenerate views does not eliminate spurious 3D symmetrical interpretations 129
4.3 What goes with what? A new kind of correspondence problem 130
4.4 Everything becomes easier once symmetry is viewed as self-similarity: The first working solution of the symmetry correspondence problem 136

5. A second view makes 3D shape perception perfect 144

5.1 What we know about binocular vision and how we came to know it 145
5.2 How we worked out the binocular perception of symmetrical 3D shapes 158
5.3 How our new theory of shape perception, based on stereoacuity, accounts for old results 160
5.4 3D movies: what they are, what they want to be, and what it costs 162
5.5 Bayesian model of binocular shape perception 163
5.6 Why we could claim that our model is complete? 169

6. Figure-ground organization, which breaks camouflage in everyday life, permits the veridical recovery of a 3D scene 172

6.1 Estimating the orientation of the ground-plane 175
6.2 How a coarse analysis of the positions and sizes of objects can be made 179
6.3 How a useful top view representation was produced 182
6.4 Finding objects in the 2D image 190
6.5 Extracting relevant edges, grouping them, and establishing symmetry correspondence 192
6.6 What can be done with a spatially-global map of a 3D scene? 198

7. What made this possible and what comes next? 204

7.1 Five important conceptual contributions 205
7.2 Three of our technical contributions 209
7.3 Making our machine perceive and predict in dynamical environments 213
7.4 Solving the figure-ground organization problem with only a single 2D image 216
7.5 Recognizing individual objects by using a fast search of memory 218

Note Added in Proofs: Symmetry, The Least-Action Principle, and Conservation Laws in Psychology 221

References 229

Index 237

ACKNOWLEDGMENTS

We are very grateful to Joan Bossert and Miles Osgood for editorial assistance and for their strong encouragement from our proposal to the completion of this book. We thank Travis Scott Rother, who helped us with several of our demos. Finally, we acknowledge the support of our research provided by the National Science Foundation, the Air Force Office of Scientific Research, the U.S. Department of Defense, and the U.S. Department of Energy.

1

How the Stage Was Set When We Began

1.1 Introduction

Why did we write this book now? We wrote it now because it tells an unusual story. It is unusual because actually *Making a Machine That Sees Like Us* does not happen every day. The computer vision community tried to do this for more than 60 years without success. Modern interest in making a machine that sees as we do began more than 70 years ago, shortly after the first electronic digital computer was built in 1941, but trying to make machines that can emulate other human capacities has a much longer history. All of these early attempts concentrated on emulating motor skills and human thinking. They did not try to emulate human visual perception as we did. Attempts to make such machines go back almost to the beginning of recorded history. A written account of Chinese *automata* appears 2300 years ago and this account includes a claim of a still earlier success almost a thousand years earlier. Machines resembling human beings appeared in the early Mediterranean cultures and spread into Western Europe as societies developed there. Leonardo da Vinci made his mark here around 1495 by including, in one of his notebooks, a design for a mechanical knight in armor, based on his anatomical studies. The goal of making machines that act like us heated up after René Descartes (1596–1650) launched modern European science near the end of the 17th Century. There were major developments in mechanics at this time and the beginnings of what is now called *biomedical engineering*. Julien Offray de la Mettrie (1709–1751) was a prominent proponent of this endeavor. He insisted that human beings were actually quite ordinary machines and that their performance could be emulated without the intervention of Descartes's *vital spirit* (a special life force). When the Industrial Age began at the beginning of the 19th Century, automata came into widespread use in what came to be called *industry*. By the middle of the 19th Century Charles Babbage had designed an analytical engine, operated by punch cards, that performed arbitrary mathematical computations, and George Boole had invented a new type of symbolic logic that was essential for the development of robots and computers. The major landmark on the road to making the kind of machine described in this book possible was Alan Turing's (1912–1954) development of a theory of computers. This development provided the basis for contemporary computer science, the science that made developing a machine that sees like us practically, as well as theoretically, possible. Our machine can locate objects, distinguish them by their shapes, and recognize open pathways among them. These pathways can be used to navigate effectively within the kind of natural environments that we humans live and work. In its present state of development, our machine *sees* our world much as we do. This book was also written to (1) show how a complete computational model can be made and explain, in the simplest possible terms, how such a model works; (2) provide an example of a successful application of Inverse Problem Theory in human and machine vision; and (3) help those advocating the use of computational modeling who have had a hard time finding successful examples before this book was published.

1.2 What Is This Book About?

It starts with the first public explanation of the need for, and the possibility of, actually developing this kind of model. This claim was first made at the 2006 European Conference on Visual Perception that was held in St. Petersburg, Russia. It was made only 4 months after the manuscript for the first book ever devoted entirely to the nature of *3D Shape* went to press (Pizlo, 2008). The next to last paragraph in this book raised this possibility. It went like this:

> .... attempts to understand shape outside of the context provided by psychophysical results on shape constancy, led investigators astray. Keeping this in mind as our research proceeds should, in time, allow us to understand how: (i) the human visual system achieves shape constancy with real objects in natural scenes and (ii) to make a machine visual system that works as well as ours (p. 184).

This book's story ends when the first working, computational model, which could see like us, was demonstrated at the Vision Sciences Society Meeting on May 9, 2011, in Naples, FL, USA.

The model works in the sense that it emulates the way we humans see in our natural environments. The book describes the mistakes and the successful moves made as we progressed rather rapidly toward the goal of making this machine. It took only 5 years to get to where we are today. The mistakes were included because they illustrate the kinds of decisions that must be made when modeling in both naturalistic and synthetic environments with a wide variety of stimuli.

This book is intended for a relatively diverse audience with only modest formal training in both math and science. Its story is told without technical details that would impede the story's flow. All of the technical material included in this book has been published in specialized journals so any reader who wants to know more about what we did should consult the source papers listed in the Reference list. This book *must* contain a lot of technical material because explaining why and how the machine works as it does, like explaining human vision, is much more complicated than explaining why and how a ball accelerates as it rolls down an inclined plane or when it falls from a leaning tower, but every effort will be made to explain all of the critical computations simply. Demos showing progress and new problems encountered at each stage of the model's development will be provided throughout the book. They should be run whenever attention is called to them in the text. They are designed to make even relatively subtle technical material available to most, hopefully even all, interested readers. Whenever possible, each chapter will begin with one or more demos illustrating where we are and where we want to go.

Some of the novel ideas described in this book, like those presented in the first book on the nature of 3-dimensional (3D) shape, will be controversial, but now that we have a machine that actually sees almost as well as we do, these controversies can and should be dealt with thoroughly, rather than tactfully, as they were handled previously. This should be done because understanding them sheds light on important differences in underlying assumptions and on important theoretical differences. Put simply, the pros and cons of our and other approaches to the study of shape will be explained in detail. We will be able to do this with an appreciable advantage now because having a working computational model forces skeptics to choose between the evidence given by their own eyes when they view demos showing what our model can do and their own results, theories, and models, none of which can come even close to producing a machine that can "see" like ours. If one was asked to point to a single aspect of our approach that was critical for accomplishing so much so fast, it would be the recognition of the fact that the successful functioning of the human visual system depends on a number of abstract, but very effective *a priori* constraints (operations built-in to the visual system and elaborated throughout its evolution). It is surprising, but true nonetheless, that these *a priori constraints are often more important than adding additional visual information.* Using *a priori* constraints permits the veridical perception of 3D objects and 3D scenes. Saying that human perception is veridical simply means that human beings see the 3D shapes and scenes in the physical world as they really are "out there." It seems unlikely that veridical perceptions can be produced in any other way. Technically, *veridical visual perception is a very difficult computational problem, so difficult that there is probably only one way that veridicality can be achieved.* So, when a machine's perception is as veridical as ours, it is likely that the machine is operating according to the same principles that our visual system uses. Appreciating this allows us to answer an important question that Hochberg (1987) asked, namely, should machines see the same way that people do? Our answer is that they almost certainly must if they are going to be able to see veridically as we do. You can visualize what we mean when we say that our machine sees 3D objects and scenes as we do by showing you how our machine sees a relatively natural, but cluttered, 3D scene we set up for this purpose in our laboratory. Look at Figure 1.1.

Using a number of *a priori* constraints allowed the machine's perception of the 3D objects in the 3D scene to be just like ours. Both our and the machine's perceptions were veridical; they really reflected what was present in the room. The machine's view of the scene showed all of the objects in the room as separate objects, despite that fact that their 2-dimensional (2D) images partially overlapped. It also showed where each object was located within the scene. Not everyone, who has studied or is studying the perception of 3D shapes and scenes, accepts our claim that the human beings' perception of 3D objects and 3D scenes is veridical. This claim appears controversial to many, but it should not. If there are actually two objects in front of you, you always perceive two, not one or three or more. The number of objects in natural scenes is *never* illusory, providing none is inside another or hidden from view by a larger object in front of it. Furthermore, there are *never* illusions of the shapes of objects in our natural environments. If you look at a TV set, you see a TV set, not a fox or a box or a bird. Illusions of the shape, the number of objects, and their arrangements within natural scenes are very rare; actually, they are probably *never* encountered in everyday life. Common sense tells us that our vision *is* veridical. It works so well that anyone trying to teach visual perception has a very difficult time convincing the students that there is any problem to be solved when it comes to explaining how we see the world, as accurately as we do, with the visual equipment we have. Common sense is actually a very useful concept in visual science, despite the fact that it can make it hard to teach, because many of the things we say are intuitively obvious are said to be obvious precisely because we can visualize them. We will capitalize on this important commonsensical observation throughout this book. This will be done by explaining almost *all* operations of our machine in two ways: for readers with mathematical background, our *technical* readers, we will provide the gist of the mathematical and computational aspects in the text and refer them to published papers listed in our Reference list for details, and, for those without such background, our *intuitive* readers, we will provide demos and interactive animations throughout the text that illustrate what each computation means and how it is done.

Now that you know what this book is about, and how the material it contains will be explained, we will describe a number of controversies that confront anyone who sets out to do what we did. We begin by considering what we, and others, mean when we talk about an object's shape and how the meaning of the word *shape* has been used since Plato called attention to the importance of this abstract property.

FIGURE 1.1. A natural scene perceived by our machine. Top: furniture arranged haphazardly in our laboratory. Middle: outlines of each piece of furniture (their convex hulls) drawn by the machine. Bottom: machine's top view of the relative sizes and positions and pathways among the 3D convex hulls. Gray rectangles represent the actual positions and sizes. Black rectangles represent the positions and sizes as estimated by our machine.

1.3 Analytical and Operational Definitions of Shape

Shape is one of those concepts that seem intuitively obvious, but proves to be surprisingly difficult to define when called upon to do so. In this section, we will describe what seemed to be an almost insoluble definitional problem when we started working on it and then explain how we developed two satisfying, as well as effective, complementary solutions. This will be done first by presenting a new and novel analytical definition of shape. This will be followed by an explanation of how this analytical definition provides a mathematical justification for the operational definition of shape that had guided our research on shape up to now. We start by describing the conventional analytical definition of shape. This definition is derived from concepts widely used in mathematics and physics. Our analytical definition of shape will be different. It is unlike all prior analytical definitions of shape in which shape is defined by using the *similarity of one object to another object*. Our new definition uses the *similarity of the object to itself*. This is done by using the object's symmetries (its self-similarities).

It has been widely assumed that all objects and *all* patterns exhibit the property called *shape*. This assumption raises some questions. Can we talk about the shape of the spatial arrangement of points in space? According to conventional definitions we can. Specifically, most shape theorists agree that the property we have in mind when we refer to some visual arrangement as shape refers to something that is *invariant under transformations*. What do we mean when we use such technical language? Consider first, an example of what is probably the most appropriate transformation we can use when we try to define shape analytically. This transformation is produced by the rigid motion of an object within a 3D space. Pulling a chair away from a table would be a good and familiar example. The position of the chair within the room has changed (this is what we mean by the transformation), but the chair, itself, did not. We call this kind of transformation a *rigid motion* because all of the geometrical properties of the chair (what the conventional definitions call the chair's shape) stayed the same. These properties were invariant. The size of the chair stayed the same, as well as all the distances and angles between the individual parts that made it up. The legs were not broken or bent, and the individual parts were not stretched by this kind of transformation. It follows that if there are two identical chairs in the room, we would say that they have the same shape.

Note that this conventional definition of shape often goes a little further than simply a rigid transformation when it includes a 3D reflection of the object and the change of its overall size in what will be permitted and still allow us to say that two objects have the same shape. Technically, in these cases, the transformation that results is called a similarity transformation (Figure 1.2). According to the conventional analytical definition of shape, all

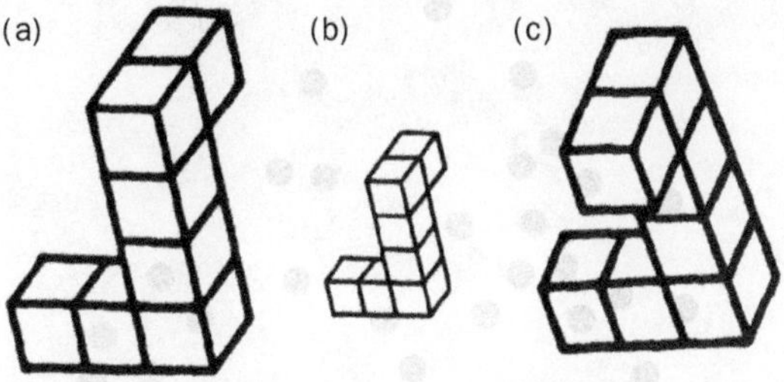

FIGURE 1.2. The object in (b) is identical to the object in (a) except for its overall size. The object in (c) was produced by computing a 3D reflection of (a). According to the conventional analytical definition of shape all three objects have the same shape (From Shepard, R.N. & Cooper, L.A. (1982) Mental images and their transformations. Cambridge, MA: MIT Press. With permission of The MIT Press.)

three objects seen in Figure 1.2 have the same shape. Repeating this claim in technical parlance will not add much to this explanation for most readers, but it will be done here for those who will feel cheated if we leave it out: namely, all angles remain the same in a similarity transformation, so an angle formed by two line-segments is an *invariant* of this transformation. If all corresponding angles in two objects are equal, one object can be produced by transforming the other using a similarity transformation. These two objects are said to have the same shape because such a transformation is possible.

This is by far the most commonly used analytical definition of shape.[1] Recall that this definition was derived from concepts routinely used in physics and mathematics. It implies that *all* objects have shape, providing only that they have at least three points. Three points allow at least one angle to be specified and measured. Intuitively, even commonsensically, something seems to be missing from this strong claim. One does not have to think deeply to figure out what is wrong. A big problem emerges as soon as you realize that we know that there are patterns and objects that actually have no shape at all. Not even the hint of one. Asking someone about the shape of the pattern of randomly generated points, like the one shown in Figure 1.3, simply makes no sense. Common sense tells us that there is no shape in Figure 1.3. We also know that shapeless common objects exist in everyday life. A crumpled piece of paper, a bent paperclip, or a rock before it is shaped by a human hand do not have what we really mean when we refer to an object's shape. All these objects, as well as random patterns like the one in Figure 1.3, are called *amorphous* or *shapeless*.

---

[1]See Pizlo (2008) and Li et al. (2013) for other, less common definitions that use other types of transformations. Among them, geodesics are particularly interesting because they can handle the articulation of parts and non-rigid objects. But, geodesic lines do not convey any volumetric information. This information is essential for characterizing 3D shapes, so there is really a problem if you base your definition of shape on geodesics because all origami objects have the same shape, namely, a flat piece of paper.

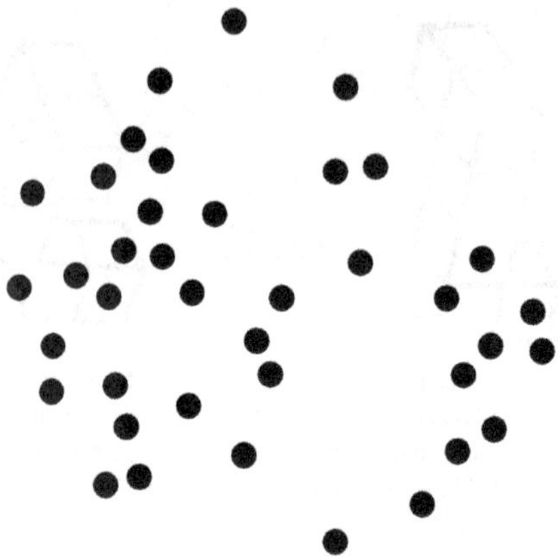

FIGURE 1.3. An irregular set of scattered points. (From Li, Y., Sawada, T., Shi, Y., Steinman, R.M. & Pizlo, Z. (2013) Symmetry is the *sine qua non* of shape. In: S. Dickinson & Z. Pizlo (Eds.), Shape perception in human and computer vision, Springer (2013). With kind permission of Springer Science+Business Media.)

Why? They are amorphous because they are completely irregular. Some regularity is missing.

This observation makes it clear that the term shape makes reference to some spatial regularity, or some self-similarity possessed by an object. We have all had lots of experience dealing with such regularities in our everyday life. Biological shapes permeate and regulate our lives. The bodies of most animals are mirror-symmetrical. By mirror-symmetrical we mean that one half mirrors the other half. Technically, one symmetrical half is the mirror image (the reflection) of the other with respect to the animal's plane of symmetry. But there is more to symmetry than mirror-symmetry and reflection. Limbs of animals, trunks of trees, and stems of flowers are characterized by what we call *translational symmetry*. Technically, translational symmetry can be illustrated by taking a planar shape and sweeping it through a 3D space using rigid motion along an axis and overall size scaling (see Figure 1.4). Figure 1.5 shows examples of several very different shapes that were produced with translational symmetry. Such shapes were called *generalized cones* by Binford (1971).

In Figure 1.5, all cross-sections of each of the 8 objects are *similar* to each other. The technical meaning of *similar* here is that the members of any pair of cross-sections in a single object are related to each other by a similarity transformation. If, in addition to translation and size scaling, we use rotation around the translation axis, we will obtain what is called spiral symmetry, the kind of symmetry characteristic of the shells of snails (Figure 1.6). We can use rigid motion, reflection, and size-scaling of the parts within the object itself to define the shape of the object as its spatial self-similarity instead of using rigid motion, reflection, and size-scaling of an entire object in 3D space to define the shape of this object (as we did with the similarity group of transformations,

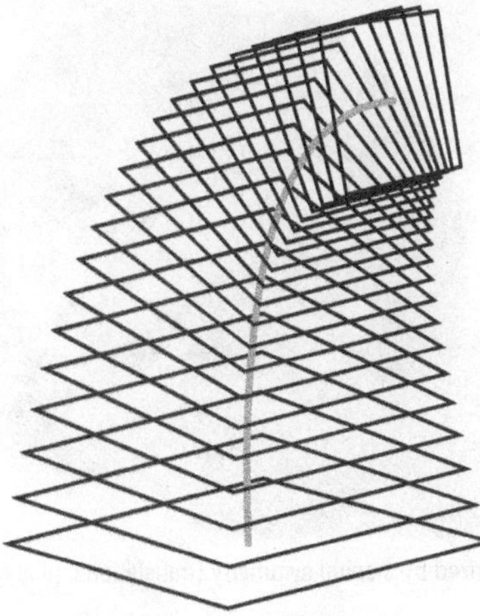

FIGURE 1.4. This shows how a square swept along a parabolic axis produced a generalized cone.

just above). ***Shape is an intrinsic characteristic of an object because it refers to its self-similarity, rather than to the similarity of one object to another.***

Self-similarity of biological forms seems to be an inherent characteristic. It is the result of the natural process called *growth* (D'Arcy Thompson, 1942). Growth explains why all flowers and plants are characterized by one or more types of symmetry. They have the shape they have because of *how they grow*. Most animal bodies are mirror-symmetrical because of the *way they move*. A dog without a mirror-symmetrical body could not run straight along a straight path. *All biological forms have shape because all of them are symmetrical.* Some biological forms, such as trees, are usually only approximately symmetrical, but they never are completely devoid of all symmetry. The branches of each tree are generalized cones that exhibit a high degree of translational symmetry. Inanimate objects, such as rocks and crumpled papers, that have no trace of symmetry are obviously shapeless. Mountains,

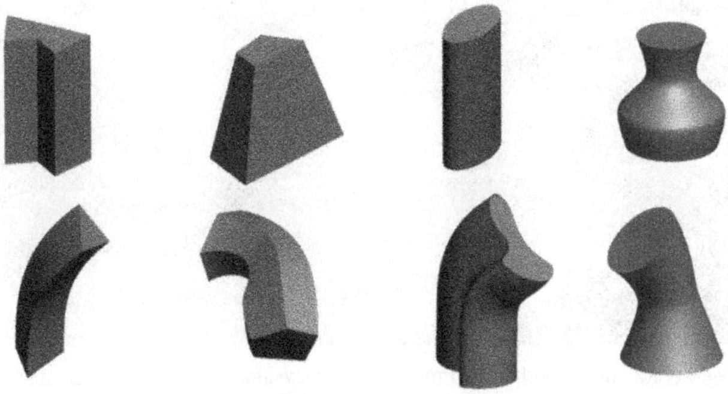

FIGURE 1.5. Eight differently shaped meaningless objects characterized by translational symmetry. (From Pizlo, Z. (2008) 3D shape: its unique place in visual perception. MIT Press. With permission of The MIT Press.)

FIGURE 1.6. Shells are characterized by a spiral symmetry (translational plus rotational symmetry).

on the other hand, always have some degree of regularity resulting from natural forming processes related to tectonic forces. These forces include volcanoes. The formed mountain is then subject to erosion caused by water, wind, and glacial processes. Both of these processes, formation and erosion, operate under the influence of gravity, which provides the mountain with some of the abstract property most people call shape. Figure 1.7 shows a view of K2, the second highest mountain in the world. This 2D view of K2 looks triangular.

FIGURE 1.7. A view of K2, the second highest mountain in the world. This 2D view of K2 looks triangular and it has considerable mirror-symmetry, but this symmetry is not perfect. K2 as well as most other mountains will have shape measures considerably less than one.

It has considerable mirror-symmetry, but this symmetry is obviously not perfect. The same is true of other 2D views of this mountain, as well as of its actual 3D shape. The fact that the regularities of this, and other mountains, are never nearly perfect implies that mountains will tend to have shape measures considerably less than one. It is also important to note that many important inanimate objects actually do have shape. All objects that serve some useful function, such objects as furniture and tools, have one or more types of symmetry, without which they would probably be dysfunctional.

There are three intriguing, and perhaps even surprising, implications of the powerful role played by symmetry (self-similarity) in our new analytical definition of shape. First, when shape is defined by self-similarity, rather than by the similarity of one object to another, it becomes much easier to talk about the shapes of *non-rigid* and *piece-wise rigid* objects. If an object is non-rigid, like the stem of a flower, bending the stem does not remove its translational symmetry. All of the flower's cross-sections are still circular. Bending only changes the curvature of the axis of the flower's stem. If an object is piece-wise rigid, like the body of a dog, changing the articulations of its legs distorts the mirror-symmetry of the dog's body, but it does *not* eliminate the symmetry altogether. After all, the dog still has two legs on the right side of his body and two legs on the left side. This obviously applies as well to your body as to your dog's body. Our new analytical definition of shape removes all of the fundamental difficulty inherent in all other conventional definitions of shape. None of them can deal with the non-rigidity of objects, objects that are common throughout our natural environment. Three types of non-rigid symmetrical shapes are shown in Figure 1.8. The animations of these three non-rigid transformations showing how natural objects like these, in real environments, would appear in action can be seen as DEMO 1.1.[2]

Second, we know from our work on the recovery of the shape of a 3D object from only one of its 2D images (described later) that 3D symmetrical objects can be recovered veridically from a single 2D perspective image. The shape recovered is said to be *veridical* because it is the same as the object's shape out there. But 3D objects devoid of symmetries cannot be recovered from a single 2D perspective image, which means that amorphous objects cannot provide us with useful information about conditions in our visual world. Symmetry, which is ubiquitous in our visual environment, plays a critical role in the veridical recovery of 3D shapes, so it is symmetry that provides the basis for the perceptual achievement called *shape constancy*.

[2] All demos are at the following address: http://shapebook.psych.purdue.edu. In the electronic version of this book, the address has a link to the demos, so simply clicking your mouse on the address will take you there. If you are reading a hard copy version, type the address in your browser and then choose individual demos which are identified by numbers. To go directly to Demo 1.1 click here: http://shapebook.psych.purdue.edu/1.1

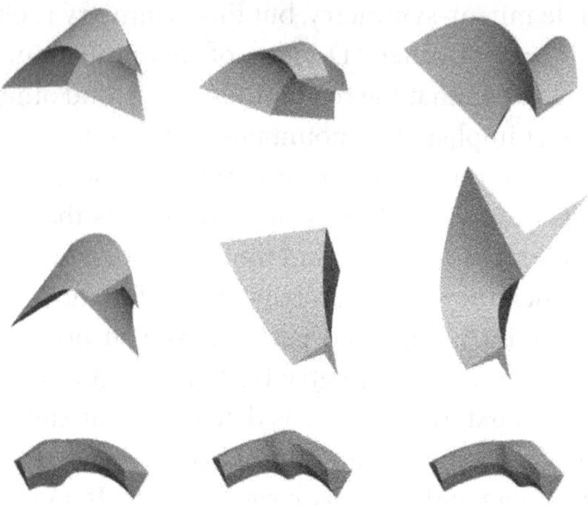

FIGURE 1.8. Three snapshots from a range of articulations of non-rigid objects: Top—the shape of the cross-section is changing, but the axis is not (this looks like a flying bird). Middle—the axis of a GC is changing, but the shape of the cross-section is the same (this looks like a gymnast on horizontal bars at the Olympic Games). Bottom—the local size of the cross-section is changing, but the shape of the cross-section and the axis of the GC is constant (this looks like a snake digesting a large belly bulging prey). (From Li, Y., Sawada, T., Shi, Y., Steinman, R.M. & Pizlo, Z. (2013) Symmetry is the *sine qua non* of shape. In: S. Dickinson & Z. Pizlo (Eds.), Shape perception in human and computer vision, Springer (2013). With kind permission of Springer Science+Business Media.)

Finally, once the object's shape is defined by its symmetries, it should be easy to compare (recognize) the 3D shape presented to the observer to the shapes in the observer's memory of previously seen 3D shapes. This can be done by using the object's symmetries as the address in one's memory that can be used to recognize the specific shape. Until now, the recognition of shapes has required checking *all* familiar shapes. Recognition required performing an exhaustive search through all possible shapes, a very time-consuming as well as laborious task. Our suggestion of limiting the search required to recognize a specific 3D shape to a specific symmetry address that is a property of the 3D physical object is analogous to how Biederman (1987) envisioned his *geons* mediating fast shape recognition (see Figure 1.9). According to Biederman, once the observer identifies the geons possessed by a 3D object, the geons themselves, elements that resemble an alphabet for 3D shapes, will tell the observer important things about the type of object that must be recognized. For example, is this shape an elephant or a watering can? Both are common objects with quite different geons. A search restricted to quadrupeds will be much faster than an exhaustive search of all 3D shapes. Biederman's geon approach never worked with real images of real objects because the set of geons he used is too small and his geons are too simple. Note that the set of symmetries being proposed here is smaller than Biederman's set of geons, but our relatively small set of symmetries allows a *unique* description of each of the infinitely many possible 3D shapes. This can be done simply by specifying which symmetries are to be used and providing the values of their parameters (this will be explained more fully later).

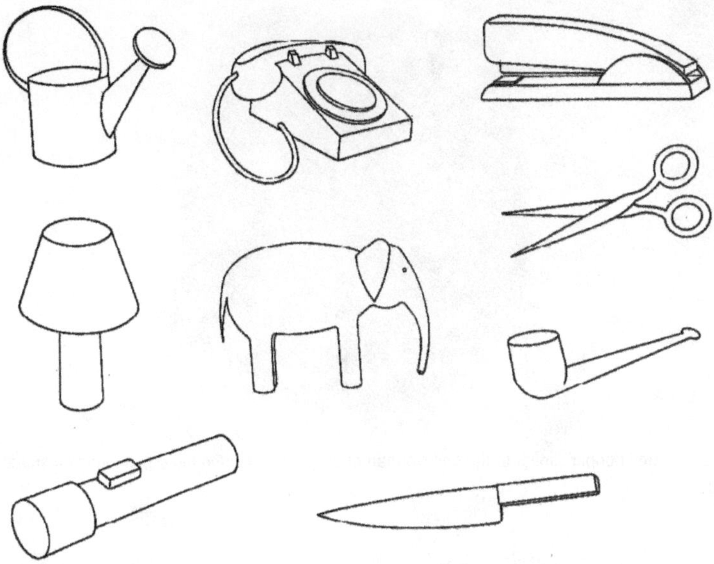

FIGURE 1.9. Objects composed of Biederman's geons. (From Biederman, I. (1987) Recognition-by-components: a theory of human image understanding. Psychological Review, 94, 115–147.)

Before our analyses, the conventional analytical definition of shape, rooted in physics and mathematics, was unsuccessful in all attempts to define the abstract property Plato called *shape*. Realizing this led us to develop the analytical basis for distinguishing an amorphous object from an object that actually has a shape. Removing crumpled papers, bent paper clips, and potatoes from the family of natural objects that can be said to have shape does not restrict our analytical definition very much. Despite restricting shape to objects with demonstrable symmetries, we are still able to apply our new definition to most, probably even all, living organisms and to inanimate objects that serve useful functions. Amorphous objects are neither common, nor particularly important in everyday life, nor do they play an important role in human affairs. Amorphous objects have been taken more seriously and used too often as stimuli in the vision laboratory than they should have been. Furthermore, whatever we took away from irregular rigid objects by applying our slightly restricting analytical definition was replaced by our ability to generalize our definition to the family of non-rigid objects. Finally, our new analytical definition of shape explains how, from a mathematical perspective, shape constancy can be achieved. Until now we have only been able to use shape constancy as our operational definition of shape. This operational definition allowed us to know which experiments were actually able to tell us something about shape and which could not. We made a lot of practical progress by using shape constancy as our operational definition of shape and we will continue to do so, but, as of now, this useful practical tool has acquired a solid mathematical and computational foundation.

FIGURE 1.10. Bell pepper similar to the one Norman et al. (2012) used in his experiments on shape constancy.

At this point both of our formal definitions of shape can be stated ***technically*** as follows: **Our *operational* definition of shape states that *there are no stimulus properties that can be attributed to shape beyond those that can be demonstrated in a shape constancy experiment.*** Said succinctly, shape constancy is the *sine qua non* of shape (*without which, there is no shape*).

Our *analytical* definition of shape states that *the shape of an object refers to all of its spatially global symmetries (its self-similarities) as measured by the group of rigid motions, reflections, and size-scaling of the parts within the object itself.* This definition can be elaborated quantitatively—a 3D object has as much shape as there are symmetries within it. Once this is accepted, shape can be measured on a scale from zero to one. Objects whose shape can be completely characterized by one or more symmetries have a *shape measure equal to one*. Human and animal bodies, including human faces, will have shape measures very close to 1, not exactly 1, because there are always some small, random perturbations of the symmetry of real objects. Other natural objects like the bell peppers, used by Norman et al. (2012) in his shape constancy experiments, will probably have shape measure close to 0.5 because natural peppers are quite irregular (see Figure 1.10). The pepper looks like a generalized cone with a straight axis (analogous to the cones in the top row of Figure 1.5), but the cross-sections of a real pepper like this one do not have the same shape.

Objects with very little or no trace of symmetry, when this quantitative definition is used, can be said to have shape but their measure of shape will be zero or close to zero. So, if we use this quantitative elaboration, what we have called an amorphous object until now, such objects as a random set of dots or a crumpled paper, can be described as having some, albeit negligible, shape. When and why should this be done? As far as we can see, it should be done whenever one wishes to discuss 3D shape with researchers who have been studying what they thought was shape with amorphous objects. We have found that if we simply tell the truth and call an amorphous object *amorphous*, our message falls on unreceptive minds. There is an additional advantage in using our analytical definition, namely, once we know that symmetries can be systematically degraded by adding random noise to an object, it is desirable to be able measure this kind of degradation. Our definition makes this possible. For example, you buy a box of breakfast cereal, open it, and use it for a week. By the end of the week, the box, which arrived pristine with all its corners square, is a distorted remnant of itself. But, it is still a rectangular box, albeit only a shadow of its former self. There is place for such transformations of shape in the real world and the branch of Applied Mathematics called *Information Theory*, and its rubric called *Minimum Description Length*, seems to be ideally suited for this purpose. By doing this we will be able to provide a valuable basis for making meaningful psychophysical measurements of 3D shape perception because the shape measure we are proposing provides a physical scale that can be compared to human performance in the natural world where the shapes of objects are often far from perfect. Note that when the shape measure is substantially lower than one, we should expect shape constancy to be far from perfect. This is precisely just what Norman (2012) reported with his bell peppers. Note that when shape constancy is not perfect, the observer cannot recognize objects on the basis of their shape. In such cases, abstract labels, colors, sizes, weights, surface texture, and stiffness will be needed to recognize particular objects.

Finally, the emphasis placed on symmetry in our analytical definition of shape should remind the reader of the concept called *Platonic solids* (Figure 1.11). This family of basic 3D shapes has stimulated the imagination of both mathematicians and artists interested in shape and symmetry for thousands of years.

1.4 Shape Constancy as a Phenomenon (Something You Can Observe)

We start with an example drawn from your daily life: imagine you are walking around in your apartment or in your house. When you do this, you will see all of your furniture and the objects on and around it from different viewing directions. But, you never see the shapes of any of these objects change as you move about. They always look the same. Naively, this does not seem to present a problem because we all know that all of the 3D objects in our physical world do not change their shapes unless we do something to modify them. But as soon as you realize that *all* of our information about what is present in

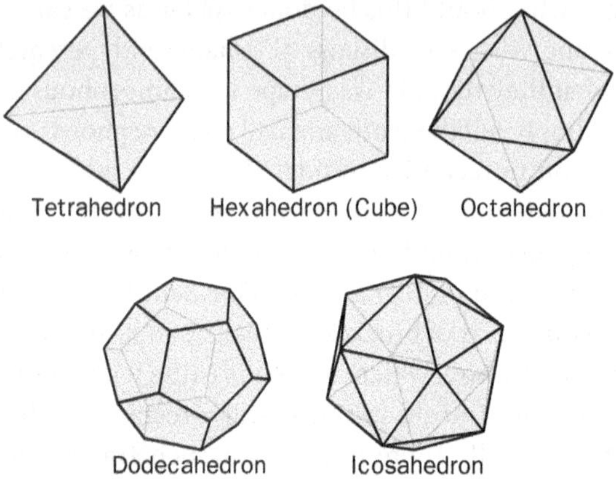

FIGURE 1.11. The Platonic solids.

our 3D world, beyond the objects we can touch, is conveyed to our brain by 2D representations on our retinas, it becomes difficult to ignore the problem raised by the fact that there are only 2-dimensions at our mind's interface with the external world. This inconvenient fact, which was established by Descartes and others more than 350 years ago, presents a huge problem because the shapes of the 2D images of all of the objects out there change as our viewing directions change when we move from room to room and from position to position within each room. But our perceptions of the shapes of all of the 3D objects out there do not change despite the changes of their 2D retinal images. This is the phenomenon called *shape constancy*. Technically, *shape constancy is said to occur when the perceived shape of an object is constant (and veridical) despite changes in the shape of its retinal image.* Shape constancy is illustrated in Figures 1.12.

The importance of contour for the perception of shape is illustrated vividly in Figure 1.13 where the 3D shape is only obvious when contours are shown. It is completely absent when only the corners are represented by dots.

The perceptual constancy of *shape* is not an isolated phenomenon in visual perception. Shape constancy is a member of a large family of perceptual constancies. This family includes size, position, lightness (white, gray, black appearance of an illuminated surface), color (hue, brightness & saturation), depth, and speed constancy. Shape constancy is unlike all of the other constancies because it is virtually perfect. All of the other constancies are only more or less successful. All of these perceptual constancies are nontrivial perceptual accomplishments because the visual system only has access to the 2D retinal image that often confounds some object's property with the viewing conditions, namely, 3D shape with 3D viewing direction, albedo (% reflected light) with the intensity of the illuminating light, an object's size with the viewing distance, and surface color with the spectrum of the illuminating light. How the visual system is able

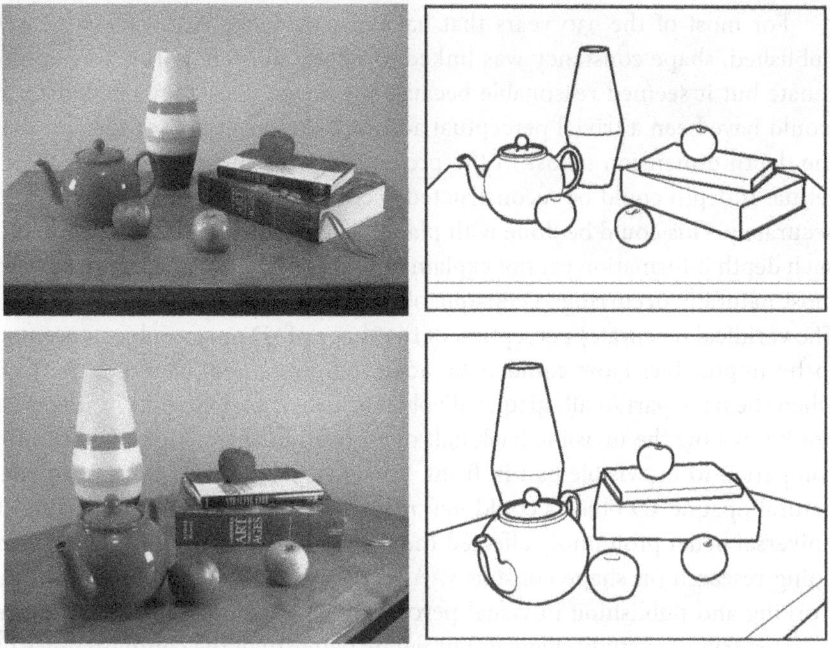

FIGURE 1.12. Two views of the same scene. Clearly, surface, texture and grey-scale are not required for shape constancy. Shape is obviously in the contour (from Pizlo, 2008). (From Pizlo, Z. (2008) 3D shape: its unique place in visual perception. MIT Press. With permission of The MIT Press.)

to reconstruct the object's property from the retinal image, and how it achieves veridicality in the case of shape, is arguably the most important question in vision. In fact, shape is the *only* visual characteristic that allows us to perceive the outside world veridically. Shape by being both complex and symmetrical is the *only* communication channel that provides us with accurate information about our external world. We, as humans, probably would not even be here as we are if shape did not permit us to perceive our environment veridically. The importance of many of the perceptual constancies was recognized very, very long ago. Alhazen, an Arabian physician/scholar, discussed this problem in a variety of the perceptual constancies, including shape constancy, in an influential treatise on vision published in 1083 CE (this really is a zero, not a typo).

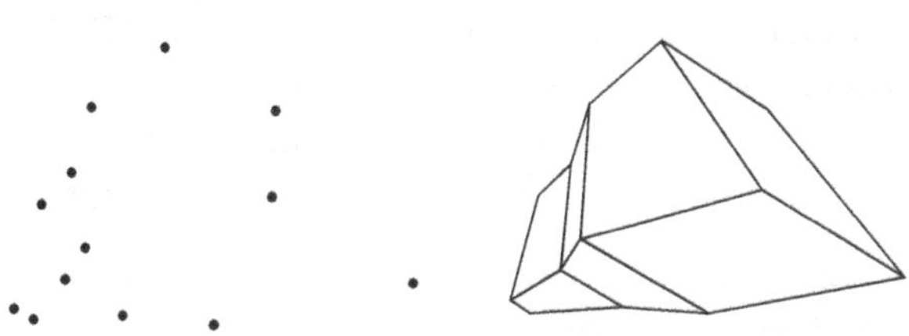

FIGURE 1.13. Left: Scattered dots. Right: these dots connected (From Pizlo et al., 2010).

For most of the 930 years that have elapsed since Alhazen's work was published, shape constancy was linked to depth constancy. This was unfortunate but it seemed reasonable because the shape constancy phenomenon would have been a trivial perceptual accomplishment if not for the fact that the depth dimension is lost in the projection from the 3D scene to the 2D retina. If depth could be reconstructed accurately, shape could be perceived accurately. This could be done with planar (flat) figures slanted in depth, but such depth information cannot explain how shape constancy is achieved with most naturally occurring 3D opaque objects in our natural 3D environment. The veridical (accurate) perception of the shape of 3D opaque objects seemed to be impossible. How could it be achieved, much less be nearly perfect, when the back part of all opaque 3D objects is invisible? Obviously, if you do not know how the invisible back half of an opaque object looks, you cannot compare it to the visible half in front. This question seemed to be insoluble, natural opaque 3D objects could *never* be perceived veridically. This almost universal belief profoundly affected the entire history of thinking about and doing research on shape constancy. Apparently, it did not occur to anyone working and publishing in visual perception that the common sense of the scientist trying to study shape might *not* be better than the common sense of the man in the street who made use of shape constancy every waking hour of every day of his life (we leave speculation about its presence in dreams to our clinical colleagues). It is very difficult, well-nigh impossible, to explain the fact that *veridical shape constancy is impossible*, as most visual scientists claimed, to a lay person who has been living with it so well in his daily life. Why would anybody expect to find it difficult to recognize the same object when it was viewed from different viewing directions? DEMO 1.2 (jeep)[3] shows that our computational model can, like a lay person, achieve virtually perfect shape constancy in the case of this 3D jeep. Note that the visual system of this machine is much simpler than any human being's and it has no sensors that provide it with any information about absolute distances. It also has been given no knowledge about the nature or probability of finding one or another 3D shape in its environment. Note that our model as shown in DEMO 1.2 recovered the entire 3D shape of the object accurately. It recovered the invisible parts on the 3D object's back as well as the visible parts in front. It also did this with an abstract, random, polyhedral object (DEMO 1.2, polyhedron[4]) and with real objects such as the chair (DEMO 1.2, chair[5]) and jeep shown in this demo. We will explain how this was done in the next chapter. The point being made here is simply that achieving veridical shape constancy is far from an impossible problem once you appreciate what the

---

[3] http://shapebook.psych.purdue.edu/1.2/jeep

[4] http://shapebook.psych.purdue.edu/1.2/polyhedron

[5] http://shapebook.psych.purdue.edu/1.2/chair

problem actually is. Furthermore, understanding the nature of the problem prepares the way for figuring out how it might be solved.

Unfortunately, once everyone expert in the study of visual perception actually believed that veridical shape constancy was impossible with opaque 3D objects, shape research could not make significant progress. Almost without exception, prior research on shape constancy concentrated on working with amorphous stimuli, stimuli devoid of shape, or on studying objects that had shape under viewing conditions that precluded their showing shape constancy. The long list of so-called experiments on shape includes studies that used too simple objects, such as ellipses and triangles; and amorphous objects, such as crumpled paper, bent wire objects, random sets of 3D points, and amorphous volumetric objects explicitly designed to resemble potatoes. Studying such shapeless objects and proving that they did not manifest shape constancy had a hidden virtue when developing computational models began to become commonplace. A computational model predicting that shape constancy would fail with amorphous stimuli or with viewing conditions chosen to make shape constancy impossible made modeling quite simple. It is not difficult to develop a model that *fails* to demonstrate this important perceptual phenomenon. Making a model that can achieve shape constancy is quite another story.

Was there any other motivation for performing such experiments? Were the authors looking for something else when they performed experiments on shape with stimuli that had no shape and what did they do after they discovered that shape constancy fails with amorphous stimuli? They turned their attention to trying to find out whether the perception of shape could be derived from the perception of depth. They studied this relationship in two ways: first, by measuring the role of depth cues in the perception of slanted ellipses and triangles and, second, by studying how the visible 3D surfaces (not the shapes) of objects were perceived. It is easy to demonstrate that depth cues affect the perceived aspect-ratio (height to width) of an ellipse or a triangle. But, this fact tells us absolutely nothing about shape constancy or anything else important about some other aspect of shape.[6] Similarly, the accuracy and precision of perceptual judgments about the distance and orientation of a 3D surface are strongly affected by the availability of depth cues. But, technically, because visible surfaces are usually described in a *viewer-centered coordinate system*, the percept of the visible surfaces will tell us nothing about perceived shape because shape requires using an *object-centered coordinate system*. Put simply, shape is a property of the object residing out there and surface orientation and distance are properties of the viewer's relationship to the object. So, such research has little merit because it is comparing apples with pears, which is

[6]See Pizlo (2008) for an extensive review of the limitations inherent in this large body of research.

often considered somewhat less than optimal anywhere in science. This comparison also calls attention to why performing a shape constancy experiment during all research actually designed to study shape is so critical: it is the only way you can be sure that you are studying shape, not surfaces. If a shape constancy experiment is not performed during a series of experiments purporting to be on shape, you cannot know whether you are studying the shape of your stimulus, which is object-centered, or some viewer-centered characteristics of stimulus. Changing anything other than the 3D viewing direction, the critical manipulation in a shape constancy experiment, such as the illumination falling on your stimuli, their shading, or the texture of your surfaces is not likely to have anything to do with shape regardless of how the results come out. One simply cannot ignore the fact that once we know that the perception of 3D shape is *not* derived from the perception of visible surfaces, studying surfaces cannot produce any useful information about the perception of shape.

Another way people working in visual perception made a living by studying something they called, but never proved, was actually shape, was to try to explain the phenomenon called shape constancy on the basis of learning. This seemed to be a much easier tack to take because it did not force one to understand the structure and function of the visual system itself. The idea is really quite simple. We see the shapes of common objects veridically because we have seen them many times in the past. Most objects in the adult human's environment are familiar. More formally, once we have seen a given object from a number of viewing directions, we could form an explicit representation of all parts of the object. This will, in time, permit us to see it veridically even if we only see its front surfaces because we remember the other views. Unfortunately, this intuitively pleasing kind of explanation does not explain how the 3D percept of the visible surfaces was formed initially. Faced with this obvious limitation, the proponents of this learning (empirical) approach to shape perception adopted the position advocated by Hermann von Helmholtz (1867). Knowing that the retinal image is 2D, Helmholtz assumed that the visual representation (the representation in the mind) should also be 2D. Helmholtz's approach to this problem became the basis of what we call *multiple view* theories of shape today. In machine vision, this is called *appearance based* shape models (Dickinson, 2009). Surprisingly, despite the phenomenologically obvious and compelling fact that we see the 3D world as 3D, an awful lot of excitement has been provoked by the idea that we might actually see the 3D world as 2D. Claims like this are greeted as intriguing, even cool in undergraduate classes on Sensation & Perception. They have also taken hold in the world of science. This somewhat less-than-obvious claim that our perceptual world is two-dimensional has kept both the human and machine vision communities active for at least two decades, during which dozens, perhaps even hundreds, of articles based on this assumption have been published in peer-reviewed journals. Human and machine vision communities have only recently, in some measure because of what we have done, come to realize what non-academicians have known for a long time, namely, the problem of how we perceive real 3D objects in real 3D scenes will not be solved by denying the reality of the 3rd dimension. Put at a simpler level of analysis, the Earth really is not flat.

If you think that this diversion into alternative worlds represents the outer limits of a scientist's imagination, you are wrong. How about the claim that visual perception, more precisely, visual representation of the external world does not exist at all? Why should it? According to the Radical Behaviorists (1913–1958) the only thing that matters to a really objective scientist are the input-output behavioral relationships. There is no need to assume that the mind actually exists or that it is doing anything useful. Edward C. Tolman, a cognitive psychologist, writing in 1930s–1940s preferred to assume that there was a scientifically useful mind, acting as an *intervening variable* in his terminology. This is by no means all ancient history as evidenced by recent publications of Hoffman (2009) and Pont et al. (2012). These two groups refer to an interface theory of the mind, which claims that Darwinian evolution rewarded the development of efficient mating behavior rather than the development of veridicality in visual perception. What they seem to be saying is that we do not need to assume that the observer has an accurate representation of a particular stimulus in his mind in order to explain the fact that the agent can produce an adequate (effective) reaction to a stimulus. They are encouraged to do this because they believe that producing veridical perceptions would take limited computational resources away from what is really the most important factor in evolution, namely successful mating. Such ideas have become quite popular in a new offshoot of Psychology called evolutionary psychology. Evolutionary psychology is not in the mainstream of either Vision or Cognitive Science today, and hopefully never will be. Denying the reality of perception does not seem to be the best way to study perception. It seems more reasonable to assume that the veridical perception of 3D shapes and 3D scenes is possible now that we have a working machine that does just this.

We can offer two additional arguments for the veridical perception of the 3D world for those who do not find watching our machine perceive veridically sufficient evidence. These arguments should convince even those who have commitments to: (1) surfaces, (2) learning, (3) a 2D perceptual world, and (4) a world completely devoid of perception. Consider the shapes of animal bodies. Most, if not all of them, are mirror-symmetrical. How do we know that they are mirror-symmetrical? Because we see them as such. Seeing a mirror-symmetrical object as mirror-symmetrical is not possible unless the two symmetrical halves are perceived as having identical shapes. Now, note that this is remarkable because: (1) we only see the front, visible surfaces of each of the two halves, and (2) we see the two halves from viewing directions that are 180° apart. Unless shape constancy is a real phenomenon and unless it is close to perfect, we would not even know that symmetrical shapes actually exist. Without shape constancy, we would not all see each other as we do.

The second argument is much more abstract but important, nonetheless. It begins by pointing out that most human actions are *purposive* (or *goal directed*, another concept promoted by Tolman). Purposive means that an agent (human or machine) takes an action now to achieve some desired outcome in the future. I turn on the coffee maker to make and drink coffee. I chose to go to a graduate school for a purpose, to become a scientist. But we know from our physical science classes that the future event (having coffee) cannot affect the present; it cannot *cause* me to turn on the coffee maker. So, how can my current purposive behavior be explained? How can the coffee 5 minutes down the road lead to my turning the coffee maker on now? Such a causal relation cannot exist in the real world. The only generally acceptable way to explain the purposive behavior of animals and humans (and machines someday) is to assume that the agent's action now is caused not by a future event, but by the agent's model of the future event. In the case of spatial behavior, a useful model must provide a visual representation of our 3D environment. It is not possible to conceive the successful evolution of animals, and the success of their natural selection without providing for planning and purposive behavior. Without effective planning, actually without optimal planning, it is hard to imagine successful hunting that often requires the collaboration of an entire group. How about the human's plan to plant seeds and then plan to harvest them? Can any of this be done without a *veridical representation of the 3D environment?* It seems very unlikely that we would be where we are today without inheriting the ability to construct veridical 3D representations of our environment, particularly now that we have found a way to give this skill to a simple inanimate machine. You will discover, when this story ends, that using veridical representations of 3D shapes and scenes is essential not only for achieving future goals: it is also essential for acting now. A human's now is always a prediction based on what was going on a short time back because of unavoidable delays in his physiological machinery. Seeing is not what is there, but what will soon be. This will be discussed in depth in our last chapter where work is in progress to provide our machine with the capacity to predict the 3D dynamical environment we share. We already know that predicting the future in both space and time can be done with the same kinds of computations that we found worked well for predicting the invisible back sides of objects.

So far, we have gone to considerable lengths to try to convince you that all human beings, as well as our machine, achieve almost perfect shape constancy, namely, we see the shapes of the objects veridically. This statement will probably not be accepted by almost all scientists who are studying perception now and by most who worked on shape perception in the past. Our claim will not be accepted because the common wisdom, developed and supported in perception empirically since Descartes' day, is that perceptual constancy is never perfect. This has been taught for centuries and is still taught this way today. It has some merit because most perceptual constancies are never even nearly perfect. This is true of size constancy, lightness constancy, color constancy, and binocular depth constancy. The percept in all of these constancies is known to be a compromise between the retinal image and the actual object. This compromise is typically quantified by measuring either Brunswik's or Thouless's constancy ratios. These ratios are always less than one and sometimes even zero. Why should shape constancy be different from color and all other constancies studied to date? Why have an exception to what seems to be a very general theory in perception, a theory that is supported by the repeatedly observed fact that perception tends to be inaccurate, rarely as high as 80%, rather than veridical (100%) in so many constancies. There is a very good reason to qualify this generally accepted belief that constancy is never perfect because the visual property called *shape* is unique. Shape is different from all other characteristics of objects in the physical world that can stimulate the visual sense. Its special status is recognized by artists, architects, and mathematicians but until now the basis for its uniqueness has not been understood. It had no formal basis. The next section discusses the mathematical complexity of shape and shows how this complexity provides the basis of shape's uniqueness, the quality that permits shape to be perceived veridically.

1.5 Complexity Makes Shape Unique

Our explanation of what is meant by complexity and how it applies to shape begins by counting the number of dimensions (parameters or measurable factors) that are needed to describe several perceptual characteristics known to be important when we study vision. In a typical experiment on size constancy, the observer is asked to judge the *length* of a line. This requires assigning only a single number to the stimulus whose retinal image size is being varied. So, it follows that linear size is a one-dimensional characteristic. The same is true of the speed of a stimulus, its depth, and its lightness. They are all measured by varying a single parameter. The color of a stimulus is different: color is a 3D characteristic. Three numbers must be assigned, one for its hue, a second for its brightness, and the third for its saturation (the proportion of hue to achromatic color, grey).

So, color is only slightly more complex than size, speed, depth, and lightness. The difference between one and three parameters in the subjective perceptual world is not large when it is compared to the number of parameters available to describe characteristics present in the physical world. For example, color, a perceptual property, is much less complex than the physical stimulus (the visible portion of the electromagnetic radiant energy spectrum), which is largely responsible for its appearance. There are many wave-lengths in the

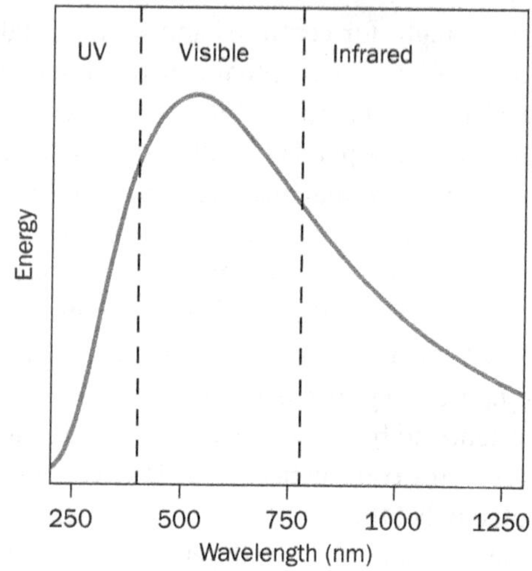

FIGURE 1.14. Spectral energy distribution of our sun.

electromagnetic radiation that are able to excite the 3 types of receptors that transduce (translate) the physical stimulus into the language used by the visual nervous system that has evolved to provide the human being with its experience of color.

The physical stimulus shown in Figure 1.14 is much more complex than the color experience itself. The physical electromagnetic energy spectrum can be represented by a function that assigns energy to individual wavelengths. If this is done for the minuscule portion of the physical spectrum we can see and call light, the visible region ranges between 400 nm and 700 nm ($400 \cdot 10^{-9}$ m and $700 \cdot 10^{-9}$ m). How many physical wavelengths are in this visible range? There are as many wavelengths as there are real numbers, infinitely many. So, the energy spectrum of light and reflectance of a surface (both physical characteristics) are *infinitely* dimensional characteristics. To represent them geometrically, one can draw a *function* like the one shown in Figure 1.14. Alternatively, one can plot a single point in an N-dimensional Cartesian coordinate system, with N being infinitely large. Think of the individual axes (the dimensions) in this space as individual wavelengths within the visible range with one wavelength per axis. The coordinates of our point in this space are the values of the light energy assigned to individual wavelengths. The concept of infinitely dimensional spaces, described here, is obviously not intuitive, but up to now, it has proven to be a very useful mathematical tool for solving problems in physics and engineering. We will now show that it has an important place in psychology, too. The perceptual correlate of the physical stimulus called light is only 3D. Specifically, the percept of light can be represented as a point in a 3-dimensional subspace of the infinitely dimensional space of light's physical stimulus. So, the transformation from the physical stimulus called an energy spectrum to the psychological percept called color can best be thought of as a projection from a larger to a smaller space. Note that this is the same kind of transformation found in the formation of the retinal image where there is a projection from a 3D space to a 2D retina, a projection from a larger to a smaller space.

Before going on to explain how this kind of thinking applies to shape, we will summarize what we said about the low dimensionality characteristics of the visual stimulus described above, namely, size, depth, speed, lightness, and chromaticity. Such a summary is needed to avoid confusions among geometrical spaces. First, consider the line-length example that we used when we began this discussion by considering a one-dimensional physical stimulus. All possible lengths of a line can be represented on a single axis and there may be as many different lengths as there are real numbers (infinitely many). Similarly, all possible wavelengths of light can be represented on a single axis (see Figure 1.14), and there can be infinitely many of them. So, what makes a line-length a 1D stimulus and an energy spectrum an infinitely dimensional stimulus? The *critical* difference is that the *physical* stimulus used in a single trial of a line-length perception experiment corresponds to only *one point* on our axis, but the physical stimulus used in a single trial of a *color* perception experiment corresponds to *infinitely many points* on our axis, namely, the energy spectrum.

The physical stimulus used to study shape perception is like the physical stimulus used to study color vision: it is infinitely dimensional, but shape constancy is very different from all the other constancies, including color, because the number of dimensions (parameters) needed to describe *perceived shape* is much larger than those needed to describe the percepts produced by other visual characteristics. Perceived shape is much more complex. A technical explanation of this claim begins with Figure 1.15.

FIGURE 1.15. Leonardo had to move infinitely many points to transform a circle into an outline of a man. He had to take each point on the circle and move it an appropriate distance in a particular direction. (From Pizlo, Z. (2008) 3D shape: its unique place in visual perception. MIT Press. With permission of The MIT Press.)

How might one go about describing the physical stimulus to make it useful for the study of shape perception? One might start by choosing any arbitrary point on the curved contour of the man in Figure 1.15 as your starting point and then walk around the curve representing the man inside the circle, plotting the orientation of the line tangent to the curve as a function of the distance from the starting point. This will produce a function that has the same properties as the Spectral Energy Distribution shown in Figure 1.14. Specifically, the shape of these curves, like the energy spectrum of visible light, contains infinitely many points. So, a *geometrical* stimulus that can be said to have shape is as *complex* as the *physical* stimulus called the *Spectral Energy Distribution* (see Ballard & Brown, 1982, and Pizlo, 1994, for a technical explanation of how this is done). But note that the percepts corresponding to these two characteristics, shape and color, are not equally complex. Namely, the color of a physical light stimulus is transduced at the physical-physiological interface within the eye by only 3 kinds of receptors, called L, M, and S cones. There are at least one million of each of the 3 types of cones in the retina. But, for the purpose of color vision, it does not matter how many cones of each type one has in his retina; the only thing that matters is the number of the *types* of cones, namely, 3. The shape stimulus, unlike color, is served by many cones, many more than 3. It follows that the perceptual *complexity* of a curve representing shape can be quite high. Pizlo (2008) estimated it as having as many as 400 dimensions. This implies that if one wants to describe all of the exact and approximate symmetries of a curve like the man in Figure 1.15, the visual system might have to use a space with as many as *400* dimensions. Furthermore, every natural 3D shape contains multiple curves, not just one. It follows that an object which occupies the central 20 deg of the visual field may stimulate more than half of all of the cones in the retina (about 3 million[7]). This huge number represents the number of samples potentially available to the visual system for processing the shape of a 3D object. The perceptual dimensionality of a 3D shape can be as large as three million. The 3,000,000 dimensionality of a 3D shape, or even the 400 dimensionality of a 2D shape available for processing, is much larger than either the 1 or 3 dimensions available for all other visual characteristics. Quantitative differences as large as this provides the main basis for our claim that shape is unique. The uniqueness of shape, stemming from its complexity, offers unique advantages in using it, but it also poses unique challenges when it comes to computing it. You will read more about this later.

If you have stayed with us to here, you should be both willing and able to appreciate the fact that shape is completely different from any other perceptual

---

[7]Using a log polar transformation from the retina to Area V1 in the cerebral cortex of our brain, described by Schwartz (1980), the number of samples in the retina between 1° and 10° of eccentricity is about the same as the number of samples between 10° and 90° eccentricity (log10−log1=1; log 90−log10=0.95). So, of the 6 million cones in the human retina half fall below 10° of eccentricity.

characteristic. This difference, despite its obvious importance, has been overlooked, or deemed unimportant for most of the history of research in visual perception. Why is this difference so critical and why do we feel compelled to call shape unique, not simply different? The reason is not complicated. The complexity of shape makes it possible for us to detect even small differences among the shapes of objects. There are many objects whose sizes, weights, and colors are the same or very similar, but the shapes of these otherwise similar objects are frequently very different. An elephant may be the same size and color as your car but the difference in their shapes will surely disambiguate them. Pears and apples and peaches and lemons can have similar colors but one will rarely be confused with another. Similarities of shape also carry information about the nature and use of objects. Most chairs are perceived as similar to one another. The same is true of all quadrupled (4-legged) animals. Such commonsensical observations have a couple of important implications for understanding the role of complexity in the perception of 3D shape, namely: (1) 3D objects with different shapes are never confused, and (2) the shapes of the 2D retinal images of different 3D objects are never confused regardless of the direction from which they are viewed. At this point you should be able to anticipate where this argument is going. Shape constancy should be easy to achieve in everyday life *because of its complexity*. Other perceptual constancies will be much more difficult to achieve *because of their simplicity* (low dimensionality). Note that this conclusion about shape constancy was reached by combining common sense with a rational argument. Once this is possible it becomes difficult to understand why the very existence of shape constancy has been almost universally denied by students of vision who performed dozens, if not hundreds, of psychophysical experiments that failed to demonstrate shape constancy despite its obvious presence in their everyday life experience. How did this come about?

Previous researchers started and continued their research working exclusively with the family of ellipses and triangles, the worst possible stimuli. These stimuli were obviously too simple to be used in experiments intended to look for the shape constancy phenomenon. The shapes they chose were simply not appropriate. Ellipses are characterized by only one parameter, their aspect ratio, and triangles by only two of its three angles. These stimuli were not even as complex as color. It is a simple fact of projective geometry that two different ellipses out there can always produce identical ellipses on the retina. Similarly, two different triangles out there can always produce identical triangles on the retina. Ellipses and triangles were used because their simplicity made them seem as simple as the stimuli used to study size, depth, lightness, speed and color. But, by using these stimuli they managed to lose all of the information about shape. The shape of an ellipse is completely lost in its retinal image. The same is true of the information about the shape of a triangle, the length of a line, the depth or the speed of an object, and the lightness or the color of the surface. Once critical information about the physical (weight, reflectance, etc.) or geometrical (length, shape, etc.) characteristics of a stimulus out there (technically a *distal stimulus*) is lost in its retinal image, perceptual constancy will be difficult to achieve, if possible at all. With impoverished stimulation, the visual system will have to use information about the context in which the stimulus appears to disambiguate it. All of these physical and geometrical stimuli must be reconstructed by using other information about the stimulus such as the slant of the surface on which the ellipse resides[8], the physical distance to an object whose size, depth, and speed is to be judged, the intensity and spectrum of the light illuminating an object whose lightness and color is to be judged. But, context is often not very useful because it often varies independently from the stimulus itself. Using context to judge the stimulus often leads to unreliable perceptual inferences. Once this is appreciated one should not be surprised to find a literature full of papers showing that perceptual constancies are never perfect and often fail completely. There is no alternative.

Shape is never a problem. The perceived shape of a 3D object is different from other visual perceptions in two ways. First, there is never a problem of disambiguating different 3D shapes on the basis of information provided in a single 2D retinal image because both geometrical and perceived shape are complex characteristics. Second, once a 3D shape is defined by its symmetries, namely the geometrical self-similarities within the 3D object, these 3D symmetries never disappear completely in a 2D retinal image of a 3D object. Once these symmetries are detected in a 2D retinal image, they can be used to recover the 3D shape of an object without using any information about the context within which the 3D shape appears. This explains why shape constancy can be, and actually is, perfect. No other visual characteristic has sufficient complexity to manifest this characteristic. When a 3D object is complex, but completely lacks symmetries, shape constancy is bound to fail. Amorphous (shapeless) objects, such as bent paperclips and crumpled papers, have often been used to prove that shape constancy fails. We hope that this persistent claim will be put to rest now that we have an analytical definition of shape, which predicts that constancy will fail and now that almost perfect shape constancy has been demonstrated in experiments with appropriate stimuli.

1.6 How Would the World Look If We are Wrong?

Now that you know why shape is unique and how this property makes it possible for a human being to function effectively, we will consider how the world

---

[8]Slant is the angle by which a planar (flat) figure such as an ellipse is rotated away from the frontal plane. When slant is 0°, the retinal image of a figure has the same shape (aspect-ratio) as the figure out there.

would look if our novel approach was replaced by the conventional approach we have criticized up to now. How would 3D shapes and 3D scenes look if veridical shape constancy could not be achieved and if symmetry did not play an important role in our visual perceptions? Note that we are not doing this to be fair to those we think have gone astray. We are doing this to make it clear that much of what is taught as common knowledge today is simply wrong. So far, we have used mainly common sense to encourage you to accept our way of thinking. You have had the carrot. Now you get the stick. Here, we take an entirely different tack. We will let you explore our professional adversaries' alternative visual universes. The universes they build primarily on amorphous stimuli and degenerate views; universes without symmetry where shape perception is not veridical.

Once one appreciates the important role symmetry has played in art, math and science for centuries, it is hard to understand why symmetry was ignored by so many scientists who have worked on visual perception. A possible reason for this neglect might be the desire to enhance one's scientific stature by imitating what is going on in the hard sciences. This clearly was the case when the modern study of perception began in the last quarter of the 19th Century. It began when Wilhelm Wundt (1832–1920), a student of Helmholtz, established Psychology as a separate discipline by launching a doctoral program called *Experimental Psychology* at the University in Leipzig in 1879. Wundt and the members of his school, modeled their new science on the physics of their day. They devoted a good deal of effort to the study of Sensation and Perception where they concentrated on measuring simple mental states they called *sensations*. Sensations were unrelated mental points of colored light that came to be perceived as objects with shapes through learning. The idea of building complicated things from small simpler elements has been popular in human thought since ancient Greece. By the time Experimental Psychology had been launched, John Stuart Mill's (1806–1873) approach had taken hold and the idea that simple elements, such as sensations of color, contours, odors and tastes could be used to build up complex mental states like thoughts of apples, memories of eating them, and even the concept encapsulated in the thought of fruit was universally accepted. Mill's approach, in vogue in Wundt's day, is often described as mental chemistry. This was considered complimentary back then because it likened the new Experimental Psychology to Chemistry, which had made a lot of progress in the 19th Century. Dmitri Mendeleev (1834–1907) captured this progress in his periodic table of elements. By the time Wundt retired in 1919, he had awarded 186 doctoral degrees (Tinker, 1932), and by 1899, when the Periodic Table had 84 elements, Wundt's school had become preeminent in academic Psychology. Wundt's preference for studying perception bottom up by building a 3D object from bits of 2D mental states, was thought to be the best way to do science at the time. This approach has persisted. Today we find individuals interested in machine and human vision trying to construct

3D objects from 0-D (zero dimensional) dots called pixels, 1D line-segments called edges, 2D color patches called appearances, and 3D dots called voxels. The tendency for perceptionists to try to gain credence by aping real hard science has not been confined to a preference for small elements over 3D objects or for empirical (learning) over nativist (instinctive) explanatory mechanisms. It also applies to attitudes about the use of common sense in science. A movement called *Positivism* in the mid-19th Century credited to August Comte (1798–1857) played down the role that common sense should play in serious science. Comte's Positivism held that laboratory measurements were always superior to common sense and that they should be used whenever possible. This tendency reached its apogee in Vienna, just before WWII, and it reemerged full force after the war when Logical Positivism came into vogue. This new emphasis on positivism profoundly influenced the study of visual perception just after WWII. Logical Positivism saw little need or room for common sense in science and, as you should expect, this had a detrimental effect on visual perception research. A particularly influential example of its influence can be found in Rudolf Luneburg's (1903–1949) theory of binocular space perception that he published in 1947.

So far we have only considered how 3D shapes will be perceived in the alternative universes of our professional adversaries, universes without veridical shape constancy, filled with amorphous objects and with the role of symmetry played down. Here, we move on to consider the perception of the space in which these objects, including the observer, reside. The first modern study of this problem was done by Rudolf Luneburg, who was a Professor of Mathematics and Optics at Dartmouth University. Like many of his intellectual ancestors, he was influenced by what was going on in physics in his day. This encouraged him to use non-Euclidean geometry to study space perception probably because it had played such an important role in Einstein's Theory of General Relativity. By way of reminder, in a Euclidean space, a 2D box (a square) has 4 equal 90° angles but the angles of a square (i.e., a quadrilateral with straight and equal sides) in a non-Euclidean space are not equal to 90°. Alternatively, if the four angles are all 90° angles, the sides are not straight line-segments. Luneburg probably thought that if visual science used such new sophisticated mathematics, this relatively young specialty might be able to produce the kind of scientific revolution that had been accomplished with non-Euclidean geometry in physics. Luneburg assumed that binocular visual space is a non-Euclidean space with a negative curvature. He began his work by taking some psychophysical results on space perception, published early in the 20th Century, seriously. The results that Luneburg (and others since) used came from what was called Blumenfeld's (1913) alley experiment. Blumenfeld's experiment was surely motivated by the illusion discovered in the 19th Century that railroad tracks do not look parallel when they can be seen to be going off in distance. They appear to be converging. This illusion must have been perceived much earlier, as soon as ancient human

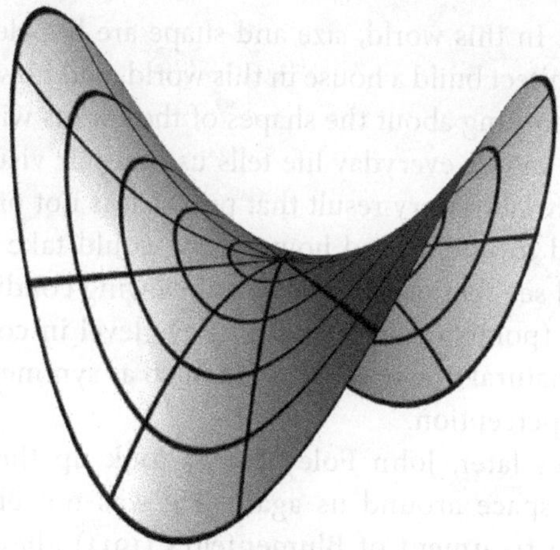

FIGURE 1.16. The saddle surface representing the binocular percept of the plane in front of the subject. This space has negative curvature, which means that if you draw a triangle on this surface, its three angles will add up to less than 180°.

settlements had long straight alleys. In Blumenfeld's experiment, the subject was asked to adjust the position of points of light (4 at a time) that were shown at eye level in total darkness symmetrically with respect to the subject's plane of symmetry. The points were arranged to form (1) parallel alleys, or (2) equidistant alleys. In Euclidean geometry, such pairs of lines must coincide, whenever they have at least one pair of points in common. When the subject finished his adjustments, the two pairs of alleys were not straight lines and the equidistant alleys did not coincide with the parallel alleys. They were outside the parallel alleys. This encouraged Luneburg, as well as those who replicated his result, to conclude that visual space is non-Euclidean. Technically, this non-Euclidean space is hyperbolic; it has constant negative curvature. This kind of space can be represented by the saddle shown in Figure 1.16. Intuitively, this kind of saddle-like surface represents the percept of the physical space in front of the subject. So, in Luneburg's alternative universe, the visual space looks quite different from what you might suspect.

The technical explanation of Luneburg's theory can be summarized simply by realizing that the sum of angles in a triangle is *less* than 180°. This happens on a flat surface only when the sides of the triangle are curved, rather than straight. But there is more to this story. In such curved spaces, objects with different sizes cannot have the same shape. Can you imagine such a world? In this world, there would be no scaled-down model of a car for a child. Changing the car's size will change its shape. Simply put, Luneburg's idea of using *non*-Euclidean geometry in visual perception cannot describe, much less explain, objects that we see and activities we perform, things that we see and do *all* of the time. It does not apply to real objects in our natural environment. The non-Euclidean world produced is not only absurd, it is also unfriendly. In this world, size and shape are hopelessly confounded. How could an architect build a house in this world, and how could it stand up to gravity, to say nothing about the shapes of the rooms with different sizes? Everything we do in our everyday life tells us that our visual space must be Euclidean, and any laboratory result that proves it is not probably should be ignored. It is hard to understand how anyone could take this kind of stuff seriously. You will see that using stimuli and viewing conditions that are not ecologically valid (points of light shown at eye level in complete darkness) prevents critical, natural innate constraints, such as symmetry, from contributing to veridical perception.

Three decades later, John Foley (1972) took up the problem of the geometry of the space around us again. He was not enthusiastic about Luneburg's (1947) treatment of Blumenfeld's (1913) alley experiment. He thought that the theory was sound but that Blumenfeld's experiment was not sufficient to fully justify Luneburg's interpretation. He saw two problems with it. First, large individual variability was observed across the subjects and even when the experiment was repeated with the same subject. Variability is not uncommon in visual experiments, but here, the nature, as well as the size of the variability, implied that the mind's representation of geometrical space changes from a saddle surface to a sphere and even to a flat surface (Euclidean). Foley's second concern went even further. He was concerned because he thought that although Blumenfeld's result, used by Luneburg, could be used to justify the claim that visual space is curved, it did not permit the experimenter to choose the sign of the curvature. Foley went on to design his triangle experiment to provide the kind of experimental evidence that, unlike Blumenfeld's, actually was suitable for testing Luneburg's theory except that he failed to use stimuli and conditions that had ecological-validity. This will prove to have been an important mistake because we discovered that Foley's results can only be obtained under unnatural conditions. See Figure 1.17 for an explanation of Foley's experiment.

Foley did the following experiment: a binocular subject, whose cyclopean eye is represented by O, is asked to adjust the point A so that the triangle

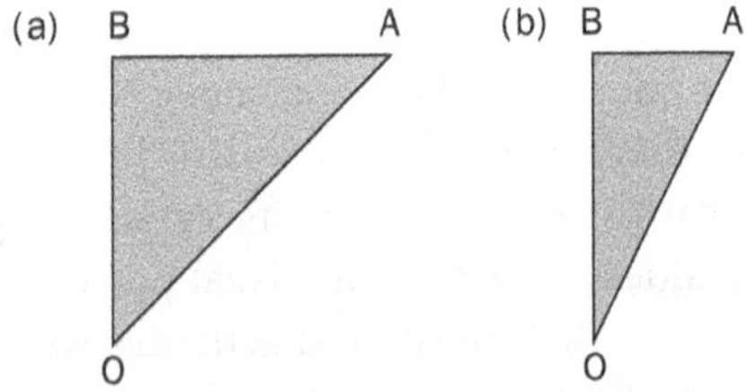

FIGURE 1.17. (a) A right (90°) isosceles triangle. (b) The triangle as adjusted by the subject.

OBA is a right isosceles triangle (OB=BA, ∠OBA=90°). The adjusted triangle looked like the one shown in (b) when the subject finished his adjustment. The angle OBA was still a right angle, but OB was twice as large as BA. This indicates a large compression of visual depth. However, when the subject was asked to judge another angle, namely angle AOB, he correctly judged it as 30°, its actual size. If visual space is Euclidean and if the triangle OBA is perceived as an isosceles right triangle, the angle AOB must be perceived as a 45°. If this angle is perceived as smaller than 45°, this visual space is non-Euclidean with a negative curvature. A triangle in such a space would look like the funny (curved) triangle shown in Figure 1.18.

Curved triangles like this can be constructed easily by using geodesic lines, like those used on globes. The fact that this is possible convinced Foley that visual space is non-Euclidean with a negative curvature as Luneburg had claimed. Note that Foley accepted a non-Euclidean explanation of the nature of binocular visual space that was based on an experiment in which completely *unnatural* stimuli and viewing conditions had been used. There is another, Euclidean, way to interpret his results. Foley's data can be interpreted in a much simpler way, once one realizes that Foley used results based on two very different kinds of psychophysical judgments to draw his conclusions. Binocular length discriminations and monocular judgments of an angle are very different kinds of judgments and there is no *a priori* reason for assuming that such judgments can be represented by a single triangle. This concern is compounded by the fact that there are very different difficulties inherent in these judgments. A judgment of the angle AOB is easy because the visual system can estimate it based on a single retinal image. A binocular length judgment is different. It is difficult because it requires the observer to reconstruct the depth dimension based on information provided by retinal images of both eyes, plus the extraretinal information, that is, information about the orientation of the eyes within their orbits and about the distance between the two eyes. So, accepting Foley's improvement on Blumenfeld's experiment does not force us to agree

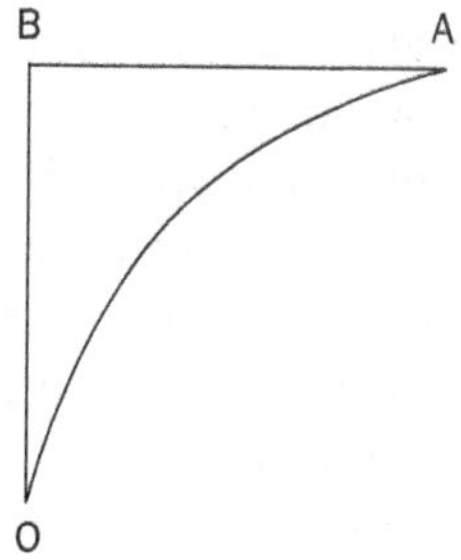

FIGURE 1.18. A right isosceles triangle as it would be in a negatively curved non-Euclidean space. Angles in this triangle do not sum up to 180°.

that visual space is curved. There is a much simpler alternative. We just need to acknowledge that such different visual judgments could lead to inconsistent results. Once this is acknowledged, the claimed non-Euclidean distortion of human space perception is more likely to reside in the mind of the experimenter than in the mind of the observer. Foley was not the first, nor the last, to make this error. Whenever anyone confuses the geometry of the stimulus with the percept of an observer, this is likely to occur. We saw this problem before with Thouless' (1931) experiment in which he used ellipses in his studies purporting to be on shape; stimuli that are much too simple to allow one to study shape. We will see it again when it was made more recently in an experiment on 3D surfaces that will be described next.

Twenty years after Foley published his paper on the non-Euclidean perception of space, the problem was picked up by Koenderink, a physicist by training, who is credited with solving a number of difficult problems in computer vision and image analysis. Koenderink's model of the visual space is not as distorted as Foley's and Luneburg's, but it is very different from the world as we normally perceive it. Koenderink's world is not curved, but it is compressed. Technically, such a model of space is called *affine*. Before we tell you what an affine space looks like, we will explain how Koenderink got started in this work. It is likely that Koenderink noticed Foley's confusion because he took Foley's underestimation of depth seriously, but ignored his curved-space interpretation. Koenderink, who had interest, as well as expertise in art, may have been inspired to do this by *bas relief* art in which the observer often perceives fully volumetric objects and scenes despite the fact that depth is dramatically compressed in the carvings. Koenderink et al. (1992) developed a theory of visual shape and space that was based on Felix Klein's (1939) revolutionary concept of a hierarchy of geometries. It included our familiar Euclidean geometry, as well as several more general geometries. Klein pointed out that Euclidean Geometry, which had served us so well for millennia, is actually a special case. There are several other more general geometries and they can all be described by a single mathematical language, the language of what is called group theory. Koenderink et al. argued that despite the fact that our environment can be described very well by Euclidean geometry, our perception of this space can be described better by affine geometry. In affine geometry, distances and angles are not meaningful in the sense that two objects with different angles and pairwise distances (such as line lengths), may be considered to be identical. A group led by Koenderink published experiments that led them to conclude that human observers are only able to perceive the affine properties of 3D shapes. In plain English, they claimed that despite the fact that a straight line is perceived as a straight line and despite the fact that parallel lines are perceived as parallel, we never perceive the extent of objects in depth veridically. If they were correct, rectangular chairs and tables would not be perceived as rectangular, and the horizontal floor would not be perceived as horizontal.

You do perceive all of these objects as rectangular and the floor surely looks horizontal to you. So, even if this affine model describes their experimental results adequately, it cannot explain the perception of real objects in our natural environment. We have an additional problem with this work, namely, the way in which these authors measured their subjects' percepts makes it possible to show that their results can be explained without claiming that visual space is distorted.

The flawed step in their reasoning lies in the way they did their computational reconstruction of the 3D shape percept. They did it from *local* perceptual judgments of *local* 3D surface orientations. In their psychophysical experiment, the subject was shown a 3D surface produced by using one or more conventional depth cues, that is, motion parallax, binocular disparity, texture, shading, or simply by showing a line drawing that looked like a 3D surface. The experimenter superimposed a small *elliptical* probe on the 2D image. The ellipse looked like a slanted circle, which made it possible to see the probe as if it were lying on the 3D surface. When the subject said that it did, the experimenter concluded that the percept of the 3D orientation of the circle was the same as the percept of the local orientation of the 3D surface. This method assumed that the perceived 3D orientation of a surface could be measured by using the orientation and aspect ratio of the elliptical probe. Both the subject's and the experimenter's tasks were fairly easy, but this simplicity is deceptive. Using the shape of an elliptical probe to measure the shape of an object *cannot* work because the *percept of a slanted circle does* depend on depth cues, whereas the percept of the shape of a 3D object *does not* depend on depth cues. The authors apparently were unaware of this difference, so they were able to convince themselves that this kind of measurement was appropriate as well as very useful for measuring the perception of the shape of a 3D surface. It is not. Geometrically, if the 3D surface's slant and tilt is known at many points of the surface, one can integrate these local measurements geometrically to produce an estimate of the entire 3D surface at least the front, visible part of it.[9] Once you know that this can be done geometrically, why not assume that it can be done perceptually, too. If both of these assumptions would be true, *and they are not*, the experimenter could reconstruct the subject's percept of the 3D surface from his percepts of such elliptical probes. But, the fact that this can be done *geometrically* does *not* imply that this is how the visual system actually perceives a 3D shape. This geometrical fact is *not* the percept and by putting multiple perceptual judgments into one geometrical structure, and examining the result of this collage, Koenderink *et al.* made the same mistake Foley had made earlier. There is nothing ambiguous or uncertain about our claim,

---

[9]Tilt is the direction of slant. Tilt specifies the axis around which the plane is rotated in depth and away from the frontal plane, and slant specifies how much the plane is rotated.

because we have experimental results showing quite clearly that 3D shape perception is not based on the integration of local judgments of 3D surface orientations. The perception of 3D shape is accomplished by recovering the 3D shape on the basis of an *a priori* constraint that makes use of symmetry (Li, 2009). We will explain what is meant by an *a priori* constraint soon.

Note that support for all of the theories discussed so far used impoverished stimuli or an inappropriate probe, stimuli that bore little or no resemblance to any objects normally present in our natural environment. Egon Brunswik (1903–1955) would have been as unhappy, as we are, with these stimuli because in his terminology, such stimuli are not ecologically valid. Brunswik was sure that such stimuli could not provide much useful information about how human beings actually see in their real world. We agree. One cannot but wonder how these scientists, who worked so diligently in this distorted world were able to reconcile their conclusions with their perceptions. The traditional way people deal with this problem is to assume that (1) what you actually perceive is an illusion, that is, your perceptions outside the laboratory actually do not agree with the way the world is out there, and (2) you are not aware of the fact that these perceptions actually are distorted. We think that they got this backwards. They are projecting what they are finding with unnatural stimuli in the laboratory onto the world in which we all live. This reasoning ignores the fact that perception in everyday life depends critically on the operation of *a priori* constraints. When impoverished stimuli are used, these constraints are not effective and perception will fail. The only way to ensure that the laboratory study tells us how the visual system operates under natural conditions, that it is ecologically valid, is to design stimuli and to use conditions that make it possible to apply these constraints.

1.7 What Had Happened in The Real World While We Were Away

Now that you should be convinced that common sense, and only common sense, can lead an investigator to perform useful studies of veridical perception, we will describe where and how this dogma was developed. This dogma is not new. It goes back at least to the 18th Century when it was proposed and defended vigorously by the founder of the Scottish School of Common Sense Philosophy, Thomas Reid (1710–1796). Reid published two books primarily written as responses to the Bishop Berkeley's (1709) skepticism about the reliability of the knowledge provided by one's visual perceptions. Berkeley stressed that vision, a distance sense, cannot guarantee accurate information. A single stimulated point on the retina could be an image of infinitely many points out there. You cannot be certain about what you can see unless you are able to touch it. He claimed that this ambiguity will always be very difficult, perhaps even impossible, to resolve. Reid's commonsensical response was that he "never saw a skeptic walking into fire because he did not trust his senses." Reid not only emphasized that our percepts are veridical; he also made a fundamental distinction between sensations and perceptions. This distinction is much more important than you can possibly imagine. Its implications extend down the present day where it explains why making a distinction between *direct* and *inverse problems* has become timely, as well as critical, in contemporary vision research. This technical language came into use in 1985 in vision research, 221 years after Reid made his important distinction between sensations and perceptions. This distinction paved the way for using it in vision research in what is called the Theory of Inverse Problems today. We will begin our explanation of this development by describing what we mean by a direct problem. A direct problem is said to have occurred when an earthquake somewhere below the Earth's surface causes vibrations that you can measure on the Earth's surface. An inverse problem is said to have occurred when we infer that an earthquake has occurred and where on the basis of measurements made on the surface of the Earth. Now, let's take this explanation from geophysics to psychophysics. Acquiring a 2D camera image of a 3D shape is a direct problem. Veridical recovery of the 3D shape from the 2D camera image is an inverse problem. Direct problems in natural sciences are easy in the sense that they are solved by Nature, herself: the observed (measured) effect is a *physical* result of the operation of physical forces and energies. Inverse problems are different. They are always difficult because they require making inferences about unknown natural causes from what will always be incomplete data. An inverse problem can only be solved if you have some knowledge about what might be going on because some information about the actual cause has been lost. Solving an inverse problem always requires some useful knowledge before you start, but you cannot know, in advance, exactly what knowledge will be both necessary and sufficient to solve the specific problem. Technically, the knowledge needed but not certain is called *a priori* knowledge.

We will now trace out how Reid's insights in the 18th Century helped us get to the point we are today. Without them, we could not have made the machine that sees like us. According to Reid, *a perception always refers to an object.* We perceive a rose or a tree or the Sun. *A sensation never refers to objects.* For example, the sensation described as feeling pain need not be associated with the object causing the pain. In some cases, one can experience both. For example, when the smell of a rose allows us to recognize that a rose is present even if we cannot see it. Reid's distinction between sensation and perception makes a lot of sense. In today talk, we would say that Reid's sensation refers to sensory coding, such as experiencing the brightness and the color of a light, or the pitch and the loudness of a tone whereas perception refers to recovering (estimating) the true physical characteristics of the distal stimulus, such as, the color of a surface, or the shape of an object. Reid's observation that perception always refers to an object, and that perceptions, unlike sensations (also known as sensory coding), are always veridical is potentially very useful. Unfortunately, the way Reid distinguished sensations from perceptions disappeared in the scientific literature more than 250 years ago. It was lost when Thomas Brown (1778–1820) changed Reid's definitions. Brown's definitions have been used almost universally ever since. Brown assumed that *sensations* were the elementary mental elements from which the more complex *perceptions* were built by means of a learning process much like Aristotle's. Bright red spots (unrelated sensations) will build the percept of a red apple if they appear together frequently enough. Unfortunately, Brown's empirical definition of perception was not replaced by Reid's when the Gestalt Psychologists successfully discredited Brown's empirical definition of the percept in the first half of the 20th Century. They may have known about Reid's distinction, but they ignored its potential importance because they were not sure that perceptions were veridical despite the fact that they were convinced that what Brown called sensations were abstractions, rather than the elemental building blocks of the human mind (see Koffka, 1935, for a discussion of this issue). In Reid's day, John Locke's (1632–1704) assumption about the mind of a newborn baby being a blank slate still held sway. It provided the backbone, as well as the starting point, for the long line of skeptics who built on Locke's commitment to empiricism that had been the foil to Descartes nativism in Locke's day. Brown's, Locke-based, empirical position makes it difficult to understand how the visual system could learn how to perceive veridically. So, when Reid said that veridical perception was important, as well as possible, he was poking a finger in Locke's eye, so it is not surprising that he was ignored until the reign of Empiricism in perception ended near the turn of the 20th Century when the Gestalt psychologists brought it under attack. Reid knew that the intuitions about space, time, and abstract geometrical concepts that had been emphasized by Descartes could go a long way toward understanding how veridical perceptions could be achieved, but he did not know how they actually worked. Reid's contribution to nativism was ignored throughout most of the 19th Century, but his insistence on their importance might have influenced the philosopher, Immanuel Kant (1724–1804), who is often credited with bringing innate ideas back into perception. Reid's ideas were in print 17 years before Kant's book, *Critique of Pure Reason*, which made a big deal about intuitions, was published in 1781.

The importance of something like innate ideas in visual perception has been influential since the Gestalt psychologists encouraged many perceptionists to put Brown's views aside, but Reid's emphasis on the role of common sense in formulating theories of perception and his insistence that perceptions are veridical and different from sensations have always been downplayed. There are two important exceptions. Machine Vision people working in the infancy of this specialty in the 1950s tried to make veridical 3D reconstructions of objects, and in the 1980s, a group at MIT led by Poggio brought what is called the Theory of Inverse Problems into the study of visual perception. In this theory sensations and perceptions in Reid's terminology can be handled separately, sensations can be treated as direct problems and perceptions can be treated as inverse problems. The formal basis of this theory goes, like so many cutting edge technologies today, back again to the 18th Century when Thomas Bayes (1701–1761) formulated Principles of Inverse Probability. In Section 1.9, we will see how Bayesian inference comes into play and its strengths and weaknesses when it is used to formulate the theories in visual perception.

1.8 Perception Viewed as an Inverse Problem

When a 2D retinal image of a 3D object, say a chair, is formed, we call this a direct (forward) problem. This retinal image is produced *automatically* by light reflected from the object and refracted by the optical elements of the eye (cornea and lens). This problem is *well-posed* because there is always a unique 2D image when the position of the 3D object, relative to a camera with known optical power, is used. Whenever this applies, the 2D image will always be *unique*. When such a 2D image is shown to an observer who perceives a 3D chair, we can say that the observer's visual system *solved* an Inverse Problem. This kind of Inverse Problem is *ill-posed* because its solution is *not unique*. It is not unique because there are many 3D objects that could have produced this 2D image of the 3D chair. A very well-known and striking visual illusion, called the Ames's chair, is a very good example of what happens when the observer is presented with this kind of ill-posed problem. The stimulus responsible for this illusion is a haphazard collection of several unconnected rods and one plate shaped like a parallelogram. To create the illusion, this collection of elements is arranged in 3D space in such a way that when it is viewed from one particular viewing direction, it produces the same kind of retinal image that would be produced by a real chair. This would be a good time to look at our Ames's chair demo (DEMO 1.3).[10] Use your mouse to look at this stimulus from various directions. This shows you the 5 rods and the plate that were used to construct what looks like a chair when you view it from one special direction. It should be obvious to the reader by now that both the 2D image of a real chair and the 2D image of Ames's illusionary chair is always ambiguous. All 2D images are always ambiguous, so there is nothing surprising about what you can see. The difference between a real chair and Ames's chair is that a real chair looks like a chair from all viewing directions, whereas Ames's chair looks like a chair from only one viewing direction. From any other viewing direction, Ames's chair looks like a meaningless mess. The fact that a 2D image of a chair

[10]http://shapebook.psych.purdue.edu/1.3

can be produced by a real chair or by other stuff was anticipated 300 years ago when the Bishop Berkeley called attention to the problem inherent in the fact that there are always infinitely many potential visual 3D interpretations of any 2D retinal image produced by 3D objects in our 3D world. He pointed out that each point on the retina could have been produced by any of the infinitely many points that lie on the line emanating from this retinal point. Given this *geometrical* fact, it is actually amazing that the visual system is almost always able to choose a unique, veridical 3D interpretation. In our example, the shape of the real chair could be perceived veridically from almost all viewing directions. The veridicality of 3D shape perception was apparently so amazing that, after Berkeley published his observations, most people studying human vision refused to accept the veridicality of what they could see. They persisted in this nonsense for hundreds of years despite what they could see with their own eyes. Strange as it seems, almost everybody since Berkeley's day, down to today, preferred to believe that 3D shape perception simply cannot be veridical. Now that you have seen a good example of the kind of ill-posed Inverse Problem that your visual system must solve all of the time, we will explain how this system does it.

It is generally accepted that the only *effective* way to solve this kind of ill-posed Inverse Problem is to use *a priori* knowledge (Tikhonov & Arsenin, 1977). How can this be done? *A priori* knowledge can be used to formulate constraints that can then be imposed on the family of possible solutions. How would you do this with the example of a chair? The first thing we must do is to define the family of all possible solutions. We must know this before we can choose *a priori* constraints that might help us solve the problem. Berkeley did this for us by pointing out that each retinal point determines infinitely many 3D points on the line emanating from this point. DEMO 1.3 can be used to illustrate a portion of the family that includes these rods and the plate. The 6 sliders in bottom allow you to change *only* the depth of the 5 rods and the plate, not their left-right or up-down position in space. The 4th from the left moves the plate. Check this out by moving the sliders—the image of the chair does not change. This illustrates what Berkeley pointed out when he said that changing only depth does not affect the retinal image. Now, use your mouse to change the direction from which you are viewing the chair. When you do this, it is obvious that you are not looking at a normal chair. Instead, you are looking at a haphazard arrangement of 5 rods and one plate that happen to look like a chair when you look at it from only one direction. Do not try this at home by breaking up one of your chairs and then trying to arrange them so that it looks fine from only a single viewing direction, unless you are prepared to devote as much time as Ames did to make this impressive demonstration work. You can always return to the original viewing direction by clicking on the default bar on the lower right. To actually see how the depth of the 5 rods and the plate change when you move the sliders, change the viewing direction with your mouse and use the sliders on the bottom left to change the depth position of one or more of the 6 elements. You will be able to assemble a real chair by adjusting the 6 sliders. Once you have aligned all the elements properly, use your mouse to change the viewing direction any way you want and the chair will always look like a real chair, rather than as a haphazard collection of 6 elements. There are a number of important points we want you to take away from the fun we had with this demo. It is important to appreciate that this demo explained everything you need to know about how images are formed on the retina in the back of your, or the machine's eye, and how these images change as your line-of-sight scans around from 3D object to 3D object in the natural 3D scene. With the demo of the Ames's chair you just enjoyed, you were able to learn that (1) information about depth is completely lost in the 2D retinal image, (2) shape information is not lost in the 2D retinal image, (3) Berkeley was right when he pointed out that each retinal point could be produced by infinitely many points out there and (4) some viewing directions are very unusual because what you see is not what is there; such directions are called degenerate. We will build on what you learned in this demonstration by elaborating this treatment of the relationship between objects and retinal images in the natural environment where things can be close by as well as far away. We will be talking about differences between *perspective projection* and *orthographic projection* of visual stimuli on the retina. These new terms will be explained and used in the upcoming demos just like this one.

Once we have Berkeley's description of how the family of possible solutions is formed in a 6 element family you just got to know well, the next step is to choose an *a priori* constraint that will select one member from this family. When this constraint is chosen well, we will have recovered the 3D chair from the single 2D image containing the 6 elements. We can then say that what began as an ill-posed problem has been changed into a well-posed problem. We can also say that the problem has been *regularized*. Now we will choose what we think could be an effective constraint. You should not be surprised if we decide that our initial constraint will be that the 3D interpretation should be a *symmetrical* object. We are going to let symmetry guide our model's choice of the 3D percept. When the symmetry constraint is applied to family of 3D arrangement of the 6 elements, this chair will be the *unique* solution. The reader should note that we started with a symmetry constraint because our analytical definition of shape is based on symmetry. This symmetry constraint will appear throughout this book; its application seems to be virtually universal. Symmetry provides the foundation for our Theory of Veridical 3D Shape Perception.

The idea of applying *a priori* constraints to solve Inverse Problems has a long tradition in science. Collecting scientific data on the motion of objects in the presence of gravity is a Forward Problem. A scientist can drop an object from various heights and record the time it takes to hit the ground. Inferring the underlying natural law for falling bodies from experimental data is an Inverse Problem. In this example, *inferring* that the body falls with constant acceleration, as Galileo did, represents his solution of this Inverse Problem. It should come as no surprise to anybody who has used regression analysis to fit a regression curve (function) to a set of data points that there is always more than one theory that can account for a given set of data. There is always more than one curve that can approximate the data points that represent the observed relationship between the time it takes a ball to fall from different heights. Scientists have been using William of Occam's (1285–1349) *razor*, for choosing among the various functions at least since Francis Bacon's (1561–1626) day. This criterion simply says that the simplest curve should be chosen. In our example, we would choose a quadratic curve ($f(x) = ax^2 + bx + c$), despite the fact that polynomials of a degree higher than 2 would have produced slightly better fits of the curve to our data. This is done because a quadratic curve is *simpler* than other polynomial curves and we decided that simplicity is more important than accuracy. So, once we realize that symmetry is a form of simplicity, the observer's recovery of the 3D shape of a chair can be seen as an example of our visual system applying Occam's razor to the perception of 3D shape.

We are assuming that the distinction between direct and inverse problems is now clear. It should also be clear by now that this distinction resembles Thomas Reid's (1764) distinction between sensations and perception, and the distinction between retinal image formation and visual perception. Here the reader might ask whether the introduction of the new terms *direct* and *inverse* accomplished anything special. Could we have used more familiar terms such as deductive vs. inductive reasoning equally well? Why do you want to use these new terms? We use these terms rather than the older, more common, terms, simply because they are the terms used in a modern branch of Applied Mathematics. This modern branch of mathematics provides a set of powerful computational methods to solve inverse problems (Tikhonov & Arsenin, 1977). These modern methods are very important because they actually allow us to solve what many thought were impossible problems, such as recovering 3D shapes and 3D scenes. There are two classes within these methods, one is called the Regularization method and the other is called the Bayesian method. As our work on making the machine that sees progressed, it became clear that these two methods actually represented two quite different kinds or classes, an insight that until now had not been appreciated by us or by anyone we know. This new distinction makes it possible for us to add something new to the discussion of what has been called the *nature–nurture problem* ever since Descartes' day. This distinction allows us to contrast the role of learning with the role of built-in *a priori* processes in perception in a quantitative way.

1.9 How Bayesian Inference Can Be Used for Modeling Perception

We already pointed out the connection between the regularization (deterministic) and Bayesian (probabilistic) methods when we described the nature of Inverse Problems and the role of *a priori* simplicity constraints in solving them. The deterministic approach, which uses the Regularization method with its cost function and *a priori* constraints, was used first in perceptual modeling. The probabilistic approach, which uses Bayes's rule with priors, was tried later. Now, almost everyone believes that these two methods are conceptually and mathematically equivalent (e.g., Chater, 1996). But, are they really equivalent? We think not. There is an important conceptual difference.

Recall that the *Bayesian methods* recognize the importance of what Bayesians call *priors*, but they try to minimize the effect of their priors on the final solution of Inverse Problems by adding a sufficient amount of data to obtain the solution. They assume as little as possible and use brute force, not finesse, to solve their Inverse Problems. Priors in the Bayesian approach, have only a supplementary status. They do not provide the basis for the solution. Their initial assumption, perhaps only a bias, seems to be that, in the best of all possible worlds, the inference underlying the problem's solution can be based on the likelihood function, itself. The priors are needed *only to improve* the inference. The priors are not the mechanisms required for a veridical solution. In contrast, *a priori* constraints play a primary role in our *Regularization method*. They are essential. *A priori* constraints are used *not* to refine the solution; they provide the basis for the solution. Without them the inference problem remains ill-posed. It cannot be solved at all.

With this large conceptual difference on the table, consider the issue of updating priors in the Bayesian method. Updating priors is an essential element of the Bayesian method because in most Inverse Problems the first prior is chosen without having any information about it, whatsoever. So, the Bayesian prior is usually non-informative. Consider first the case in which there is only a small number of hypotheses (possible solutions). Take for example an ordinary die (half a pair of dice) that you suspect might be loaded (one face is more likely to come up than the other 5), but you do not have any information about which of the 6 faces is more likely to turn up than expected by chance. If we assume that the die is symmetrical, it means that the probability of observing any one of the six outcomes 1, 2, 3, 4, 5 or 6, is 1/6 (the priors are equal). We then roll the die 70 times and the frequencies with which individual faces turn up are: 10, 12, 9, 8, 10, 21, respectively. The face 6 was observed approximately twice as often as any of the other faces. We may conclude that the die is loaded with the face 6 being two times more likely than any of the other faces. This conclusion is not guaranteed to be accurate because we only rolled the die a few dozen times. But, this conclusion (posterior in Bayesian terminology) is probably closer to an accurate description of the die than our original uninformed guess that was based on the assumption of equal priors. If we roll the die a few more dozen times, we can refine our description of the die. But now, we can, and will, use the *posterior* from the first set of rolls as a *prior*, and the new set of results will produce a new *posterior*. The more times we roll the die, the more accurate our description will become. Note that our conclusion that the die was loaded came from making observations of its performance; we *learned* what it tended to do by rolling it repeatedly.

In contrast, when a *Regularization Method* is used in 3D shape recovery, informative *a priori* constraints are used when we start, and they are not updated (modified) as data are collected. In other words, learning is neither natural, nor essential, in the Regularization Method we use. By way of explanation, consider how a 3D shape can be recovered from a single 2D retinal image. You already know that all natural shapes are symmetrical or nearly symmetrical. So, symmetry seems likely to be an important *a priori* constraint. There is no need to learn anything about the object to form an *a priori* constraint of symmetry because symmetry is defined as the self-similarity of the object. Put differently, symmetry is defined by using geometrical transformations not by learning from particular examples. As Plato would surely say, *symmetry existed before objects came into existence*. He would also expect symmetry to continue to exist after all objects disappear. Abstract concepts are permanent as well as insubstantial (lack substance). The problem with Bayesian priors becomes even more apparent when infinitely many solutions are possible. An infinity of possible solutions is the rule, rather than the exception, in the recovery of 3D shapes and scenes. The Bayesian method requires assigning an *a priori* probability to each interpretation (3D shape) even when there are infinitely many possible 3D interpretations for any given 2D retinal image. Technically, there can be no uniform prior in this case, because such a prior would have to assign a small positive number to each solution. But, were this done, the sum of all these probabilities would be infinitely large, a clear violation of the axioms of probability. So, one must use a non-uniform prior, not a uniform one. This is tricky because in the absence of any information about the priors, it is not easy to decide which solutions should be considered to be the more-likely *a priori*. There is a theory of how to assign such priors (Solomonoff, 1964; Rissanen, 1978; Li & Vitanyi, 1997), but doing it in practice leads to problems. In the case of 3D shape recovery, it is not clear how such priors could actually be computed and then updated for *infinitely* many 3D shapes in a *finite* amount of time. How do you construct a prior probability density function that can be used with *all* possible shapes, including shapes that have never existed? How do you construct a single prior density function that would adequately handle such a variety of objects as human and animal bodies, coffee cups, needles, cars, crumpled papers, houses, lamps?

The answer is *not* to assign priors to all possible 3D shape interpretations, but to assign them only to some abstract aspects of 3D shapes, such as symmetries. So, the *priors used in the Bayesian approach are conceptually quite different from the kind of a priori constraints we need and use in our computational model of 3D shape recovery.* The mathematics are the same but these tools are used quite differently in each approach.

The Regularization Method we use is much simpler than the Bayesian Method conceptually as well as computationally. There are only handful of relevant symmetries, namely, mirror, translational and rotational. So, instead of assigning *a priori* probabilities to infinitely many 3D shapes, we only have to assign *a priori* probabilities to only 3 types of symmetries. One can recover the 3D shape veridically by applying one of these 3 types of *a priori* symmetry constraints to a 2D retinal shape. Furthermore, *all* 3D shapes can be recovered by applying one of only 3 *a priori* symmetry constraints to any 2D image produced by the object's 3D shape. Recall that the symmetry of a 3D shape refers to its self-similarity. As such, symmetry is an intrinsic property of an object independent of our experience with it. To put this claim in a broader context by paraphrasing the Aristotelian axiom: *not everything that is in the mind must be in the senses first.* Particular objects are instantiations of the *universal* mathematical concept called symmetry: symmetry is *not* abstracted from particular objects. The most natural, perhaps even commonsensical, way is to think about symmetry as an *a priori* simplicity constraint, rather than as a prior related to the likelihood of the object being present or the amount of experience we have had with it. We believe that the difference we have pointed out between the Bayesian and Regularization approaches to solving Inverse Problems is as profound and as likely to engender controversy as the Nature vs. Nurture controversy that has consumed philosophers and scientists ever since Descartes' and Locke's day.

To summarize, a great deal of effort has been put into formulating mathematical foundations for solving ill-posed inverse problems since the 1960s. Mathematicians have worked hard to make their methods as general as possible by establishing the equivalence of deterministic and probabilistic approaches. They did this by showing how both can be applied to all infinitely many objects and events, even to those that do not exist now and can never be observed. These efforts have been valuable, but one must not stop with what we have now. A visual system like ours has to function effectively. It must provide the observer with fast and accurate information about his environment. It follows that a theory of our visual system must take the form of a working computational model, or even better, a machine that can actually see like us. The next section will explain, in detail, exactly what we mean when we talk about a model.

1.10 What It Means to Have a Model of Vision, and Why We Need to Have One?

Obviously, a machine that sees like us can perform many useful tasks. It can do almost anything that we can do under visual guidance. This includes tasks that are fun as well as tasks that are dangerous or boring. It can play games with us, even games without formal rules like chess or solitaire: it can play games based on imitating what it sees us do. The machine can even baby-sit our children because it sees the world as we do. It can know when a child is hiding behind some object because it can see the back, invisible parts of all objects, as well as the open spaces among them. There is also scientific merit in having a machine like this. It is not all fun and games. It can serve as a computational model in psychophysical experiments where the machine's performance can be compared with a human being's. When used this way, the model's free parameters can be estimated and the psychological plausibility of the model can be evaluated simply by comparing the model's performance with the human being's. This idea is not new; computational models of visual functions have been used before. Kenneth Craik (1914–1945) proposed using machines and algorithms to simulate human performance 70 years ago when the ancestors of today's computers could barely do fast multiplications and divisions, much less solve difficult computational problems. Unfortunately, the word model no longer has the unambiguous meaning in the vision community that it had in Craik's day (1943). Today, the word model can refer to many different things. Model can be a synonym for a (1) verbally stated theory, (2) mathematically stated theory, (3) hypothesis or a speculation, (4) 3D object or class of objects used by an algorithm for object recognition, and (5) cause to be inferred from data in Inverse Problems Theory. We prefer to use the term model differently. We use it in a way that is very close to what Craik had in mind. The best way to explain this is to begin by describing how Brindley (1960) dealt with the burgeoning new knowledge about visual neurophysiology that became available shortly after WWII. New data obtained by recording from single units in the retina by Kufler and Hubel & Wiesel and others had generated a lot of interest at that time and Brindley wanted to know how human psychophysical data, the behavioral data he liked to use, could be used to make valid inferences about these exciting new physiological phenomena. He started by defining two types of psychophysical experiments. He called them Class A and Class B. In Brindley's words: "Class A observations.... include the results of matching experiments and of determinations of thresholds, both absolute and incremental." (p. 145).

In a Brindley's Class A experiment, the observers might be asked to match two slightly different stimuli. For example, they could be presented with two line-segments and their task was to match their lengths. Their ability to see differences in line-length (the variability associated with their average setting) was estimated by a difference threshold (DL). Several psychophysical methods can be used to perform Class A experiments, namely, the Method of Adjustment, Constant Stimuli, or Signal Detection. Brindley considered Class A experiments the only ones that can be used to make *valid* claims about the physiological underpinnings of the stimuli perceived. He explained this claim by pointing out that if two percepts are different, the underlying brain states must also be different. But, if two brain states are identical, the resulting percepts must identical; they cannot be told apart because there cannot be a mental state without activity in the brain. Brindley called this logical construction his linking hypothesis.

Brindley went on to say that: "Any observation that cannot be expressed as the identity or non-identity of two sensations will be called a Class B observation. Class B observations include all those in which the subject must describe the quality or intensity of his sensations, or abstract from two different sensations some aspect in which they are alike.... The most completely satisfactory way of using a Class B observation to test a physiological hypothesis is to convert it into one belonging to Class A" (p. 147).

Brindley's emphasis on Class A experiments has passed the test of time. Much of what we know about sensory coding today is based on thresholds measured in Class A experiments. Thresholds can be measured reliably and since the introduction of (1) the Signal Detection Method for measuring Receiver Operating Characteristics (ROC), (2) methods for establishing the Speed-Accuracy Tradeoff (SAT) and the Attention Operating Characteristics (AOC) have been developed. These relatively new methods can actually separate the observer's percept from the variability in his data contributed by decision processes (response biases). The methods used for threshold measurements before these techniques were developed were introduced by Gustav Fechner's (1801–1887) in a book he titled Elements of Psychophysics, published in 1860. So, today, we can say that we really know what is going on when an observer says that two line-segments are different. But, despite the merit of such Class A experiments, a big problem remains. Class A experiments can only be used to answer a single question, namely, can two stimuli be discriminated (told apart). There are many more important questions in perception. We often want to know how things look and why they look as they do (the underlying perceptual mechanisms). Phenomenology (how things look) can be answered simply by asking observers to describe their percepts. As pointed out earlier, Brindley called these kinds of observations Class B experiments. In Class B experiments, there is no established way to separate the observer's percept from his response bias on the basis of their verbal descriptions. Brindley dealt with this problem by recommending that Class B questions should be answered by reformulating them to make it possible to use a Class A experiment to answer them. This suggestion was useful but it only goes so far. Brindley's suggestion permits us to understand the relationship between a physical stimulus and its sensory coding (what Reid called sensations) very well, but this tells us nothing about the relationship between what Reid called perceptions, and the properties that reside in objects out there. We believe that progress can be made toward filling in this gap by elaborating Brindley's classification. The properties of objects out there can be incorporated into how we perceive real objects in natural environments. This can only be done by using a model, a computational tool that solves the ill-posed Inverse Problem of recovering 3D objects and scenes. One can think of our proposal as adding a third kind of experiment, called Class C, to Brindley's classification. Class C experiments will use a model to understand how the visual system solves ill-posed Inverse Problems.

What do we mean by a model? First, consider what a 3D shape perception model would be like. It is a machine, usually in the form of a computer algorithm that recovers a veridical 3D shape from 2D images. Once such a model is at hand, it is easy to figure out how a 3D shape looks to the model. One can then ask an observer to reconstruct a 3D shape from 2D images by using standard computer graphics tools. We already know how to use such tools in this kind of experiment (see, Li, 2009; Li et al., 2009; 2011; Sawada & Pizlo, 2008). Once a 3D shape has been recovered by the model and a 3D shape has been reconstructed by the observer, we can compare these two shapes to determine whether the model and the observer are actually seeing the same thing. If they are, we are entitled to say that we have a "model of human 3D shape perception." But, note that great care must be exercised when claiming that a model is explaining how an observer perceives a given 3D object. Recall that a percept represents an object's *permanent* properties out there. If this is not the case, the percept *cannot* be veridical. Said slightly differently, one has to be careful to verify that the model actually models how the object looks unconfounded with the viewing conditions. This cannot be emphasized too much nor said too often. So, when anyone tries to develop a model of 3D shape perception, the developer *must* verify that *both* the model and the observer achieve *shape constancy*. They must see the 3D shape veridically from any viewing orientation. The failure to use this kind of verification by demonstrating shape constancy in what is meant to be a shape experiment can lead one astray. Unfortunately, it often has.

Once our model is in place, we can claim not only that it can see like us, we can also claim that the model is sufficient to explain the underlying perceptual mechanisms. Technically, we would say that the model explained how the visual system solves the Inverse Problem by showing which *a priori* constraints are used by the human visual system to solve this ill-posed problem, as well as how these constraints are used.

1.11 End of the Beginning

We set out to develop a machine that can see like us because, at present, the best way to test a theory in vision is to develop this kind of machine. This was done in two stages. We started by developing a computational model that had the ability to see the world as we do. We, then, implemented this model in an autonomous machine. The basic idea here was that the machine's ability to see the 3D world as well as we do would be a particularly convincing way to demonstrate the success of our efforts. What could be better than being able to compare the machine's visual recovery of a real 3D scene with what you see when you look at it with your own eyes? This approach has seldom even been attempted by others working in vision today. We know of no example of anyone having been even partially successful when it was tried. More often than not, contemporary researchers studying vision put together a more or less coherent set of hunches in plain English and then treat them as though they were a theoretical treatment of some visual process or mechanism. Even when mathematical, rather than verbal tools or a computational model are used, its success is often tested with artificial visual images or with a handful of natural images selected because the math was chosen or the model was developed specifically to handle them. Such verbal theories and skimpy quantitative models add little or, more often than not, nothing to our knowledge about any important problem in vision. This kind of science, which was the best one could do some years ago, no longer passes muster. Theory, experimental methods and instrumentation have advanced sufficiently for us to insist that researchers studying vision should be much more ambitious. These days, a rather complete, working theory of some obviously significant aspect of visual processing should be required of anyone wishing to contribute to this specialty. These requirements can be met by insisting that any theory published now satisfies at least two criteria, specifically, the theory must be relatively complete, and it must not have any implicit or any unjustified, explicit assumptions. The best way to meet these criteria is to build a machine that actually sees as we do. This is not an easy task and the challenges it provides can be appreciated by considering some of the insights that prepared the way for doing this.

It started in Descartes' day when he pointed out that the visual, and other sensory systems, were separate as well as different from the motor systems. The mere fact they were different encouraged our scientific forbears to study them separately. The main justification for their doing this was simply that it could be done, but toward the end of the 19th Century, it began to become clear that the sensory and motor systems are not nearly as independent as their treatment up till then warranted. The actions of one system *always* had important influences on the other. Once this issue was raised, attempts began to be made to study the sensory and motor processes working together, rather than separately. Dewey (1896) inspired this movement by emphasizing that perception is not a distinct and passive process in a publication about the reflex arc. Dewey described perception as only one part of a closed, continuously active sensory-motor system. Dewey said that the arc was more like a circle or a loop. He called this loop the perception-action cycle. In this cycle, perception and motor actions follow one another and interact continuously as the human being goes about his daily life. This claim is not only more than 100 years old, it was accepted and elaborated often since it was proposed by Dewey, who credits William James (1890) for pointing him in this direction. Hebb accepted and built this idea into his physiological theory of vision on it in 1949, and Gibson gave this interaction an important role in three books in which visual perception was viewed as an active process, published in 1950, 1966, and 1979. Gibson's treatment of interactive vision is called ecologically valid vision today. Note that this integration of sensory and motor actions is not only hallowed by time, it also makes a lot of sense. Unfortunately, this insight tends to be de-emphasized, and even completely ignored today in vision, despite its obvious importance. Such neglect is unfortunate because the observer (human, animal, or machine) must seek information about its environment actively. It does this by using more than one viewing direction. In the real world, this must be done if only to verify that the initial viewing direction allowed the scene to be perceived veridically (accurately). Veridical perception is critical for planning effective behavioral acts, acts that achieve desired goals. Such acts cannot succeed if the perception of the scene is not accurate. The best way to study interactive processing is to develop a machine that sees and acts like us. Studying vision in a disembodied eyeball or in an immobilized human or machine cannot add much to what we know about seeing.

Making a model that sees and acts like us has both theoretical and practical implications. Appreciating the theoretical importance of making such machines is not new. It is important because it is the best, perhaps even the only way, to be certain that you really understand what is going on. This claim can be traced back at least to a proposal by Miller, Galanter & Pribram (1960), who pioneered the development of what is now called cognitive science. They said that, "The creation of a model is proof of the clarity of the vision. If you understand how a thing works well enough to build your own, then your understanding must be nearly perfect" (p. 46). Stephen Hawking (2001) reported that Richard Feynman had a similar proposal on his blackboard at the time of his death in 1988. It said what I cannot create I don't understand. These claims make a lot of sense. They did, however, present us with a huge challenge, as well as encouragement, when we set out to develop our machine. Accepting this challenge meant that our machine would have to perceive its 3D world as well as we could. Finally, the machine that will be described in this book can deliver food in hospitals and trim grass as well as any off-the-shelf machines you can buy today, but these machines are not at all like ours. They do not see the world as we do. The tools they use to navigate are not like ours. The machine we made does see like us. This difference is important because it means that our machine can emulate visually guided human activities within natural human environments. The rest of this book explains how we made this machine and how it does what it does so well.

2

How This All Got Started

2.1 Controversy About Shape Constancy: 1980–1995

Our work on 3D shape, which led to making the machine that sees like us, started in 1995 when we set out to resolve an important, longstanding controversy. Investigators were arguing about whether the phenomenon called *shape constancy* actually existed. Both sides on this issue had some support. Rock & DiVita (1987), and others, had shown that we do not have shape constancy, while Biederman & Gerhardstein (1993) had shown that we do. Very different stimuli had been used in their experiments. Rock used what we now call *amorphous* bent wires. Biederman used much more complex objects composed of the highly symmetrical elements called *geons* (Fig. 1.9). Geons were designed to represent the kinds of shape elements that could be used to construct familiar 3D objects, including animal bodies, simply by putting them together in appropriate configurations. Geons were meant to serve much as our alphabet and morphemes serve for language. Despite the glaring difference between the stimuli that led to this controversy, nobody had taken the trouble to try to reconcile the controversy before we took it on. Shape constancy was on the back burner at this time because most people were working on other perceptual problems such as mental rotation, visual representation (2D vs. 3D), perceptual learning, viewpoint invariance, and perceptual similarity. Despite the obvious importance of shape constancy, it was probably being ignored simply because, at that time, like now, the need to publish papers and get grant support encouraged almost everyone to work on what everybody thought were the cutting edge topics of the time.

Biederman's conclusion was startling, as well as unique, because all prior research on shape constancy, as well as on all of the other constancies, indicated that constancy was far from perfect even when it was demonstrated convincingly. Biederman showed clearly that shape constancy is a robust, compelling visual phenomenon, hardly the kind of phenomenon that would be hard to show. Everyone, including Biederman, underestimated how easy it would be to show and how big this effect would be. Despite what he had found, he stopped short of claiming that shapes are perceived *veridically*, as they really are out there. He was only willing to commit himself to saying that his subjects recognized his shapes rather well on the basis of the qualitative features provided by his geons. Even this modest conclusion came under massive attack from all sides. Edelman and his associates at MIT criticized Biederman's neglect of metric features, such as the aspect ratios, angles, and curvatures of his stimuli. They also did not like his assumption that we see 3D stimuli as 3D (you heard about this before). Another group led by Tarr at Brown attacked Biederman for his claims that shapes can be recognized from different viewing directions (viewpoint invariance) and for his outrageous assumption that visual perception is three-dimensional (3D). A third group, led by Todd at Ohio state and Koenderink in Utrecht did accept Biederman's assumption that there *could* be 3D visual representations, but they did not like Biederman's geons or his claim that the shape was perceived as the same when it was viewed from different directions (viewpoint invariance). Durgin and Eagle attacked Biederman's attackers by showing that 3D shapes *can* be perceived veridically and by calling attention to a number of methodological flaws in the work of those attacking Biederman. Clearly doing shape research back then was a risky undertaking. One could say back then that the academy was more jungle than ivory tower. This situation continued for about 10 years before it subsided. It never actually died out completely but it lost most of its force for two reasons. The younger generation was discouraged because it made it hard to publish papers and get grant support. The then younger generation was either forced out of studying shape perception or overwhelmed by boredom. We remember members of the younger generation freely admitting that they had stopped working on shape simply because the rancor was so great that it had become impossible to build a career. By 1995, when we started working on shape, almost no one else was. The word *shape* had disappeared from the titles of sessions at conferences, as well as from all undergraduate textbooks on Sensation & Perception. This was not entirely bad news. There were fewer people around to argue with us, but those who were around were convinced that the shape constancy phenomenon simply did not, could not, and would not exist if they could do anything about it.

We had an entirely different view. For us it was clear that it was *shape constancy* that made shape special. If a chair actually did change its shape when it was viewed from different viewing directions, one simply could not function. Shape perception *must* be veridical. How could we prove this claim? Biederman's side of this argument was obviously much more plausible than its alternative. The only way we could see to *prove* this was to show that Biederman, and only Biederman, was actually studying shape. Rock must be studying something else. Looking at the stimuli used in the two experiments suggested that the bent wire might not have "shape." Biederman's stimuli obviously did. Common sense told us that there was a real difference between these stimuli but understanding what was going on was hard because we did not have a formal definition of what we meant by *shape*. We needed a formal definition or at least some operational criterion to take the next step. The operational definition, explained in Section 1.3, did the trick. We began our research by introducing the concept of *symmetry* because it is a very common property of our natural world. This seemed to be the most direct and simplest way to bring *a priori* constraints into a formal definition of shape, the kind of definition we needed to explain shape constancy. We had no idea when we started just how important symmetry would ultimately prove to be. We shared a gut feeling that some kind of built-in mechanism would work better than learning for explaining constancy but we had little more to work with. Symmetry, when we started, had been neglected in perception since the Gestalt Psychologists' influence had waned in the 1960s. It had received some attention from Julesz at Bell Labs who was using random dot patterns to study what he called *texture segregation* (how a boundary appears between two regions of a textured pattern). He noticed that the mirror symmetry of a dotted pattern can be detected easily even with complex patterns of dots, even when the pattern had *thousands* of dots. A little later, Barlow at Cambridge took up this topic and showed that not all dots in such stimuli are equally important for the perception of symmetry. Unfortunately, neither of these studies of symmetry had bearing on the perception of shape. The role of built-in machinery, *a priori* constraints, had been emphasized by the Gestalt Psychologists in their heyday, but by 1990, the importance of their simplicity principle had almost faded completely. Now that you know what was going on, we will describe the experiment that proved that Biederman was studying shape and Rock was not.

The stimuli used in our 1995 experiment were designed to satisfy several criteria. The objects should be ecologically relevant. They should represent the types of objects we regularly deal with in our everyday life. Such stimuli will ensure that our laboratory experiment has relevance for how shape perception operates under normal conditions. It will also guarantee that shape constancy is achieved because we knew that everyone sees shapes veridically under these conditions. The stimuli should also be complex because complexity is what makes shape unique. Next, they should not resemble familiar objects, like animals, airplanes, teapots, chairs and tables, as they did in Biederman's first experiment. We wanted to be sure that familiarity played no role in our experiment. We wanted to exclude the possibility of a contribution from learning as much as possible. Finally, we wanted to be able to change our naturalistic stimulus, simulating Biederman's, in such a way that it could resemble Rock's bent wire; the amorphous stimulus that should cause shape constancy to fail completely. All of these criteria were met with the truck-like stimulus shown in Figure 2.1. We all perceive trucks and similar objects the way they are *out there*. If we did not, driving around a busy parking lot would be impossible. We used the truck-like stimuli in our experiment in part

FIGURE 2.1. Our truck stimulus. The wheels shown in this figure were not present in the stimuli used in our experiments.

because we could remove all familiarity from our truck simply by removing its wheels. We generated each truck-stimulus with a lot of random variability of its 3D structure. We were careful to preserve all important aspects of its structure when we did this, specifically, its mirror symmetry and its overall geometry. The truck-like shape we used had the following features: (1) it had a small box in front that represented the driver's cabin, (2) it had a larger box in back that represented the part used to carry cargo, and (3) both the large and smaller box always rested on a common plane. It was easy to satisfy all of these requirements because it is not hard to write a computer program to generate such stimuli. Furthermore, simply looking at a few made it clear that they would allow perfect, or near-perfect, shape constancy to be achieved. Recall that we wanted to replicate not only Biederman's results showing perfect shape constancy, but also Rock's showing complete failure of constancy. We did this by connecting the 16 vertices of the truck by a polygonal line (bent wire) in a random order (Figure 2.2). We also presented intermediate stimuli whose regularity varied systematically.

Our experiment was ready (Pizlo & Stevenson, 1999). The two authors served as subjects for several weeks to be sure that their performance had reached its asymptote: more practice would not make performance better. We wanted to be sure that we had achieved as much constancy as we possibly could. Once we knew that this had been accomplished, we ran two naïve subjects to verify that knowing what we were trying to do had no effect on the results we got. All of the subjects achieved a lot of shape constancy and naïveté did not matter. For our technical readers, shape constancy, as measured by the signal detectability measure, d′, was close to perfect with the symmetrical polyhedral

(a) 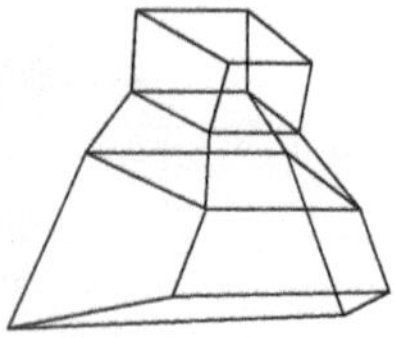 (b) 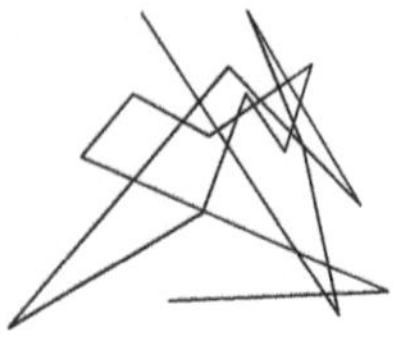

FIGURE 2.2. Stimulus to test Biederman's result (a) and Rock's result (b). (From Pizlo, Z. (2008) 3D shape: its unique place in visual perception. MIT Press. With permission of The MIT Press.)

objects, but failed completely with the bent wire objects. Furthermore, the degree of shape constancy achieved could be manipulated by varying the degree of geometrical features, namely, the symmetry, the planarity, and the topological relationships among the faces of the polyhedron. For our other readers, the amount of constancy achieved depended on the amount of shape in the particular stimulus: the more the shape, the more closely the percept resembled the shape out there.

We did not stop here. By the time this study was published, we had replicated it with different viewing conditions. We used different cues for depth, substituting binocular disparity (slightly different views in each eye) for motion parallax (slightly different views obtained from a single eye by moving the stimulus) and got the same results (Chan et al., 2006). This was a breakthrough because these experiments *resolved the shape controversy unambiguously; a controversy that had raged for 20 years.* So, shape constancy can, in fact, be achieved reliably, providing only that the object actually has shape. It cannot be achieved if it does not. We were extremely pleased with these findings. As you also might expect, not everyone shared our enthusiasm. One reviewer called our paper "the worst study he has ever seen." Another reviewer dismissed our results because "he was never able to achieve shape constancy in his lab," ignoring the obvious fact that he had used amorphous stimuli, a problem made clear in our manuscript.[1] It became clear at this point, at least for us and a handful of other scientists, that shape constancy *is* a real phenomenon, and that *a priori* constraints are essential. But this did not happen overnight: it took 3 years to publish the first paper and 7 years to publish the second. This delay was not caused by disruptions in the postal system. It would take just as long today because it is difficult to get clear evidence for controversial ideas into print.

Despite of all the fussing and quibbling required to get this stuff published, it was clear to us that it was important, even essential, that we continue to study shape. We needed a theory of shape perception to do this, but we did not know which, if any, of the contemporary approaches would

[1]This reviewer is now on board. He has demonstrated reliable shape constancy with naturalistic stimuli.

work for us. The framework provided by the Theory of Inverse Problems and Regularization were in the air when we faced this problem. Fifteen years had elapsed since Poggio et al. (1985) had brought the Theory of Inverse Problems to the attention of the vision community and Knill & Richards (1996) had just published a book summarizing what was known about the role of constraints in vision. The theoretical framework of Inverse Problems was known to many, but there were only a few examples that showed that it could be used in human vision. The field of vision, at the time, was still heavily under the influence of Marr's view of *vision*. According to Marr, the primary function of vision was to reconstruct 3D surfaces. In other words, for Marr it did not matter whether the surface belongs to a TV set, a fox, a box, or a bird. It was the surface, not the shape, of an object that mattered. Once the surface, not the shape, was important, it was clear that you had very little to work with. Only surface smoothness and rigidity were tried as *a priori* constraints. These constraints can be easily implemented in computational models, but, once this was done it was not clear what could be done next. Furthermore, it was not clear how to test these simple models in psychophysical experiments. The smoothness of a surface cannot predict much about visual perception. The only known psychophysical result that suggested that this constraint was actually used by the visual system was the well-known underestimation of the slant of a surface. But this trivial perceptual result had already been explained by several other models, so it was not clear that another model was needed. The bottom line is that despite the theoretical appeal of the Theory of Inverse Problems, it did not stimulate research in vision because this theory can only be as interesting as its underlying *a priori* constraints. There cannot be a useful theory of *shape perception* formulated within this framework, unless the theory uses *a priori shape* constraints. The reader surely knows by now that our theory of shape perception uses a symmetry constraint. Poggio, who called the vision community's attention to the potential of the Theory of Inverse Problems, was among those who showed how mirror symmetry can be used to reconstruct a 3D shape from a single 2D image (Vetter & Poggio, 1994). Unfortunately, he overlooked the fundamental importance of his observation for a general theory of shape perception. Had he appreciated what symmetry could do for shape perception, he might have advanced the acceptance of the Theory of Inverse Problems and our understanding of shape perception before we did.

So, when we were finally ready to use the Theory of Inverse Problems to explain human vision, no one was even interested in hearing about this, much less in doing it. It had been pretty much discounted a few years before we started. This was not without practical consequences. This became painfully obvious when one of us submitted a review on Inverse Problems, intended to alert the vision community to what we thought was a new and exciting way of modeling human vision. Initially, it was rejected because "everyone knows about this and everyone is doing it." This came as a shock. Fortunately, it was not hard to convince the Editor, who had rejected the paper on the basis of this claim, simply by pointing out that there were hardly any "Inverse" papers published in her journal, or anywhere else, for that matter. The review on the Theory of Inverse Problems was published in 2001 and we began to use this formalism to develop our new theory of shape perception at that time (Pizlo, 2001). It was novel because it was the first time that the solution of a perception problem was assumed to rely primarily on *a priori* constraints, rather than on visual cues.

We used the psychophysical results of the truck experiments, which had established the existence and robustness of the shape constancy phenomenon, to formulate our first shape model. The fundamental importance of symmetry was not obvious in 1995–1999, when these studies were run, so our first model solved the Inverse Problem of recovering a 3D shape from a 2D input by using only two constraints, namely, planarity (surfaces look flat) and the minimum variance of angles (all angles are similar to each other). Symmetry was not used. These two constraints had been used by others for about 10 years when we started our work. The planarity constraint works by restricting the family of possible interpretations of a line drawing of a typical 3D polyhedral object (our truck) to just three. Take a cube as an example. Even though the cube has 8 vertices, only 3 of them can be independently changed if you want to change the 3D shape but keep the faces planar (flat). This means that the planarity constraint, used alone, still allows infinitely many 3D interpretations. The 3D shapes in this infinitely large family have different angles among their faces and the faces have different aspect-ratios. We are searching for only one of these 3D interpretations. How can we select a *unique* 3D interpretation? This is done by choosing a 3D object that has a minimum variance of angles (all angles are similar to each other). This measure tends to maximize the 3D object's volume, as well as its symmetry. It was clear from the start that this first model had serious limitations because these two constraints (planarity and minimum variance of angles) can only be applied to synthetic 3D objects like our truck. They cannot be applied to the 2D images of ecologically-significant natural objects, like animal and human bodies. There is no meaningful way of defining the angles around and within the body of a horse. Our trucks do not present this problem, so, in 2003, one of us[2], looking for a master's project, decided to fix this by substituting a maximum 3D compactness constraint for the minimum variance of angles constraint and used it to recover 3D boxes from single 2D images.

[2]Li.

Maximum 3D compactness is better than the minimum variance of angles because it can be applied to *any* 3D shape. This works because maximizing 3D compactness is equivalent to maximizing the volume of the 3D object. The preliminary results were not particularly encouraging. The maximum 3D compactness constraint was not substantially better than the minimum variance of angles constraint. It was also not clear how this model could be applied to natural objects that were not like our truck. Working with objects that were not polyhedral was not possible at this point because we did not know what could be substituted for the planarity constraint. We needed a constraint that could be used with natural objects. Is there another way we can restrict the number of parameters? Is there another constraint? Symmetry seemed like a natural choice, but when we had tried symmetry a few years earlier we had not been impressed with its effectiveness. It did improve the model's performance but not by very much. Also, our psychophysical results on shape constancy had not indicated that symmetry is critical. The subjects' performance in our truck experiments was similar with both symmetrical and asymmetrical truck-stimuli. It was not obvious to us at that time that symmetry is not a binary characteristic. The stimulus was either symmetrical or it was not symmetrical. For some mysterious reason, we thought that symmetry was more like pregnancy than beauty. The fact that an object is not mirror-symmetrical does not mean that it is completely asymmetrical. This issue remained open for three years. In the Spring of 2006 when the "3D shape" book was being finished, the original plan was to end the book with our original model that only worked with polyhedral objects, the model we had on hand. But when one of us[3] read the manuscript, he was kind enough to point out that if we do not have a plausible model that can, at least in principle, handle horses, as well as "garbage cans" (the way he described our truck-like stimuli), there is no book. Clearly, something better was needed. Fortunately, it did not take long before a solution was found. The solution was found in Vetter & Poggio's (1994) paper on symmetry, where they had shown that symmetry reduces the number of free parameters to only *one*.

Substituting symmetry for planarity and substituting compactness for minimum variance of angles was sufficient to provide the necessary breakthrough. Demos based on these constraints have been shown at many invited talks and conferences since then, where, more often than not, they have been effective. Now that you know what took place right before the conference in St. Petersburg, where we showed our first working model, we have reached the beginning of the story that will unfold in this book.

---

[3]Steinman.

2.2 29th European Conference on Visual Perception (ECVP), St. Petersburg, Russia, August 20–25, 2006, Where We First Proposed Our Paradigm Shift

An opportunity to let the international vision community know that big changes were on their way showed up during the Winter of 2006 when ECVP issued its Call for Papers for its annual meeting to be held in St. Petersburg that year. The timing could not have been better. When the call was made, the manuscript for the first book devoted exclusively to the perception of shape was at the publisher and we had just added a paragraph pointing out that we had a working model that could recover the 3D shape of a synthetic polyhedral object from only one of its 2D images. We submitted the following abstract to ECVP. It was accepted without comment despite its provocative claim.

> "The last 25 years of research on 3-D shape perception have been dominated by Marr's paradigm. This paradigm makes two key assumptions: (i) perceived 3-D shape is derived from depth relations represented in a viewer-centered coordinate system (called the 2.5-D sketch), and (ii) the 2-D shape on the retina, which is a perspective image of a 3-D object, does not provide useful information, implying that figure-ground organization is not used for 3-D shape perception. A review of our recent experiments shows that these two assumptions must be rejected. The paradigm introduced by Marr must be changed. Our new paradigm makes the following assumptions: (a) perceived 3-D shape is derived from 2-D retinal shape, (b) figure-ground organization is critical: it establishes the 2-D shapes on the retina, and (c) 3-D metric properties of the shape perceived, missing from the 2-D retinal shape, are produced by applying shape constraints, not by reconstructing depth relations. Shape constraints include the symmetry and compactness of the 3-D object. 3-D reconstructions, based on our new model, are consistent with subjects' 3-D percepts." *Perception* (2006), 35, Supplement, p. 182.

Two of us[4] went to the conference in August while a third[5] stayed home to prepare a demonstration that the speaker needed to convince the audience that we were not completely out of our minds. We thought our message might be unwelcome as well as novel. The book on shape reviewed the history of shape research from 1083 CE to date. It made it clear that almost all researchers had been, and were, working on anything but shape. Almost all prior work had little or, in many cases, nothing to do with shape perception. The manuscript for the completed book was under review at that time and the reviews

---

[4]Pizlo & Steinman.

[5]Li.

trickling in were not all favorable. Other reviewers understood the story quite well and had little difficulty finding ways to praise it. One of these reviewers said that, "*The work is both original and sound. Again, the originality comes from using shape perception to guide the historical review. The manuscript is sound in that the main studies have been presented and described correctly. Overall, the book that results from this manuscript should provide vision scientists with a thorough summary of shape perception over the past 100 years.*"

This is where we stood when we arrived in Russia near the end of August. When we arrived we were *almost* prepared to do battle with any skeptics waiting for us. We still needed the demos to convince any open-minded scientists that might have been in our audience that we had good reason to propose a paradigm shift then and there. The demos were still in the works back home. We knew that we could recover 3D shapes from 2D images with the constraints in use at the time but we did not know how convincing these recoveries would be when they were shown at the Conference. Our talk was scheduled for the fourth day of the meeting and more-or-less satisfying revisions of the demo traveled back and forth on the internet until day four when time ran out. We, all three of us, were surprised, really shocked, by how good the recoveries were at that time. The recoveries were much better than we had expected. Our model *really* worked.[6]

What were conditions like in Russia while the demo was being prepared in Indiana? St. Petersburg was built on a swamp, making it very hot and humid during our stay. Our suites had lovely views of the waterways responsible for St. Petersburg being known as the "Venice of the North." We could even see the flag-decked, freshly-painted and illuminated at night, *Cruiser Aurora* from our beds. The Aurora has been a national monument since the Russo-Japanese War and the Russian Revolution. On October 25, 1917, the Aurora sparked the October Revolution by firing a blank shot, calling for the assault on the Winter Palace, the event that ended the October Revolution. It helped the Bolsheviks take over the state but when we arrived in 2006 the Soviet Union had been defunct for more than 15 years and both the hotel and the Medical Academy had received little maintenance since national funds had dried up. There was no air conditioning. Both the hotel and the conference hall were sweltering throughout our stay. We had to sit next to enormous fans as we worked on the talk and when we tried to sleep. The talk was far less stressful than preparing for it. There were about 50 people in the audience and there were no signs of hostility, polite interest at best. The potential may have been there but it was probably washed out for a number of reasons. A number of people, including those who surely did not like our paradigm shift, did not come to the conference because they anticipated a variety of problems such as the less-than-ideal

---

[6]Both the originality and efficacy of our algorithm was recognized by U.S. Patents awarded to Pizlo *et al.* (2012, 2013) and there are several other pending patent applications related to all aspects of the work described in this book.

hotel and meeting conditions. They may have even been uncertain about being able to return to their homes. After 4 days of suffering in the heat and humidity, everyone in the audience who had been brave enough to attend, was wilted, as well as exhausted from lack of sleep, when we gave our talk. Only one attendee did express the kind of enthusiasm we had hoped for. He clearly understood the story and appreciated the power of the demo he had just seen. Years later we discovered that he had been one of the anonymous reviewers of the shape book. He probably provided the praise, supported with technical comments, which got the book published. Public clashes and acrimony about our claims would not crop up for a couple of years. They loomed big at the 2008 ECVP Conference held in Utrecht a few months after the shape book had come out in print. These confrontations will be described when we reach that place in our story. We will also describe subsequent private and public confrontations because they illustrate the differences between our kind of theory of shape and all others. They became increasingly intense as our work progressed rather rapidly towards its goal. This kind of progress made our plea for a new paradigm harder and harder to ignore. Now that you know what was going on in the outside world when our story began, we will return to describing what was going on inside our laboratory after we left St. Petersburg and before the acrimonious public confrontations at the 2008 ECVP meeting in Utrecht. A lot more thought, as well as action, was needed to make an autonomous machine that sees like us.

2.3 The Role of Constraints in Recovering the 3D Shapes of Polyhedral Objects From Line-drawings

In this section, we will begin to describe how the model actually works, why it works this way, and what convinces us that it can be used to explain how the human visual system works, too. At this point, you know how we formulated our first working model for the recovery of 3D shapes, and you also are familiar with the evidence that convinced us that *a priori* constraints are essential in vision. We hope that the background provided so far is sufficient to encourage all readers to stay on board as we describe the technical steps required to reach our goal in sufficient detail to convince even our most skeptical readers.

Look at DEMO 2.1 (symmetry).[7] When you start, you see a side-view of a truck. After 2–3 seconds, the truck starts rotating, and then comes back to the original stationary view. View this a few times to see how its appearance changes as it rotates. It should be obvious to you by now that this stimulus has only one side of the truck. One side looks flat because it actually is flat, so what

---

[7] http://shapebook.psych.purdue.edu/2.1/symmetry

you perceived was veridical. One side of this truck was taken off simply to make this stimulus *asymmetrical.* When the rotation stops, you see this asymmetrical object from the original viewing direction. You could not tell that it was asymmetrical when it was at the starting position. The original stimulus looked *symmetrical.* You only discovered that it actually was not after it started rotating. Seeing symmetry, whenever you possibly can, is built-in to your visual system. Your visual system has a very strong predilection towards 3D symmetry. You will always have a symmetrical percept if a 2D image allows it to be seen. This predilection is as strong as our most compelling reflexes. It is as easy to see this *a*symmetrical stimulus as *a*symmetrical as it is to commit suicide by holding your breath.

Now, go to the second part of DEMO 2.1 (planarity).[8] Again, when you start, you see a side-view of the truck. After 2–3 seconds, the truck starts rotating, and then comes back to the original stationary view. View this a few times to see how its appearance changes as it rotates. It becomes obvious that not a single face of this stimulus is flat (planar). All of its faces are twisted. When the rotation stops, you see the original 2D stationary image. So, you also have a very strong predilection for seeing flat faces even when they really are *not* flat. Finally, go to the third part of DEMO 2.1 (compactness).[9] You see a 3D box, a cube. After 2–3 seconds, the box starts rotating. We are sure that this box looks very different than you thought it would. You thought it was a cube, but obviously it is not. It is much more like the long trailer of a tractor-trailer than like an ordinary symmetrical cube that has square faces, the way it looked when you viewed it from the direction in which it first appeared. Next time you pass a tractor-trailer on a highway, note that it actually is much longer than you thought it would be when you looked at it from behind as you pulled out to pass it. How can this illusion be explained? Geometrically, the 2D view that looked like a cube could not have been produced by a regular cube. It could only have been produced by a very elongated rectangular object. Note that the geometrical differences between the 2D images of a very elongated box and of a regular cube are very small, but the differences between the 3D objects that produced these images are very large. Figure 2.3 explains this observation. The figure on the left was produced by a very elongated rectangular object, actually by an almost infinitely elongated one. The figure on the right was produced by regular cube. If a 3D object is a cube, and if we see a lot of its top and side faces, the 2D projection of the face in front *cannot* be a perfect square. It is a perfect square in (a), but it is not in (b). Note that in (b) the 2D projection of the face in front is a parallelogram, not a square. It is only very slightly different (skewed) than the square at the front of the object (a) shown on the left. This

---

[8]http://shapebook.psych.purdue.edu/2.1/planarity

[9]http://shapebook.psych.purdue.edu/2.1/compactness

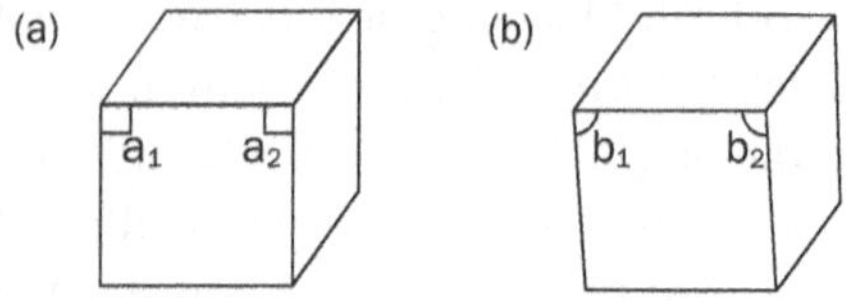

FIGURE 2.3. The front face in (a) is a perfect rectangle. Its angles, as measured on the page of this drawing are 90°. This is not the case in (b), where the two angles are slightly (by 3°) different from 90°. The rectangular brackets in (a) indicate 90° corners and the curved brackets in (b) indicate corners that are not 90°.

demo shows that the visual system has a predilection to see compact objects, rather than objects that are stretched out.

Now that you understand the geometry underlying these simple stimuli, go back to the third part of DEMO 2.1 (compactness).[10] This returns you to the original 2D image, which is *perceived* as a cube despite the fact that *geometrically* it is not a cube. These demos allow you to appreciate that your visual system has *three* very strong predilections. It favors symmetry, flatness, and compactness. Technically, 3D compactness is evaluated as V^2/S^3, where V and S are the volume and the surface area of the objects. Maximizing compactness is equivalent to maximizing volume for a given surface area. For example, a sphere is the maximally compact 3D object, and a cube is the maximally compact object built from 3 pairs of parallel quadrilaterals.

Now, that we have shown you our three *a priori* shape constraints in action, we will support our claim that using such *a priori* constraints (predilections) to make predictions about 3D shapes and scenes can be done *entirely* with the information present on the 2D retina. We will even claim that this is the rule, rather than the exception, in vision. You know this, but you do not know you know. This deliberately cryptic remark will now be explained. There is a large region in the retina of each of your eyes that has no receptors. This region is called the *optic disk*. It is there because the optic nerve, which carries information from the retina to the brain, has to get out of the eyeball to enter your brain. The optic disk is a large ellipse (6° horizontally by 8° vertically). It is located on the nasal side of each retina, 15° away from the center of the retina. We call the optic disk *large* because it is almost as big as the image of your hand held at arm's length. Another way to visualize its size is to realize that when you look at a full moon at the horizon, about *200* full moons fit into this region. Why is this big hole in your visual field invisible? Obviously, the visual system fills in the missing information, but how does it do this? Technically, the visual system uses information from around the optic disk to *predict what is likely* to be present in that part of the world out there. This relationship between the optic disk in the eye and the percept of a homogenous visual world without a hole is analogous to the relationship between the geometry of the stimulus and

[10]http://shapebook.psych.purdue.edu/2.1/compactness

how it is perceived that we just explained. The visual system's remarkable ability to make veridical predictions about spatial and temporal properties of things in the physical world provides the basis of our theory of visual perception. Its guesses about what is really out there make success in our visual world possible. Figure 2.4 is provided on the outside chance that a reader has never seen his blind spot.

Details will now be provided to explain how mirror-symmetry actually works as an *a priori* constraint. We will do this intuitively by using geometry to explain what is going on. Assume that the x-axis in Figure 2.5 represents the retinal image and the z-axis represents the direction of depth. Once this is done, recovering a 3D object from one 2D retinal image is the same as determining the z-coordinate for any given retinal point on the x-axis. In Figure 2.5, we will recover two points, P_1 and P_2, from points x_1 and x_2. Recall from our Ames's chair demo that any given retinal point determines infinitely many points out there that lie on a line emanating from the retinal point. These lines are dotted. Now take a pair of retinal points (x_1, x_2) and ask whether there is a pair of points out there (P_1, P_2), such that P_2 is a mirror image of P_1 with respect to some symmetry-axis and x_1 is an image of P_1 and x_2 is an image of P_2. The symmetry-axis is shown as a dashed axis. P_1 and P_2 are said to be mirror-symmetrical with respect to this line when the symmetry-axis bisects the line-segment P_1P_2. There are actually infinitely many such pairs of points, but only two such pairs are shown in this figure. Note that the lengths of the line-segments connecting these two pairs are different and the orientations are different, too. The pair P_1P_2, which is nearer to the retina (x-axis), forms a line-segment that is shorter and whose symmetry-axis has a larger slant (forms a larger angle with the retina). The important thing to note is that the slant is a free parameter (can take on any value), that is, it can be chosen arbitrarily anywhere within the 0° and 90° range.

Now that you know that it can be done with a pair of points, we will show you how it can be done with more than two points, as many as you will need to handle a complex object like one of our 3D trucks. Start in Figure 2.6 (top) by taking two pairs of points on the retina x_1, x_2 and x_3 and x_4 and recover two pairs of points out there P_1, P_2 and P_3, P_4, such that P_2 is a mirror

FIGURE 2.4. Close your left eye and look at (fixate) the circle on left with your right eye. At a normal reading distance the square should disappear. If it does not, slowly increase or decrease the distance between your eyes and the page. To verify that you have an optic disk in both eyes, close the right eye and look at the square. When a small object projects its image inside the optic disk of one eye and the other eye is covered or closed, the object disappears. The perceptual disappearance of an object is called the *blind spot*. This perceptual phenomenon is explained by the presence of the optic disk. The blind spot was discovered and documented for the first time in 1660 by Edme Mariotte (1620–1684).

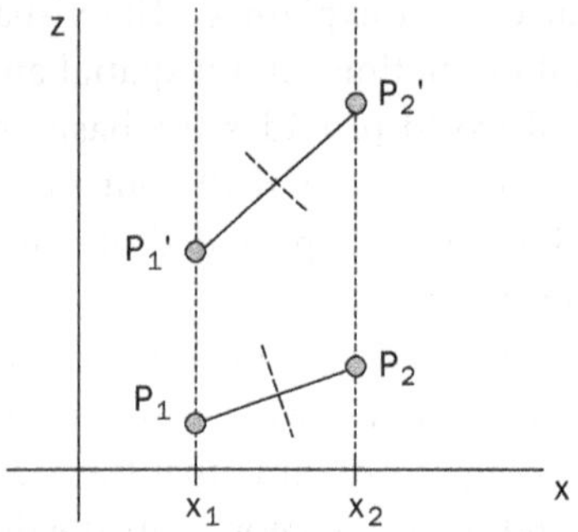

FIGURE 2.5. For any pair of image points (x_1, x_2), there are infinitely many pairs of mirror-symmetrical points (P_1, P_2), (P_1', P_2') out there. The slant of the symmetry-axis is a free parameter.

image of P_1, and P_4 is a mirror image of P_3. We want the two symmetry-axes (dashed) to have the same slant (if they do, they are parallel). Remember that this construction is possible because the slant of the symmetry-axis is a free parameter for each pair of points. So far, we have recovered two pairs of mirror-symmetrical points out there that have symmetry-axes with the same slants (they are parallel). These four points, however, do not represent a mirror-symmetrical object because the symmetry-axis of P_1, P_2 does not coincide with the symmetry-axis of P_3, P_4. They are not separated much, but they certainly do not coincide. It is easy to make them coincide—translate (slide) one pair of points out there along the depth direction. This was done in the figure on the bottom. Now that this was done, the four points P_1', P_2', P_3, and P_4 form a mirror-symmetrical configuration. This means that a single symmetry-axis exists for all four points. This kind of construction can be performed for an arbitrary number of pairs of image points, as many as you might need to describe *any* complex object.

DEMO 2.2[10] shows how we recover the 3D shape of one of our trucks from a single 2D image. This demo is analogous to the construction shown in Figure 2.6 except that now we added the third dimension to the display. The demo shows the 2D retinal image of a truck on the bottom surface. The vertical line represents the direction of the light rays that were used to form the 2D image on the retina. The 3D truck that produced this 2D image is shown above the retina. In this demo, you will see the truck changing its shape as we walk you through the family of the 3D shapes. Each truck is mirror-symmetrical and the symmetry-plane is also shown. Recall that the slant of the symmetry-plane is a free parameter. The aspect-ratio (height to base to width) of the recovered 3D

[10]http://shapebook.psych.purdue.edu/2.2

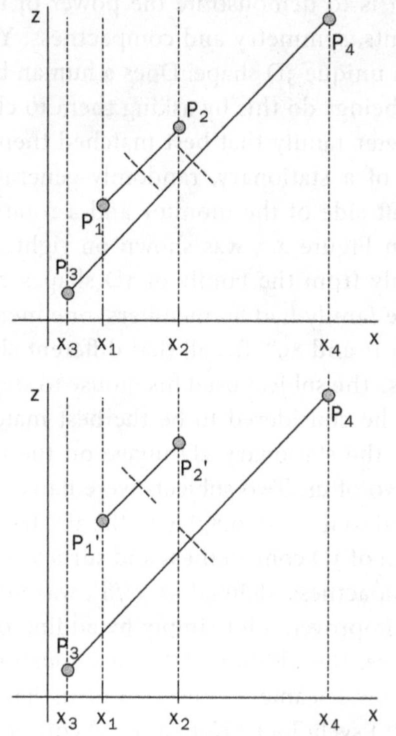

FIGURE 2.6. This figure is used to explain how a complex mirror-symmetrical object can be recovered from a single retinal image.

shape changes when the slant of the symmetry-plane changes.[11] The important thing to observe is that all 3D shapes in this family can produce the same 2D retinal image.

The next step in 3D shape recovery is to choose a *unique* 3D shape from the one-parameter family of shapes we just showed. You know that maximizing 3D compactness is the most direct way to put volume into a 3D representation and you also know that human beings have a strong predilection for maximizing compactness. Look at DEMO 2.3.[12] The 2D image in the center was used to recover eight different 3D opaque trucks. They all belong to the same family but have different aspect ratios. The most compact is the one at the 3-oclock position. By choosing this most compact 3D shape you obtained a unique solution to the 3D recovery problem.

---

[11]Some readers may have realized that we skipped over one important detail, a detail required to see the relationship between our Figures 2.5 and 2.6, and the demo. The 3D orientation of a symmetry plane, like any plane in 3D, is characterized by two parameters, slant and tilt. So far we have only spoken about slant. The tilt of the symmetry plane must be set correctly to recover a 3D shape the way we did it in our demo. How this should be done will be explained later.

[12]http://shapebook.psych.purdue.edu/2.3

Note how easy it is to demonstrate the power of two of the three of our *a priori* constraints, symmetry and compactness. You now know how our model recovers a unique 3D shape. Does a human being do it too? We showed that human beings do this by asking them to choose one member from the one parameter family that best matched their percept (Li et al., 2009). A 2D image of a stationary, randomly-generated *reference* truck was shown on the left side of the monitor and a rotating opaque 3D *test* truck, like the one in Figure 2.7, was shown on right. The rotating truck was selected randomly from the family of 3D shapes computed from the stationary image. The family had 89 members, one member for each slant in the range between 1° and 89°. Recall that different slants correspond to different aspect ratios. The subject used his mouse to step through the family and choose what he considered to be the best match to his 3D shape percept produced by the stationary 2D image on the left. We tested four subjects, including two of us. Two subjects were naïve. All of our subjects' adjustments correlated well (0.76–0.87) with the 3D shape that maximized a weighted combination of 3D compactness and surface area of the 3D shape. The maximal 3D compactness, defined as V^2/S^3, was not a good predictor, but, the fit could be improved a lot simply by adding our new constraint, called *minimum surface*. The addition of this new constraint was not entirely accidental. Here is how it came about. Two of us had many discussions about how the Gestalt Psychologist Koffka (1935) conceptualized visual perception as a conflict between a simplicity constraint on one hand and the 2D retinal image on the other. The percept according to Koffka is a compromise between the two. Hochberg & McAlister (1953) used the language of Information Theory when they applied Koffka's ideas to 3D shape perception. They showed how changing the simplicity of the 2D retinal image can determine whether the percept is 2D or 3D. According to them, there is a

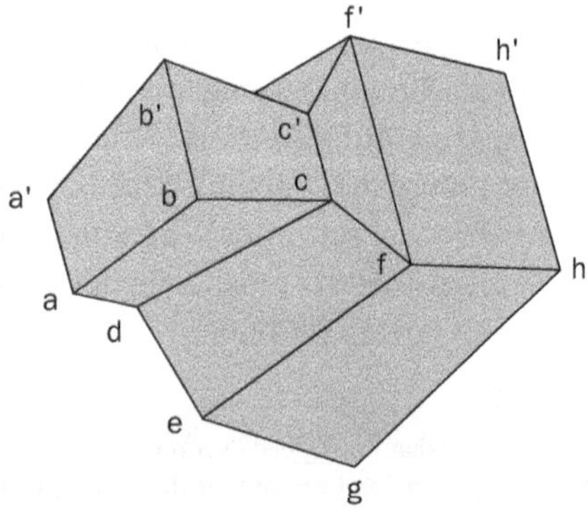

FIGURE 2.7. Filling-in the invisible (back) back parts of the 3D object. (From Pizlo, Z. (2008) 3D shape: its unique place in visual perception. MIT Press. With permission of The MIT Press.)

conflict between the simplicity of the 2D retinal image and the simplicity of the 3D percept, but this conflict does not result in a compromise (average) between the two interpretations. Instead, the visual system chooses the simpler one. The fact that the percept could actually gradually change as a function of the simplicity of the 2D retinal image relative to the simplicity of the 3D interpretation was shown by Attneave & Frost (1969) in their study of how a rectangularity constraint can explain the percept of a 3D symmetrical box. Could we use the same kind of conflict to improve our model's performance? We needed a way to describe the 2D retinal image quantitatively. During one of our debates about this way of thinking, one of us realized that minimizing the surface area S will collapse the 3D shape into its retinal image. The technical way of pulling off this trick was to combine 3D compactness defined as V^2/S^3 with the minimum surface area defined as $1/S^3$. We used the geometric mean of the two as the way to combine them.

Two important comments emerge from these results. First, we verified that the combination of maximum compactness with minimum surface area leads to a more veridical recovery than when compactness is used alone. Second, the subjects and the model adjusted only one parameter of the *test* truck to make the match. The truck stimulus actually had 15 independent parameters. This means that the remaining 14 parameters were recovered by our symmetry constraint. Symmetry contributes quite a lot. Symmetry alone is responsible for almost all of the veridicality experienced in everyday life.

But, there is still more to our story. Studying the perception of 3D shapes like our trucks turned up a number of novel visual phenomena more striking than the blind spot described earlier. We alluded to what is called the blind spot because you do not perceive it. Your visual system predicts what is likely to be present in that part of the world and somehow fills it in. This achievement is not mysterious and not unique. Filling-in missing information by making predictions is commonplace in vision. We will justify this claim by explaining how visual prediction makes it possible to see the back, invisible part of an object. In the real world, this kind of filling-in is much more important than filling in the blind spot because the blind spot only operates far away from the center fovea, where your vision is at its best. When you look at something, filling-in parts of objects you are attending to is essential for seeing them veridically. Look at Figure 2.7. It shows a truck stimulus that has 16 vertices. The vertices of the visible symmetrical half of the truck are labeled from a to h. Each of these vertices has a symmetrical counterpart, but, because the back part of the truck is not visible, not all of them can be seen from this viewing direction. Only five out of the eight, a′, b′, c′, f′, and h′, can be seen. The remaining three vertices, d′, e′ and g′, are occluded by the front part of the truck. Nobody has even thought that these invisible vertices could be seen (filled-in). Our model can do it as well as you do. If you could not, you could never perceive 3D objects veridically. Here is how it is done.

Recovering the back-invisible parts of a truck requires adding the fourth constraint, called "planarity." Consider the point, d, in Figure 2.7, which is one of the three points whose symmetrical counterpart, d′, is not visible. The first step is to find a new way to recover the *visible* 3D point, d, because symmetry is not helpful here. A symmetry constraint can be used *only* if both symmetrical points are visible. Symmetry can be used to recover points a, b, and c. Once these 3 points are recovered, d can be recovered by imposing a constraint that requires all 4 points reside on the same plane in 3D, which is one of the planar (flat) faces of the truck. Once the 3D coordinates of d are known, the invisible point, d′, can be found as a mirror-reflection of d with respect to the plane of symmetry computed from the other 3 points. The recovery of the remaining 2 invisible points can be done in the same way. With all of the 16 points recovered, they can be connected, thereby filling-in the invisible back part of our 3D opaque object.

Now that you see that our model can recover both the back invisible parts of a 3D object as well as it recovers its visible parts in front, you might wonder whether you can do this, too. You do it all the time, but you do it automatically and are unaware of this important fact. This should be no more surprising than the fact that you are not aware of your blind spot under normal viewing conditions. You must go out of your way to perceive it. Our model, like you, recovers the invisible parts of objects without any advance knowledge about the objects and without any means, or opportunity, to learn anything about their real 3D shapes. The model needs, and has, four powerful *a priori* constraints that use conventional geometrical computations. We believe that this fact should be given the weight it so deserves. Why should learning play *any* role in 3D shape perception if 3D shape can be recovered from the two-dimensional visual input without learning? It seems simpler, and much more parsimonious, to assume that these constraints are built-in, as well as effective. Scientists have used this criterion for quite a while (Occam's Razor, ~ 1287–1327). Constraints provide us with veridical percepts of the invisible backs of objects from the very start. Learning is superfluous. This claim should not seem too strong once one realizes that there is no such thing as a two-dimensional world. It is an abstraction. No animal can or has ever lived in two dimensions. The 2D world is a simplification useful for some human mental operations but nothing more than that. Our world is, and has always been, three-dimensional. Organisms that evolved to succeed within it will benefit from perceiving the shapes of objects veridically, namely, they start by knowing that everything has three dimensions, not two. They do this by predicting what is likely to be there when it cannot be seen from a particular viewing direction. Once this was done, even our simple machine could perceive shape veridically. When we started this work, we believed that recovering the 3D shape from one of its 2D images was the hardest problem we faced. It had been considered insoluble for centuries. It turned out to be relatively simple, at least with the synthetic polyhedral shapes we started with. Elaborating the model to handle ecologically valid stimuli in our natural environment remained to be done but this challenge, like the recovery of 3D shape from a 2D image proved to be relatively straightforward. The really big challenge was still way down the road. How could our machine use *a priori* constraints to separate a 3D object from its background, and do this entirely on its own? Humans do this automatically, as well as veridically, with natural objects in natural environments. It took a number of years and several false starts to figure out how this could be done. The next step on our way to this goal was to make it possible for the model to recover the 3D shapes of ecologically-valid naturalistic objects.

2.4 31st European Conference on Visual Perception (ECVP) Utrecht, NL, August 24–28, 2008, Where We Had Our First Public Confrontation

An opportunity to let the international vision community know what we had been up to since St. Petersburg turned up in 2008. We submitted the following abstract. It was accepted for an Oral Presentation at a session called "OBJECTS and SHAPES."

> "A single 2-D image of a solid (3-D) shape leads to a 3-D shape percept that is usually veridical. This achievement is remarkable because of the geometrical fact that this 2-D image cannot provide a unique description of the 3-D object producing the 2-D image. The depth of each point 'out there' is ambiguous in its 2-D image. But, when a 3-D shape is viewed, this ambiguity disappears. The image points are 'organized' into a 2-D 'retinal shape' and the 3-D shape 'out there' is recovered as a 'whole' by built-in simplicity constraints. We have identified four effective constraints: 3-D symmetry, planarity, maximum 3-D compactness, and minimum surface. These constraints explain how 3-D shape constancy is achieved and how a 3-D shape's symmetry can be detected in a 2-D image. Psychophysical tests showed that: (i) our simplicity constraints are more important than depth cues, including binocular disparity and motion parallax, and (ii) maximum 3-D compactness is the essential constraint. Ecological justification for our new simplicity principle will be discussed." *Perception* (2008), 37, Supplement, p. 85.

Two of us went to the conference in August. The venue at Utrecht University was about as different as it could be from the Russian Military Medical Academy where we had addressed this community 2 years earlier. The University was much older. It was founded in 1636, but the conference facility, which is called the *Educatorium*, was built in 1997 and it was about as modern as could be.

The session began with a big surprise. It was chaired by a Professor Emeritus who had earned his Ph.D. in visual perception almost 50 years ago. He opened his session with a lengthy introduction that was devoted *entirely* to condemning Pizlo's book on shape, which had appeared in print 4 months before. He said:

> "Pizlo, in his book, claims that shape perception is an extremely difficult problem that remains to be solved. This is strange because I, and my collaborators, have solved this problem already. So, I have no idea how Pizlo managed to have such a book published."

These remarks were entirely unexpected, as well as counterfactual, because Pizlo had actually said something different in his book. He actually presented a plausible solution of the shape problem in the book. Saying that Pizlo had claimed that the shape problem was still unsolved was hard to understand. Furthermore, the chairman had never claimed in any of his publications that he and his collaborators had actually solved the shape problem.

The chairman's attack on Pizlo's book was actually quite helpful. It encouraged everyone in the audience to pay careful attention to the talk, which was, on the whole, received well. The demos Pizlo used were effective (you saw some of them already in Section 1.4). They made it clear that recovering 3D shapes by applying *a priori* constraints of symmetry and compactness really did the trick. They produced some applause, as well as other spontaneous reactions, suggesting that many in the audience were convinced that our theory worked; it actually explained how humans see 3D shapes. Right after the session, several people who had been working on this problem for many years went out of their way to track us down to offer congratulations. Not everyone, however, was on board. The chairman of the session was not the only unhappy person in the room during the talk and while we loitered just outside the room when the session ended. One of the chairman's collaborators cornered us and tried to convince us that 3D vision is *never*, can *never*, and will *never* be veridical. He was convinced that "shapes are never perceived the way they are out there. Your new theory is completely meaningless." He was obviously not prepared to consider that there might be some small merit in our work.

2.5 Monocular 3D Shape Recovery of Both Synthetic and Real Objects

We promised in the previous section that we would show you the demo used in Utrecht that created such a stir. In section 2.3 we explained how a 2D image can be inflated to make it 3D, paving the way to make a recovered 3D shape veridical. But this is not the whole story. The time has come to explain what was missing from the previous, incomplete explanation. Run the DEMO 1.2[13] now that you know there is more to the story. You see links to 6 examples of 3D recovery, namely, a jeep, a bird, a spider, a chair, a polyhedron, and a mantis. The first four of these examples used a 2D image of a 3D synthetic model. In each of these examples you see four panels: the 3D model, one of its 2D images, 2D contours extracted from this 2D image, and the 3D contours that were recovered. In the "polyhedron" example (#5 on the menu) we used a 3D polyhedron that we generated. This allowed us to skip the step of extracting its 2D contours: the 2D contours were already there when we computed the 2D image. This is why this example has only 3 panels: the original 3D shape on the bottom-left, the 2D image on top, and the 3D shape recovered on bottom-right. In the mantis example (#6 on the menu), we used a 2D camera image of a mantis praying next to the Psychology building at Purdue. We did not have a 3D model of this mantis, so we cannot show it to you. This accounts for the fact that this example also has only three panels: the 2D photo, the 2D contours, and the 3D contours recovered by our model. Clearly, the recovery is close to perfect in all six examples. Note that the model recovered the back, invisible contours, in examples 1, 4, and 5, as well as the visible contours in front.

This demo was produced around the time of meeting in Utrecht. It clearly showed that the model can recover a wide variety of 3D shapes from single 2D images. This encouraged us to believe that we have solved what was generally believed to be the hardest problem in visual science. Note that we had accomplished this using an approach best described as backwards. We solved the second harder problem first, recovering a 3D shape from a single 2D image, by ignoring the other problem at the front-end of visual perception, namely the Figure-Ground Organization (FGO) problem. We simply gave the solution of FGO to our model and asked it to recover a 3D object from a 2D image. We did this by drawing in the contours of the objects we perceived in the 2D image, something human beings do reliably and effortlessly. How was it possible to solve the harder problem first, and was it legitimate to solve it the way we did? Even if it was legitimate was it the right honorable thing to do? Well, looking back now, 6 years later, at what we did, it seems that this was probably the *only way* it could be done.

---

[13]http://shapebook.psych.purdue.edu/1.2

Generations of vision researchers had tried to do it by working in the traditional "forward" direction. They started with contour detection and texture segregation and never got very far. They never got beyond this first stage of visual processing. Now that we had succeeded in solving both the FGO and 3D shape recovery problems by starting backwards, we feel compelled to put our approach, which some might call dumb luck, into somewhat more formal terminology. Dumb luck does not seem to be the best way to describe how we worked this out. We will begin by borrowing some functionalistic terminology used by William James (1890) and assume that one must understand the true *goal* of the visual task under study before one can explain how this true goal was achieved. In other words, understanding the output of a given process is more important than understanding its input, for explaining the underlying process. Trying to explain to students how an airplane works without ever mentioning that the airplane is designed to fly, seems unnatural, as well as likely to lead to poor test performance. Using common sense, we assumed that the goal of a vision task is to provide the observer with a veridical representation of his environment. Once this assumption was made, it was clear that we should *start* by concentrating on understanding 3D vision and shape constancy. We should not start with contour detection and segregation as others had, and were still, doing. With this in hand, it became clear that the first thing we had to do was to define the minimal input required to make the recovery of a 3D shape possible. It was easy to guess that the minimal input would be a good 2D line drawing of a natural object or scene. But simply having a good line-drawing was not enough for 3D recovery. The line-drawing had to be organized. By "organized" we mean that (1) all meaningful contours, and only meaningful contours, are present; (2) if the 3D object has parts, our model must be given information about which contours form individual parts; (3) if some faces (surfaces) of the object are planar (flat), the model must know which contours form planar (flat) configurations; (4) if several surfaces encompass volume, the model must know where the volume is located; and, finally, and perhaps most importantly, (5) the model must know which 2D contours in the image represent 3D symmetrical contours. This last element of figure-ground organization is called the *symmetry correspondence problem*. Why is establishing symmetry correspondence in a 2D image important, actually essential, for 3D shape recovery? It is essential because the model must know where the 3D symmetry constraint should be applied. The 3D symmetry constraint is our most important *a priori* constraint. Consider what the model must be able to do if it wants to recover the shape of a horse from a single 2D image. The model must know that the left legs correspond to the right legs. Specifically, they are mirror-reflection copies of the right legs. They are not copies of the horse's head or mirror-reflections of its butt. This is not a trivial problem.

The five operations listed as the processes inherent in figure-ground organization (FGO) in the previous paragraph sound like a lot to ask of our input, but common sense told us that they were essential so we simply assumed that the visual system performs them very well before it attempts a 3D shape recovery. We were confident that these operations can be performed because each of us, and everyone we knew, could do them easily for a wide range of real images of natural scenes. Even undergraduate students who knew nothing about FGO or 3D shape recovery could perform these operations as well as we did. Providing our model with a hand-drawn organized 2D image was all that was needed for us to make a successful 3D recovery. Most of our colleagues agreed that we were on the right track, but others were quite skeptical about whether our 3D shape recovery had anything to do with how the visual system works because we could not explain at this point how FGO worked. According to them, if you cannot explain the *input* to a given process, you should not even try to study subsequent processing. At the theoretical level, their belief can be said to derive from their commitment to studying perception as a *Forward Problem*, the way Fechner did, rather than as an *Inverse Problem*, which we chose to do.

Note that if our model is intended to deal with real images of real objects, symmetry will never be perfect because no object is perfectly symmetrical and no image is without noise and occlusion. Similarly, not all objects have a lot of volume, for example the Origami objects made by folding paper have almost no volume. The same is true with common objects such as chairs or tables. Look at Figure 2.8 (left). This chair occupies quite a bit of volume in 3D space despite the fact that its parts are thin. How can we measure the volume of the parts? The simplest way is to keep the chair assembled, and measure its volume the way Archimedes did. You will need a large box to pack this chair. Ideally you want a box that fits the chair very closely all around. First, make sure that the chair's cushions are made of waterproof material if they cannot be removed. Put the chair inside the box and then fill the box with water to the very top. Now, remove the chair very carefully and when it is out, measure how far the level of the water has come down. You can know the volume of the chair from the volume of water that the chair displaced. This can be done easily once you know the dimensions of the box. So which volume should our model use to measure compactness of the chair shown in Figure 2.8? The volume of the close-fitting box or the volume of the chair? Some of our readers probably have already guessed that using the volume of the chair, itself, may not be the way to go. The remainder of this chapter will explain how our model deals with both problems, namely, the fact that symmetry is never actually perfect and that some objects, which have relatively little volume in their parts, occupy large volumes in space.

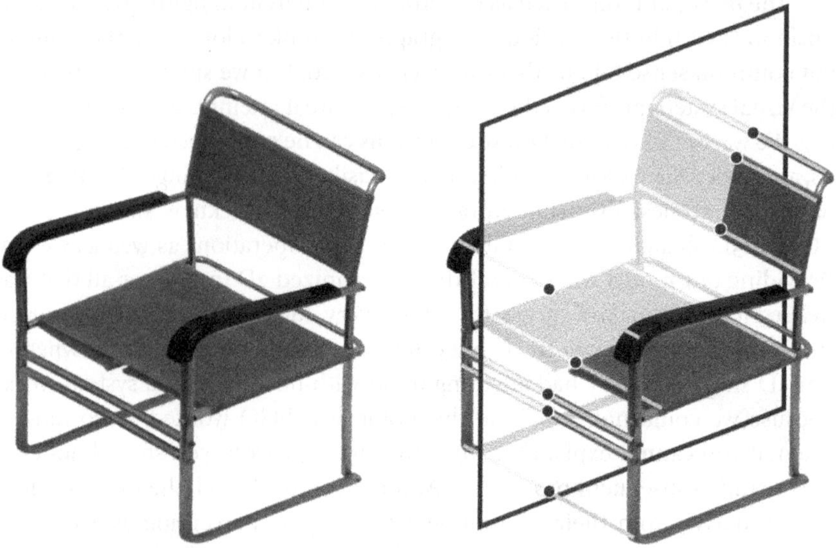

FIGURE 2.8. (left) An image of a prototypical chair. (right) The symmetry-plane is superimposed where nine pairs of corresponding-points are connected by light gray lines. The black dots show the intersections of these lines with the symmetry-plane.

You already know what mirror symmetry is, but you may not know (1) how to verify whether a given object is mirror-symmetrical, (2) whether a 2D retinal image represents a 3D mirror-symmetrical object, and (3) how to apply a symmetry constraint when the symmetry is not perfect as it always is in the real world. Look at Figure 2.8 again.

The chair shown in Figure 2.8 is mirror-symmetrical and its symmetry-plane is vertical. The symmetry-plane is shown on the right. All pairs of mirror-symmetrical points in this chair form a set of parallel line-segments because all of these line-segments are perpendicular to a common symmetry-plane. This will be true of *all* mirror-symmetrical objects, regardless of how complex they are. With this fact in mind, look at the chair again. We connected nine pairs of corresponding-points with gray line-segments in the chair shown on the right. It is easy to see that these line-segments are perpendicular to the plane of symmetry of this chair (a 3D object) and that they are all parallel to each other in 3D space. The story is the same with all mirror-symmetrical objects. Line-segments connecting pairs of mirror-symmetrical points are parallel on the human face, on the human body, on a horse's body, as well as in most pieces of furniture, including chairs, tables, sofas. So, once we are able to determine which pairs of points in a 3D object form parallel line segments, we can know that it is very likely that this object is mirror-symmetrical. If we want to verify that this actually is the case with a given stimulus, we can check whether the midpoints of the parallel lines-segments are on the same plane in 3D space. If they are on the same plane, this plane is called the symmetry-plane and we can be sure that our object is mirror-symmetrical.

Verifying symmetry in a 2D image is more difficult. The main difficulty arises from the fact that the 2D image of a 3D mirror-symmetrical object is not, itself, mirror-symmetrical. This can be easily verified with the image of the chair above. It is impossible to cut the 2D image of this chair into halves such that one half is a mirror reflection of the other half. We can, however, easily imagine cutting a real 3D chair into two identical halves, but we cannot imagine doing this with the 2D image of any chair. So, the symmetry of a 3D object is lost in its 2D image. The 3D object is symmetrical, but its 2D image never is, with only a single exception, namely when the view is degenerate. Fortunately, there is at least one property of 3D symmetry that is not lost in the 2D image. Consider a 2D image of a 3D mirror-symmetrical object. It turns out that the 2D images of the line-segments that are parallel in 3D will also be parallel to each other in the 2D image. Clearly, this is the case with the line-segments drawn in gray in Figure 2.8. So, the fact that symmetry is lost, but the parallelism of lines-segments is not, means that the parallelism of lines is an invariant of a projection. It does not change when a 3D object out there is represented in 2D on your retina. It follows that if we succeed in finding pairs of points in a 2D image that form parallel line-segments, we can be almost certain that this 2D image is an image of a 3D mirror-symmetrical object. This fact is illustrated in Figure 2.9, which was produced by placing parallel line-segments haphazardly without having any particular 3D shape in mind. We see some kind of simple 3D pattern and are sure that you see it, too. The 3D percept produced by this 2D stimulus emerges simply because these line-segments are parallel. There is no other reason for seeing a third dimension in this 2D stimulus.

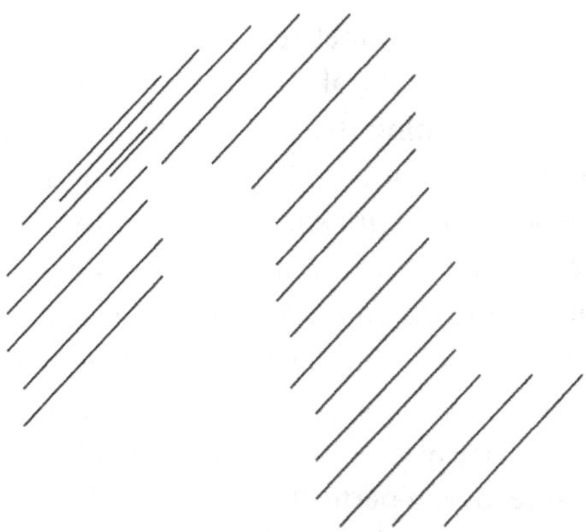

FIGURE 2.9. Producing a 3rd dimension with parallel line-segments.

Technically, this invariant is a necessary condition for a 2D image to be an image of a 3D mirror-symmetrical object. By *necessary* we mean that if lines are not parallel in the 2D image, the 3D object that produced this image is not mirror-symmetrical. If the lines are parallel in the 2D image, the 3D object *may be* mirror-symmetrical. The direction of these lines in the 2D image indicates the tilt of the plane of symmetry of the 3D shape. Formally, tilt of a plane is the direction of the projection of the normal of this plane onto the 2D image. We promised in footnote 11 in this chapter to explain how the tilt of the symmetry-plane is established when a 3D shape recovery is performed. Recall that the slant of the symmetry-plane is a free parameter in the 3D shape recovery from a 2D image, but tilt is not a free parameter because it determines the direction of the line-segments connecting pairs of corresponding-points in the 2D image.

As you know, once we leave Plato's realm and return to our own no shape is ever *perfectly* symmetrical. We are not the first to notice this. A number of critics of our work have objected to our use of the symmetry as an *a priori* constraint by claiming just this. A typical example used to support this criticism was to point out that a human face is never symmetrical. Every perception textbook and many popular magazines point this out perennially. This claim, despite its popularity, is quite surprising once one considers how one would explain what a human face looks like to an alien being who has never seen a human face. The best description surely begins with asserting that a human face is mirror-symmetrical, it has two identical halves. This would be illustrated by pointing out that it has two eyes and two ears and the lines connecting the ears and the eyes are parallel. It would go on to point out that the mouth and nose are, themselves, mirror-symmetrical and that these prominent features are located around the face's plane of symmetry. Once this was done, one would then probably add that there are always some, often only barely noticeable differences between the two halves of a real human being's symmetrical face. We all know some people who have features that violate symmetry, like a person who has one ear sticking out much farther from his head than the other ear. Two symmetrical ears sticking out a lot but equally on both sides seem much more natural. So, the moment we use the term *half* to describe a face, we are assuming that the face is mirror-symmetrical. At this point we had a model that works well with perfectly symmetrical synthetic objects. How well would it do with such objects in the real world where they can never be perfectly symmetrical? Making the model work effectively under such natural conditions turned out to be much easier than we anticipated. We simply added a front end to our model to deal with departures from symmetry. This front end works as follows: the model begins by correcting the input 2D image of an asymmetrical 3D object just enough to correct it to the point where the model can recover a perfectly symmetrical 3D shape. Once the perfect 3D shape is recovered, it is degraded in the way and in the amount that is needed to match the initial asymmetrical input. To describe what we did more succinctly: we first corrected the input and then uncorrected the output. This approach is especially well-suited for use with piece-wise non-rigid objects like the bodies of human beings and other animals. DEMO 2.4[14] shows how this is done. This demo uses a model of a human body shown with three different articulations of its limbs. In the top-left panel, the body is sitting in a 3D *symmetrical* configuration. Toggle between "original image," "drawn contour," and "recovered shape" by using the buttons available on the top-right. In this demo, we applied the model to the body's skeleton. We drew the body's skeleton by hand instead of drawing its contours as we did with our trucks. You should not be surprised that our model could recover the body's 3D symmetrical shape by using the body's skeleton because the body's 3D shape is symmetrical inside as well as outside. Symmetry is as powerful with human bodies as it is with trucks. The other two examples shown in this demo are *not* perfectly symmetrical in three dimensions, but our model recovered their 3D shapes quite well, using the method described in the previous paragraph.

We will now explain how this was done with sufficient detail to satisfy even our technical readers. Look at the standing human figure shown in the middle panel of the 3 figures on the left. Note that we marked a number of dots on this skeleton. These dots represent a few characteristic points on this body; specifically, its head, neck, torso and the joints of its arms and legs. The four points, which represent the head, neck, torso and hips, were identified and labeled as lying on the symmetry-plane. The three pairs of points on the left and right arms represent their joints. The same is true with the three pairs of points on the left and right legs. They were marked as being, in principle, mirror-symmetrical. You can easily see that the right arm is next to the body and the left arm is raised. It looks much like a student's arm when he wants to ask a question. Clearly, this model's two arms are not mirror-symmetrical in 3D space. The same is true of its legs. Now note that *you* can easily see all of this in only a single 2D image in this demo, but can our model see all this, too? It can. But how? It first verifies that the two arms and the two legs *cannot* be mirror-symmetrical in 3D space. It knows this because the line-segments connecting the pairs of corresponding-points are not parallel in this 2D image. This property was explained in Figures 2.8 and 2.9. Once the model has this knowledge, it can move the corresponding-points around in the 2D image until these line-segments are all parallel to one another. A few such parallel segments were marked in Figure 2.8. Here, it was done by moving the right arm upwards in the 2D image and the left arm downwards. There are infinitely many ways to "correct" the 2D image, so how should we, and our model, go about picking the best one to use? It seemed reasonable to apply the smallest

[14]http://shapebook.psych.purdue.edu/2.4

correction needed to meet the *parallel* criterion used to handle such problems. Our model does the correction required in the least squares sense, which simply means that the sum of squared distances by which the dots are moved to make this correction is kept minimal. The next step is to have the model recover a 3D symmetrical body. Once this is done, it moves the 3D dots representing the joints back to where they should be, that is, where they were in the 2D image shown in the demo. The reversal of this correction in 3D is not specified uniquely because the original correction was done in the 2D image. In other words, there are infinitely many ways to "uncorrect" the 3D points so that the recovered 3D shape could produce the original 2D image. Here as earlier, the model performs the required 3D "uncorrection" in the least squares sense. The 3D asymmetrical shape that results from this operation can be seen by checking the box "recovered shape." Now, click your mouse on the icon at the bottom to see another example of a recovery of a 3D asymmetrical shape by using a symmetry constraint. We conclude this section by emphasizing that the symmetry constraint, which is very effective, can be used to recover *any* 3D mirror-symmetrical shape, as well as *any* 3D asymmetrical shape, as long as it is possible to specify the nature of the violation of symmetry in the particular case. As with every step we made on our way to making the machine that sees like us, everyone working on shape, except us, *knew* that recovering 3D *asymmetrical* shapes by using a 3D *symmetry* constraint was *impossible*. Luckily, we did not know that solving this problem was impossible. This is not the first time something like this has happened in science.

Now that we have nailed down this point technically, we will explain how our model can be applied to 3D objects that do not have any volume. This will be done with a demo that you have already seen (DEMO 1.2, mantis).[15] You see a real photograph of a real praying mantis. You clearly see it sitting on the leaves of a lush plant. You can see it, but no conventional contemporary machine vision system can. Conventional vision machines try to reconstruct objects from shading and texture and they will all fail miserably with all such natural stimuli. Shading and texture, two popular monocular depth cues, convey no 3D information whatsoever about the praying mantis as it is represented in this 2D image. Furthermore, there are no other depth cues in this image that can help in the recovery of the praying mantis's 3D shape. The only way to recover the 3D shape of the praying mantis is by using our *a priori* constraints; texture and shading simply cannot do it. We knew by the time we presented our demo at the European Conference on Visual Perception in St. Petersburg in 2006 that our shape recovery model was very general in the sense that it could handle a wide variety of shapes, but not everyone who saw or read about this demo was convinced it could. Several skeptics even claimed

---

[15]http://shapebook.psych.purdue.edu/1.2 /mantis

that our model "will never generalize to any real 3D shape." The flavor and intensity of this skepticism was reflected well by one reviewer of the 3D Shape book (Pizlo, 2008) when he wrote:

> ". . . . my feeling is that this work is misleading. . . . In reality his contribution is only about the perception of 3D shape of very specific man-made objects and the algorithm he proposes only works for this restricted set of shapes."

You can surely see that his skepticism missed the mark. The praying mantis presented no particular difficulty. We handled its recovery the same way we handled the truck by marking several contours in the image. We then applied our mirror symmetry *a priori* constraint, together with our maximum 3D compactness and minimum surface area constraints. Again, we did the same thing we did with our truck. The result can be seen in the demo, but it raises a question that must be answered, namely, how did we apply the maximal 3D compactness and minimum surface area to the contour that we drew by hand? The recovered 3D praying mantis resides in 3D space, but the 3D contours representing the praying mantis's shape do not, in themselves, specify the volume or the surface area needed to apply the compactness and surface area constraints. The answer is simple. The volume and the surface area simply do not have to be specified explicitly or exactly. The model, like your visual system, knew how to fill them in. The praying mantis shown in this demo is not exceptional. There is nothing surprising about this result. The praying mantis simply does not have much volume or surface area and both our visual system and model can fill in what is needed to perceive it 3D shape. There are many other objects like this. Ordinary chairs and spiders are good, commonplace examples. Remember that the constraints of volume and surface area are needed by our model primarily to choose a unique 3D shape from the one-parameter family of shapes. These two constraints serve mainly to eliminate objects that are too long or too short. In the absence or paucity of explicit volume and surfaces, the model chooses a unique 3D shape by using the following trick. Imagine that we wrap the 3D praying mantis with a plastic wrap. This produces a good approximation to what is called a *convex hull* in computational geometry. This is the name given to the kind of box you want to buy to measure the volume of the chair in Figure 2.8. It has the closest possible fit. Technically, the convex hull of a set of points or edges is the smallest convex 3D object that contains all of the points and edges in its inside or on its boundary. It is easier to illustrate the concept of a convex hull in two-, rather than in three-dimensions so it will be illustrated this way in Figure 2.10. The polygon shown on the right is a 2D convex hull of the edges shown on the left. Technically, "convex" refers to a region in a 2D or 3D space such that for any pair of points that are in this region, the line-segment connecting these points is also in this region.

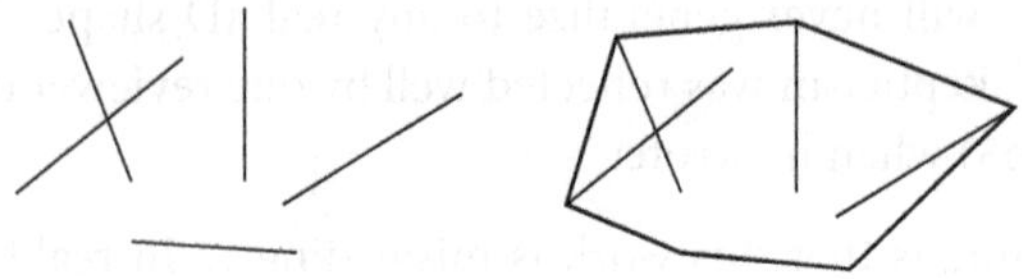

FIGURE 2.10. The convex hull on the right contains all of the lines on the left.

We can construct a 3D convex hull for all members of the one-parameter family of 3D objects produced by applying a mirror symmetry constraint. Our model simply chooses the object whose convex hull maximizes the ratio of volume and surface area raised to the third power. This is how we recovered the praying mantis, and the other 5 objects shown in DEMO 1.2.[16]

[16]http://shapebook.psych.purdue.edu/1.2

3

Symmetry in Vision, Inside and Outside of the Laboratory

Symmetry, ubiquitous in the real world, is completely absent from the laboratory. This is surprising because most perceptionists should have at least heard about the importance of the ecological validity of stimuli, the kind of validity Egon Brunswik (1956) said was needed to evaluate the merits of theories of visual perception. Brunswik introduced this concept in the 1940s and its importance was kept alive by J. J. Gibson throughout his career. Recall that using stimuli that have ecological validity is necessary if you want your laboratory results to generalize to perception in everyday life. Clearly, no perceptionist should be satisfied with a theory that *only* pertains to results obtained in his laboratory. So, the almost universal neglect of symmetry, before we picked it up, is surprising because in our natural environment, virtually all objects we encounter are symmetrical. The bodies of most animals are mirror-symmetrical; the fiddler crab is one of the very few exceptions: http://en.wikipedia.org/wiki/Fiddler_crab. Flowers and trees are characterized by their rotational- or spiral-symmetry and parts of an animal's body have translational-symmetry, the kind of symmetry used by Biederman (1987) to define his geons. Considering how common symmetry is in our natural environment, you surely suspect that scientists would have to go to great pains to keep symmetry out of their laboratories. They did. Symmetrical stimuli have almost *never* been used in perception research. Furthermore, in the few cases where symmetrical stimuli were used, they were *never* used under natural viewing conditions. They were always presented in what is technically called a *degenerate view*. The technical meaning of a degenerate view, when used to study mirror-symmetry, is the view obtained from a viewpoint located on the plane of symmetry (a viewpoint is the position from which things are viewed). From this viewpoint, a 3D mirror-symmetrical shape produces a 2D mirror-symmetrical retinal image (see the image on the left in Figure 3.1). A 2D mirror-symmetrical image cannot be used to recover the 3D mirror-symmetrical shape of the object that actually produced it. The 2D image must be *asymmetrical* if it is going to be useful for recovering a 3D

FIGURE 3.1. Two types of "degenerate images": Left: When this symmetrical automobile is viewed from this degenerate viewing direction, its retinal image is symmetrical. Right: The other type of degenerate view is orthogonal (at 90°) to the first. The side view of this automobile shows not even a hint of the automobile's 3D symmetry. Both of these views are called degenerate because an *a priori* 3D symmetry constraint *cannot* be used to recover the object's 3D shape from such retinal images.

symmetrical shape. This sounds counterintuitive, but is true nonetheless. There are, in fact two types of degenerate views of a 3D mirror-symmetrical shape. Both are illustrated in Figure 3.1. In the *view* shown on the left, the 3D *symmetrical* shape of the automobile produced a 2D *symmetrical* image on the retina. The other type of degenerate view is illustrated on the right. This degenerate view eliminated all traces of 3D mirror-symmetry because it is orthogonal (at 90°) to the view on the right and orthogonal (at 90°) to the plane of symmetry. Both views are degenerate because an *a priori* 3D symmetry constraint cannot be used to recover the 3D shape of the automobile from either of these views.

In real life, a 3D symmetrical shape almost never produces a 2D *symmetrical* retinal image and, when it does, the slightest movement of the head will make the 2D image on the retina *asymmetrical*. You must not only go to great pains to arrange the subject's line-of-sight with respect to the stimulus to produce a *symmetrical* 2D image from a *symmetrical* 3D shape, you must maintain the direction of the line-of-sight scrupulously while it is viewed. The head must be immobilized and the second eye covered. Herculean efforts are required to maintain a subject's viewpoint. One might suspect that such cumbersome procedures would mean that studies done under such conditions were not common. Fortunately, this was the case. There were only a few attempts to do them because they were so hard to do. Unfortunately, it became easy to use *degenerate views* when computers came into widespread use in shape research because the experimenter no longer had to worry about maintaining the orientation of the subject's head relative to the stimulus or to cover one eye. The computer could be used to control the orientation of the visual stimulus. Making degenerate views so easy to establish and maintain made it possible for almost any moderately skillful experimentalist to use degenerate visual stimulation. This esoteric stimulating condition is not only devoid of ecological-validity, it also *completely eliminates* the effectiveness of symmetry as an *a priori* constraint, and without symmetry there can be no shape. Scientists desirous of studying shape should go to great pains to avoid degenerate views not to establish and maintain them. Visual scientists, who appreciated this important fact, were hard to find; one might say almost nonexistent. For all non-degenerate (natural) viewing directions, a 3D symmetrical object does *not* produce a 2D symmetrical retinal image. These natural, non-degenerate images are always *asymmetrical*. These commonplace natural images were given a technical name by Kanade in 1981. He called them *skew-symmetrical* when he published his seminal research on the role of symmetry in machine vision. He called these images skewed because the angles that actually are 90° *out there* in a symmetrical figure are not 90° in its retinal image (see Figure 3.3). Unfortunately, the human vision community has not taken Kanade's pioneering work as seriously as it deserves. There have been only a handful of studies on the perception of 3D symmetry from skew-symmetrical images, the commonest stimulus, representing visual shape in everyday life. When Pizlo's 3D shape book came out in 2008, only a couple of models of the perception of *2D symmetrical patterns* from asymmetrical images were available in the literature, and there was not even a single model of the perception of *3D symmetrical shapes from asymmetrical images*, the *only natural stimulation* in the real 3D world.

3.1 Why and How Approximate Computations Make Visual Analyses Fast and Perfect: the Perception of Slanted 2D Mirror-Symmetrical Figures

Now that we know that all significant images of symmetrical objects in the real world are skew-symmetrical, what are their characteristics? Figure 3.2a shows a simple example of the image of a flat (planar) symmetrical figure. It is easy to see that this figure is symmetrical out there in the 3D representation, but it is important to appreciate that it is not symmetrical in Figure 3.2, or on your retina. This figure is perceived as residing on a plane that is slanted in 3D space relative to you. The orientation of this plane in 3D space is characterized by two parameters: the plane's slant and tilt. For a given 2D symmetrical figure we can produce a large family of differently skewed asymmetrical figures simply by varying the values of slant and tilt. Note that only the representation in (a) has contours. The type of stimulus shown in (b), which does not have contours, has been used by almost everybody working in the vision community today and in the past. You should immediately see that it is much more difficult to see that there is symmetry when only a set of points is available. Removing all contours makes it almost impossible to see the symmetry out there. The points in (b) were taken from the contours of (a). Doing this to simplify a visual stimulus is not without catastrophic consequences, a fact that practically jumps off the page when you compare (a) with (b) in Figure 3.2, so isolated points should *never* be used to represent a natural stimulus in shape research. As you should suspect by now, isolated points have been used, and are still being used, more often than not, in research putatively on shape perception. Natural

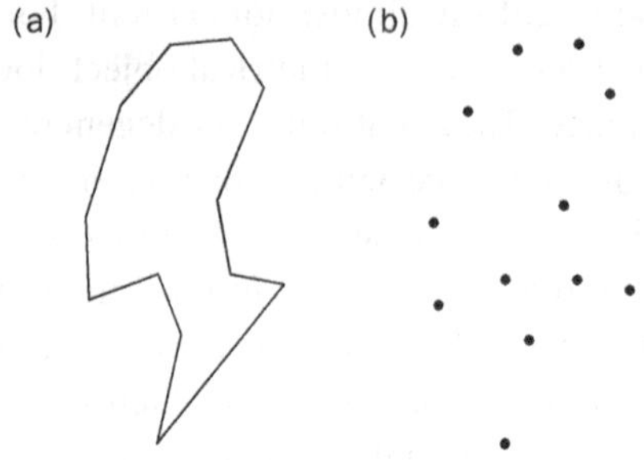

FIGURE 3.2. (a) Skew-symmetrical images of planar figures. (b) A skew-symmetrical image of a set of isolated points.

objects are always symmetrical and isolated points, such as stones on the ground or stars in the sky, are *never* symmetrical. Our constellations are drawn on the sky by connecting star-points with contours, making it relatively easy to perceive the resulting shapes as representations of 3D symmetrical objects such as Orion, the Hunter. Without these contours, you cannot see it. One cannot but wonder why anyone would ever want to use dots as visual stimuli. Unconnected dots are not only unnatural, they are also computationally and perceptually much more difficult to handle than connected dots (this claim will be explained after our computational model is described). It seems that the time-honored commitment to simplify the visual stimulus as much as possible to achieve methodological elegance has made it virtually impossible to achieve veridical perception inside the vision laboratory. Unfortunately, this obvious and easily demonstrated fact has been ignored by almost everybody studying human vision. One might think that a simpler stimulus would be simpler to perceive, but it is not. In vision, simplicity is found in *invariance*, not in the paucity of the stimulus provided to the observer. Technically, an invariant is a property that *remains constant under some transformation*. In the case of retinal image formation, there are two relevant transformations. We call them projections because the light rays, after being reflected from the surface of a 3D object, are projected onto the photosensitive surface of the retina or camera. There are two slightly different types of projections. One is called *orthographic* and the other *perspective*. You need to understand these two types of projections if you want to understand how our model recovers 3D shapes from the retinal images. These details will be illustrated by demos that will convey all the important characteristics intuitively.

We used an orthographic projection to produce the Ames's chair demo used Chapter 1. Orthographic projection means that the light rays that form a 2D image on a surface are orthogonal (at 90°) to the image. Look at the DEMO 3.1.[1] The demo starts with the image of an upside down chair with the plane of this image represented by the square. We are using the square to keep track of

[1]http://shapebook.psych.purdue.edu/3.1

the orientation of the image relative to your line of sight as well as to the 3D chair. Use your mouse to change the direction from which you are looking at the chair and its image. We put the chair inside a rectangular box that looks like a room. This room defines our frame of reference, the conventional coordinate system with three axes (x, y, and z) that are at 90° to each other. Now think about the chair's image as residing on an xy plane and about the light rays reflected from the 3D chair as being parallel to the z-axis. These light rays are shown as thin lines connecting the points on the 3D chair with the corresponding points on the 2D image. Next, click your mouse on the button *inner object*. Now use your mouse to rotate the 3D chair relative to the camera. You can toggle between *entire scene* and *inner object* to rotate the 3D object only, or to rotate the entire scene. Use the three sliders on the bottom if you want to see how things change when you rotate the scene or object around the individual axes x, y, and z. You can get a good understanding about what is going on in this demo, without thinking about x's, y's, or z's, by playing around with it for a few minutes. Also, a good way to conceptualize what is going on here is to realize that constructing an orthographic image is like taking a photo and that the same is true of a perspective projection. This assertion will be explained and illustrated in DEMO 3.2.[2]

It looks the same except for the presence of a red dot. This demo illustrates what is called a *perspective* projection. The *perspective* projection represents the actual description of image formation in both the human eye and in a camera. Use your mouse to rotate the entire scene. The projecting lines representing the light rays are no longer parallel to each other and they are no longer orthogonal to the image. Instead, they all converge at the red dot, which is called the center of the *perspective* projection. What looks like a black dot is actually the image of the 3D chair. This image is very small because the red dot is very close to the plane of the retinal (or camera) image. This red dot represents the center of the lens in your eye or in a camera. This center is fixed in your eye—it is about ¾ of an inch in front of your retina. A painter, desirous of producing a *perspective* image on his canvas, can choose the center of his perspective projection arbitrarily. This was big news in 1413 when Brunelleschi did this so effectively in Italy by providing the first correct explanation of what we are describing in this section. You can get a better feel for how this works by thinking about the image in this demo as representing a glass surface on which the painter paints, and the red dot as representing the painter's vantage point. Changing the position of the painter's vantage point can be done simply by using the slider labeled *F*, which changes the position of the red dot. You can actually see what the painter will see when he moves nearer or farther away from the glass surface. At some point, the rays will be so close to parallel that the image can no longer change. When this happens, we can say (technically)

[2]http://shapebook.psych.purdue.edu/3.2

that the center of the *perspective* projection is at infinity and that the *perspective* projection has been reduced to an *orthographic* projection.

Why are we talking at such length about what painters had to understand 600 years ago, when what we really care about is how our machine sees the world as we do? You already knew that the center of *perspective* projection is fixed in eyes like ours, so why are we interested in other projections in which the center is located at different places? The answer is practical and simple. When an object is far away (at least 10 times the object's size[3]), a *perspective* retinal image becomes practically indistinguishable from an *orthographic* image. Obviously, it is useful to know about both because we want our machine to be able to see well when things are near as well as when they are far. Some computations are easier to use with a *perspective* image, and others are easier with an *orthographic* image. A smart vision system, like ours, can take advantage of both and our machine might be able to make use of both, too.

Figure 3.3b shows a 2D orthographic image of the 2D (flat) mirror-symmetrical polygon that is shown in (a). When we say that the polygon in (a) is mirror-symmetrical, we base this on two facts, namely, (1) the symmetry line segments (shown in gray), connecting pairs of mirror-symmetrical points, are all orthogonal (at 90°) to the black axis of symmetry and parallel to each other and (2) their midpoints lie on the black symmetry axis. As you know from our discussion of the demo you just saw, in an *orthographic* image, the projecting light rays are all orthogonal (at 90°) to the retinal image. The image in Figure 3.3b is skew-symmetrical, the kind of image Kanade (1981) analyzed in his important work. The symmetry line segments (shown in gray) are still parallel to each other, but they are not orthogonal (at 90°) to the image of the *axis of symmetry of the polygon*. They are oblique or skewed. Technically, an orthographic image of the *axis of symmetry* of a planar (flat) figure out there is not an *axis of symmetry* of an orthographic image of the figure. In plain English, we can always find the image of the axis of symmetry of a symmetrical figure, but the image of the symmetrical figure is, itself, asymmetrical. There is another characteristic of a symmetrical figure that is preserved in an orthographic image. Namely, the midpoints of the gray symmetry line segments in an orthographic image are collinear (a black straight line goes through all of them) and this line is the image of the axis of symmetry. Technically, there are three invariants of an orthographic projection of planar mirror-symmetrical figures (1) parallel symmetry lines out there remain parallel in the image, (2) midpoints of the symmetry line segments remain midpoints in the image, and (3) the midpoints in the image are collinear (fall on the same line). In plain English, the invariants are what did *not* change, despite the fact that the

[3]Technically, and more precisely, at least 10 times the range of the object in depth.

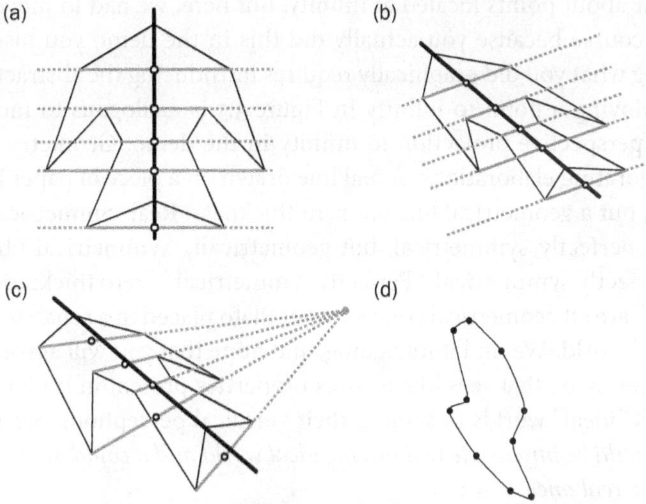

FIGURE 3.3. (a) A mirror-symmetrical polygon. (b) An *orthographic* image of the polygon in (a). The symmetry line segments shown in gray are all parallel and their midpoints are collinear. (c) Shows how this polygon is represented on the retina in the eye where the polygon is a *perspective* image. The extrapolations of the symmetry line segments shown in gray in (c) are *not* parallel and their midpoints are *not* collinear: the extrapolations of the symmetry line segments intersect at a vanishing point. (d) A skew-symmetrical smooth curve. Skew-symmetry can be verified by examining its feature points. The feature points in (d), which are marked as black dots, were determined by the curvature of the contours. (From Sawada & Pizlo, 2008, with permission of the Association for Research in Vision and Ophthalmology).

2D shape changed. These invariants apply to any planar (flat) curve. We often use polygons as examples because it is easy for the reader to see which pairs of points are mirror-symmetrical.

Now, consider a *perspective* image (shown in part (c)) of the polygon shown in Figure 3.3a, which is the situation actually present in the eye. The symmetry line segments are *not* parallel. They *all intersect at a single point, called the vanishing point.* This invariant is the *only exact* invariant of a *perspective* projection of a planar (flat) mirror-symmetrical figure.[4] Some non-technical readers will probably be surprised by this claim because in the paragraph just above, we said that an invariant is what does *not* change, but in part (c) we have a vanishing point in the image, but there is no vanishing point in (a), where the image was symmetrical. We owe the readers who noticed this an explanation. The gray symmetry line segments intersect at a point in (c), and the gray symmetry line segments also intersect at a point in (a), but this point is very, very far away. So far away that it could not be shown in any book. Technically, this point is at infinity. In most basic courses in geometry, you will probably

[4]This is the only invariant that can be used to characterize mirror-symmetrical figures. The technical reader would do well to remember that there are general case projective invariants of 2D figures, such as the cross-ratio of four collinear points and the cross-ratio of four areas.

never hear about points located at infinity. But here, we had to move beyond the basic course because you actually did this in the demo you just viewed. Explaining what you did graphically requires introducing the abstract concept *infinity*. Moving a point to infinity in Figure 3.3 is analogous to moving the center of perspective projection to infinity in the demo. Geometry is full of such invigorating elaborations. A real line drawn on a piece of paper has some thickness, but a geometrical line has zero thickness. Real symmetrical objects are never perfectly symmetrical, but geometrically symmetrical objects are always perfectly symmetrical. "Perfectly symmetrical," "zero thickness," "point at infinity" are all geometrical concepts that Plato placed in a separate and special "ideal" world. We find it intriguing, and hope that you will agree, that the machine we made that sees like us uses properties present in both our "real" and Plato's "ideal" worlds to achieve their veridical perceptions. *Seeing, as we know it, would be impossible without the ideal world and it could not be veridical without the real one.*

The vanishing point (the retinal image of a point at infinity) is not the only invariant that can be used in real vision systems. This is fortunate because this invariant, alone, would not be able do the job. The visual system also uses an exact invariant of the *orthographic* projection. This invariant is only approximately invariant in real vision systems. This approximate invariant is the colinearity of midpoints, the straight line that goes through all of the midpoints of symmetry line segments, in an *orthographic* projection. This line is shown in Figure 3.3c. Pizlo (2008), in his book on shape, emphasized the important fact that the visual system uses properties of the *perspective* projection, not of the *orthographic* projection, because a *perspective* projection is the mathematically exact description of how the retinal image is actually formed. Here, this claim will be modified because we have discovered that when the visual system is faced with the difficult problem of recovering 3D shapes from a single 2D retinal image, which it does very well indeed, it uses whatever it has available to produce a veridical 3D percept. The 3D recovery from a 2D image requires using the mathematically approximate invariant of the *perspective* projection, as well as the mathematically exact invariant of the *perspective* projection. The word *approximate* can have a pejorative connotation. It suggests that if one cannot know something exactly, one may have to settle for only approximate knowledge with the hope that approximate knowledge will be good enough. This commonplace denigration of approximate knowledge if done here will obscure an important point. The logic underlying the use of approximate information is much more interesting than this assumption implies. We will illustrate this point by presenting an example of why and how our visual system uses approximate information and approximate computations to make visual analyses fast and perfect. This discussion of the power of approximate computation will also allow us to introduce an additional type of symmetry that helps explain how we made the machine that sees like us.

In fact, this point might be one of the stronger arguments for implementing theories by building a seeing machine rather than by trying to develop models with only human subjects. You do not realize how difficult this computational problem actually is until you take a real camera and start analyzing real images, rather than analyzing toy examples. To illustrate, if the camera has 80 receptors (pixels), the number of all possible partitions is greater than the number of atoms in the universe (1 with 80 zeros after it).[5] By *partitions*, we mean regions in the retinal image that represent possible objects out there. If you have 6 million receptors, the number of partitions is greater than 1 with 6 million zeros. You had better have something "written on your slate" when you are born. If your slate is really blank, you cannot succeed. There will be no time to ever learn how to see using something like Lotze's assumption about local signs (Lotze, 1852). Your ashes will have blown away millennia before this could be done. In fact, there would not have been enough time to check all partitions in a camera with as few as 80 receptors (pixels) even if you started at the Big Bang and checked billions of partitions every second since then. Even our most prestigious scientific ancestors managed to overlook this problem. Helmholtz (1867/2000) surely never ran the numbers when he wrote his chapter on learning how to see straight line-segments. His oversight is really hard to understand because permutations were well-known back then. Hindus knew permutations around 1150 CE, and the systematic use of permutations in modern mathematics began in the second half of 18th Century and was widely known by the beginning of 19th Century. This kind of oversight not only began a long time ago, it continued until fairly recently. Hebb (1949), for example, failed to take them into account when he introduced his physiological eye movement theory of shape.

So, you must use some powerful *a priori* constraints if you want to be able to handle the veridicality of vision in a system that has 6,000,000 receptors available for processing information. You need constraints such as assuming that the object comes in a single piece, that the object is symmetrical, and that it is standing on a horizontal ground with a background behind it. You also have to introduce another type of symmetry into the representation and processing of the retinal images. This new type of symmetry, which is present in the visual system's architecture and in the visual operations (both hardware and software), is best represented as a multi-scale/multi-resolution pyramid. We will now explain what this symmetry contributes to visual processing and why it is needed. We begin this explanation by reminding the reader that the retina in the human eye has a finite number of receptors that serve the purpose of acquiring visual information and that there are *only* 6 million cones

[5]The number of partitions of a set consisting of N elements is called the set's Bell number B_N. B_N grows faster with N than 10^N but slower than N-factorial (N!).

in each retina that can do the job. We are focusing on the cones because it is the cones, rather than the rods, that are responsible for the recovery of 3D shape. It is fortunate that the retinal rod receptors do not contribute because there are 120,000,000 of them in each eye. We said there were only 6 million because this level of spatial sampling has only recently been exceeded in digital cameras. These cone receptors are *discrete* (separate and do not communicate directly with each other), which means that the visual sampling of light, a *continuous* physical stimulus on the retina, can only provide *approximate* information about the visual stimulus. The fact that the visual system obtains only approximate information from discrete receptors is actually a blessing because the larger the number of receptors, the greater the amount of visual information that must be processed. Consider the task of finding objects in a 2D retinal image. If no *a priori* constraints were used to accomplish this task, success would require checking *all* possible partitions of the receptors in the retina. In plain English, all possible patterns (groupings of the receptors) would have to be checked and verified until a partition was found that satisfied some criterion for the particular partition to be an object. Recall from what was said in the previous paragraph that if there were only 80 (yes, eighty) cones in the retina, the number of partitions would be greater than the number of atoms in the universe. So, checking all possible partitions in a human retina is not a practical undertaking. Having 6 million cones presents a huge computational problem if all, or even a miniscule fraction of all, possible partitions of receptors were tried.[6] Put simply, having and trying to use very precise visual input would not be a smart thing to do. Our visual system knows better than all of the scientists who overlooked the computational explosion inherent in using an *unconstrained* analysis based on the large number of receptors in the human eye. The system we all use that works so well for visual processing begins with a very coarse analysis of the entire retinal image, much coarser than the resolution available at the retinal image. An analysis as fine as the resolution that could be made with the individual receptors in the retinal image is not used for the analysis of the entire or even substantial parts of the retinal image simply because it would take an inordinate amount of time to do it.

---

[6]If almost all partitions are ignored, as they must be, there will be cases where we overlook the presence of objects regardless of whether the objects are small or large on the retina. This is called "inattentional blindness." Here, we are claiming that inattentional blindness is a straightforward result of a combinatorial explosion. It is not an example of some kind of "perceptual sloppiness." The fact, however, that this blindness *almost never* happens in everyday life reflects the operation of extremely efficient perceptual mechanisms, mechanisms that operate effectively despite this combinatorial explosion. There is, of course, an important exception. Inattentional blindness is a common cause of traffic accidents. Accidents do happen, more often than we would like, in today's everyday life, perhaps because evolution has not yet prepared us for the highly dynamical situations rife on our roads and highways. They were surely much less common in the life of our animal ancestors. Alternatively, it might simply be impossible to handle the combinatorial explosion inherent in such situations and we will never evolve to the point that they can be avoided completely.

Starting with and using a coarse representation also makes it easier, as well as faster, to find individual objects. Once these objects are found, finer and finer representations are made, each guided by the result of the coarser analyses. There is simply no other way to go about obtaining all of the visual information available in a retinal image that has 6,000,000 inputs. So, the real question is not whether to use an approximate representation, but (1) what should the approximate representation look like, (2) how many approximate representations are needed, and (3) how should they interact with each other. The importance of all of these questions was first recognized by Azriel Rosenfeld when he introduced pyramid algorithms to vision science (Rosenfeld & Thurston, 1971). Pyramid representations have some special properties that are of considerable significance with respect to how we detect and how we represent shapes in real images. Pyramid representations are self-similar in the sense that two neighboring levels differ with respect to scale and resolution by a constant factor (Figure 3.4). If the functional fields of the receptors on a higher level in the pyramid hierarchy are larger by some factor (say 2), their spatial resolution will be lower by the *same* factor. The resulting representations are, therefore, self-similar (symmetrical) in the scale/resolution space (see the multiple images of the woman in Figure 3.4). There is psychophysical, anatomical, and theoretical support for his kind of analysis, as well as for the significance of this kind of pyramidal architecture in the human visual system. For example, Wandell (1995) in his textbook on vision, reviewed anatomical and physiological evidence and was able to conclude that the human visual system actually has a pyramidal architecture. A decade earlier, Adelson and his co-authors (1984) put forth essentially the same conclusion when they explored the computational benefits of multi-scale/multi-resolution processing. At roughly the same time, Tsotsos (2011) used pyramids to avoid combinatorial explosion in machine vision and to model human visual attention. All of this recent work calls attention to the importance of scale/resolution symmetry in perception. It makes it clear that this symmetry plays an important role in human visual information processing. Note that this symmetry is not in the objects, but in the approximate processing of visual information.[7] This kind of symmetry in both visual and motor processing can explain such fundamental phenomena as Fitts' (1954) *speed-accuracy tradeoff*, which allows the visual system to produce fast responses to a visual stimulus when speed is needed and allows it to improve the precision of the response when more time is available (see Pizlo et al., 1995; Kwon et al., 2011, for more recent examples). It can also be used to find reliable contours of regions in the 2D retinal image (Estrada & Elder, 2006).

---

[7]Mandelbrot (1982) claimed that this type of symmetry is present in objects and called this property "fractals." At this time there is little evidence that the human visual system actually uses fractals.

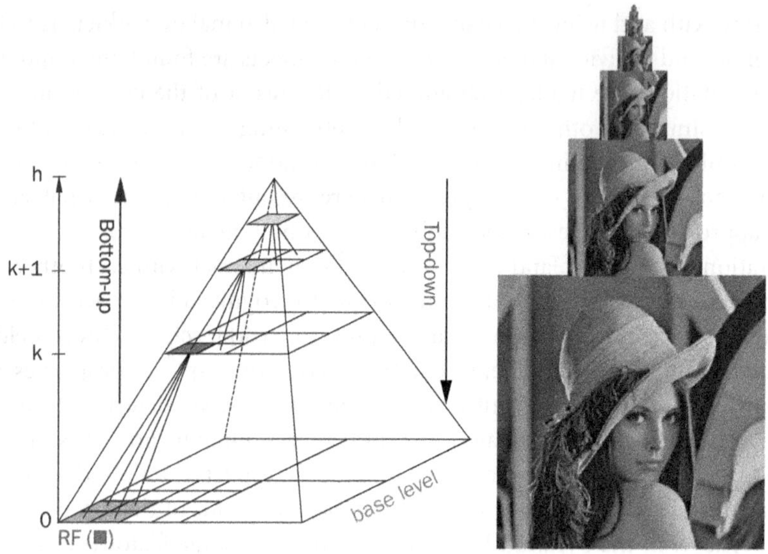

FIGURE 3.4. Pyramidal architecture (left). Illustration of self-similarity across scales and resolutions of pyramidal representation (right). Courtesy of Yll Haxhimusa.

Now that you know something about the nature and virtue of approximate computations and the scale/resolution symmetry that resides in a visual representation, we can ask whether both exact and approximate invariants can be used to detect symmetry in the skew-symmetrical shapes seen in Figure 3.2a and Figures 3.3b and c? The answer is yes. The polygon shown in Fig. 3.3b has 12 vertices, so if it is an image of a mirror-symmetrical figure, the image of the axis of symmetry must connect two opposite vertices, or the midpoints of two pairs of vertices, on the opposite side of the polygon. This means that the model has to try *only* 12 axes of symmetry. For each of these 12 lines, the model must verify that the line-segments connecting pairs of vertices, which should be symmetrical in 3D, are all approximately parallel to each other. If they are approximately parallel, the model must verify that their midpoints are approximately on the line that is an image of the symmetry axis (see Sawada & Pizlo, 2008 for details).

The important thing to remember is that when a polygon has N vertices, we have to try *only* N axes of symmetry. Not more, not less. This approach works well with smooth curves, not only with polygons. The only complication with smooth curves, like the curve shown in Figure 3.3d, is that one has to identify the feature points that will be used in lieu of the vertices before skew-symmetry can be verified. In Figure 3.3d, feature points were detected as points of maximal curvature (where the change of the direction of the curve was largest). If there are no obvious candidates for feature points, one must try all orientations of the symmetry lines when an orthographic projection is used, or all positions of the vanishing point when a perspective projection is used, and then verify whether the midpoints of the symmetry line segments are approximately collinear. By all orientations we mean a reasonably large number of orientations of a line on a plane, for example, 180 orientations with a step-size of 1. Similarly, by all positions we mean a reasonably large number of positions of a vanishing point on the surface of the retina, although it is more difficult to systematically sample points on the entire retina, than to sample line orientation in the 0°-180° range. There is no evidence suggesting that the human visual system actually tries many different orientations of symmetry lines or many different positions of the vanishing point probably simply because doing this would take too much time. It seems more likely that the visual system relies on feature points. In Chapter 4, we will provide additional arguments supporting the claim that the identification of feature points is essential.

Detecting symmetry in the image of a set of unconnected points, such as those in Figure 3.2b, is much more difficult than detecting symmetry when contours connect the points. Recall that when contours are present, as they are in Figure 3.2a, the vertices form a particular order. So, if two vertices are known to be mirror-symmetrical, the symmetry correspondence of all remaining vertices is also known. The presence of a contour and the inherent order of the vertices along the contour make it possible to perform what is called a linear search in which the number of possible symmetry correspondences is equal to the number of vertices. In the absence of a contour, the points do not form any particular order and the search becomes much more complicated. How much more? The computational complexity depends on the algorithm used, but the number of computations will be proportional to n^6, or to even a higher power of n, where n is the number of points. For 8 points, like those shown in Figure 3.2b, this means that there will be 260 thousand computational steps, when there is no contour, as opposed to only 8 computational steps, when contour is present. When as many as 100 unconnected points have to be examined, the number of computations is equal to 100^6, a number larger than the number of neurons in the human brain, so there would never be sufficient time to perform so many computations in a visual system like ours. This fact explains why we cannot see skew-symmetry in a retinal or in a camera's image of patterns made up entirely of dots, patterns that have no contours. This comparison between the computational difficulty of detecting skewed-symmetry in a polygon with n vertices, when compared to a set of n unconnected points, is completely analogous (though not identical numerically) to a lottery in which one has to guess one number out of n, compared to guessing 6 numbers out of n. The probability of correctly guessing one number out of n is 1/n (there are only n possibilities), but the probability of correctly guessing 6 numbers out of n is essentially zero for any moderately large n. Everyone playing a lottery like Powerball should know this quite well. Fortunately, this poses no problem outside the laboratory because contours are *always* present in our natural world. We never have to detect skew symmetry among n unconnected points. If we did, the probability of seeing veridically might be as likely as winning the jackpot.

3.2 How Human Beings Perceive 2D Mirror-symmetry From Perspective Images

Once we, and now that you, understand the geometrical underpinnings of mirror-symmetry, we need to formulate a model of how human beings perceive this kind of symmetry. When we started this work, there were only a few studies of the perception of symmetry of planar (flat) figures from asymmetrical images, and not even a single study of the perception of symmetry of 3D shapes from asymmetrical images, so there was no alternative to collecting the data we needed to develop our models of symmetry. This section describes experiments we did with planar (flat) shapes. The next two sections describe geometry and experiments with 3D shapes. You may wonder why, after all this fuss about the fact that real objects are always 3D, we are going to bother you with information about 2D shapes? Why should the perception of 2D shapes be included in this book once we realize that there is no such thing as a 2D object in our natural world? Such virtual objects cannot be kept out of the book because, as you already know, planarity, a 2D property, is one of the fundamental *a priori* constraints that is used by the visual system to recover 3D shapes. Planarity is critical not because things out there are flat (planar) or because they have flat parts. It is critical because planarity interacts with symmetry and compactness to make the 3D percept veridical. The simplest way to see the role of planarity is to realize that when all 3D curves are considered, the 3D curves that are (approximately) flat (planar) are simpler than 3D curves that are not (flat) planar. You already know how important the simplicity (Prägnanz) principle is in vision so, what we are simply claiming here is that the simplicity of curves and contours is an important part of the simplicity principle. For now, you will have to be satisfied with this kind of vague explanation. Much more will be said about this important aspect of 3D shape in the next chapter.

We began to acquire the data we needed to develop our computational model of symmetry perception by testing how human beings discriminate symmetrical from asymmetrical shapes based on the information provided by single 2D orthographic or perspective images (Sawada & Pizlo, 2008). Stimuli were presented briefly, only for a tenth of a second, to preclude appreciable eye movements. The stimulus was either a polygon or dots like those shown in Figure 3.2. We used these dots, a shapeless stimulus, simply to confirm that we could reproduce the chance performance obtained by others studying 2D skew-symmetry with dotted patterns. The subject's task was simple. He was asked to say whether the stimulus presented was symmetrical. Note that the *retinal* stimulus in this experiment was never actually symmetrical; it was either skew-symmetrical or asymmetrical. When the retinal stimulus was a skew-symmetrical polygon, the subject perceived it as a symmetrical figure slanted in 3D space. When the retinal stimulus was not skew-symmetrical, it was perceived as asymmetrical. We were not surprised to discover that subjects could discriminate symmetrical from asymmetrical polygons from both orthographic and from perspective images, but they could *not* discriminate symmetrical from the asymmetrical *dotted* patterns that did not have any contours. Technically, for dotted patterns without contours, performance was invariably at chance level (d' ≈ zero); with contours performance was good with d′ between 1 and 4, depending on the stimulus conditions. Furthermore, performance with *orthographic* images was slightly, but systematically higher than performance with *perspective* images. Recall that the retinal image is a *perspective*, not an *orthographic* projection of the 3D scene. In other words, the orthographic image is only an approximation of the true, perspective image. Our results show clearly that the visual system uses the tools derived from the orthographic projection and treats the true, perspective image as an approximation to this projection. We made this suggestion in Section 3.1. An orthographic projection of mirror-symmetrical patterns, which has three invariants, is potentially more useful than a perspective projection, which has only one invariant. So, as long as the perspective image is not very different from the orthographic image, it pays for the visual system to treat the image on the retina as an *orthographic* projection rather than as a *perspective* projection. This experiment shows that it does just this. This tradeoff of precision for effectiveness works well in everyday life with natural objects and natural viewing conditions. Our visual system is very clever, indeed, much smarter than the individuals who have been trying to figure out how it works since modern science began in the 17th Century. Note that we realize that this statement applies to us as well as to all others who have been trying to do this. What is important and new about what we are saying here is that our claim is completely opposite to what all skeptics, including the Bishop Berkeley, and most vision scientists today, have held. Berkeley and others were convinced that their arguments *against* the accuracy of perceptions *were* actually accurate. The thoughts supporting their arguments are mental events and they should not be taken any more seriously than the mental events called perceptions. They really had no good reason to assume that the accuracy of their arguments were any more certain than the accuracy of their perceptions.

Now that we had data characterizing how human beings perceive symmetry, we needed to explain how they do this, which meant for us, that we had to develop a computational model that can do it, too. Our model starts by searching for the direction of the symmetry line segments. This search is done by using the criterion for parallelism of the symmetry line segments and the colinearity of their midpoints that was explained in the last section. Once the direction of symmetry line segments was chosen, the *skew-symmetrical* figure in the 2D retinal image is used to recover a *mirror-symmetrical* figure in the three-dimensional space. Note that mirror-symmetry alone will not lead to a unique, veridical interpretation because a single 2D orthographic image only determines a *one*-parameter family of interpretations. This issue was discussed in Chapters 1 and 2, when we first introduced problems inherent in recovering 3D shapes. Back then, we added a 3D compactness constraint to produce a 3D veridical recovery. Here, we did this again and found that 2D compactness could account quite well for our subject's percept. We also found that with 2D figures other constraints led to similarly good results, namely, minimizing slant of the recovered shape or shearing the figure until the symmetry line segments and the line connecting the midpoints are orthogonal. Now that we have explained the perception of flat (planar) figures, we are ready for the real world of 3D shapes. This world is completely new because our study of 3D symmetry discrimination was the first in the history of this subject. This fact is puzzling because the systematic study of human vision began in the 19th Century, and the first experiment on the discrimination of the ubiquitous characteristic of 3D natural objects called *symmetry* was not done for 200 years!

3.3 Why 3D Mirror-symmetry is More Difficult Than 2D Symmetry

In this section, we will use polyhedral objects (3D analogues of 2D polygons), rather than natural objects like horses and cows, for the same reason that we used polygons in the section just above. Namely, it will make it easier for the reader to see the corresponding pairs of features in our illustrations and demos. All claims and observations that will be presented in this section generalize to natural objects as had been the case earlier. Some of the invariants of symmetry generalize from flat shapes to 3D shapes and others do not. Symmetry line segments, the line-segments connecting pairs of symmetrical points, remain parallel in any 2D orthographic image and their extrapolations intersect at the vanishing point in any 2D perspective image. This is analogous to the situation we had with flat shapes. The midpoints of the images of symmetry line segments, however, are not even approximately collinear in either orthographic or perspective projections, that is, there is no line in the retinal image that contains all of these midpoints. This is completely different from what happens with flat shapes. With 3D shapes, the midpoints of symmetry line segments are collinear in an orthographic or perspective image *only* when the 3D viewing direction is degenerate, namely when the plane of symmetry of the 3D object contains the line of sight (Figure 3.1a). This is what happens whenever you look at a photograph of a frontal view of any human face. Such a 2D photograph of a mirror-symmetrical human face is itself mirror-symmetrical. As you already know, such views are rare in everyday life because when the view is degenerate for one eye, it is very unlikely to be degenerate for the other eye and even the slightest movement of the head will remove the degeneracy from the input.

There are at least two characteristics of 3D mirror-symmetrical shapes that must be emphasized. First, take any two pairs of mirror-symmetrical points. These two pairs always form a flat quadrilateral. This is true not only with polyhedral objects, but with all objects. This means that no matter how curved the surfaces of a mirror-symmetrical object are, mirror-symmetry implies that some of the features will form flat (planar) configurations. Second, even though the images of the midpoints of pairs of mirror-symmetrical points are not collinear in a 2D image, the line connecting the midpoints *is* the image of the line that resides on the plane of symmetry of the 3D object. It follows that this line is planar (flat) out there. These are two cases where planarity can be established exactly with arbitrary 3D symmetrical shapes. By simply adding the simplicity argument presented in the previous section to the two characteristics described just above, we have already established three reasons for using our planarity constraint to recover natural 3D shapes. Later, we will add one more.

3.4 Updating the Ideal Observer: How Human Beings Perceive 3D Mirror-symmetry From Perspective Images

There was not a single study on this topic when we started studying human symmetry discrimination. The first study showing that human observers can discriminate between 3D symmetrical and 3D asymmetrical shape reliably, based on information provided by a single 2D orthographic image, was published recently by one of us (Sawada, 2010). Sawada did not include unnatural dotted stimuli, like those in Figure 3.5a, because he knew that studying such dotted stimuli had no merit and because, here, unlike in the Sawada & Pizlo (2008) experiment described earlier, there was no literature, calling for a replication of a shape experiment with stimuli that had no contours. Only shapes with contours, like the one in Figure 3.5b, were used as stimuli.

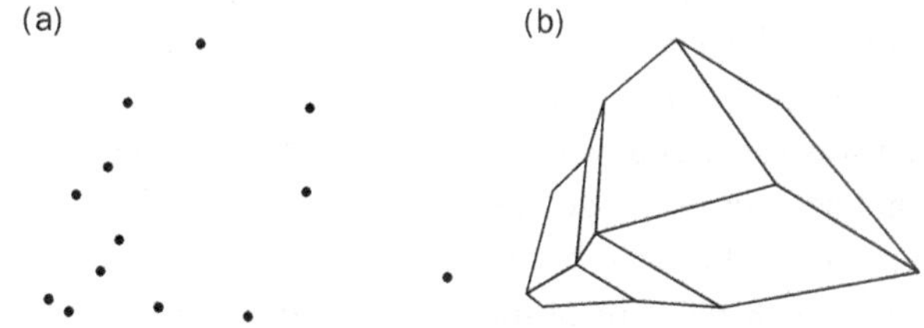

FIGURE 3.5. (a) Dots located at the vertices of the 3D symmetrical polyhedron seen in (b). It is impossible to see the points in (a) as residing in a 3D space or as representing a 3D symmetrical object. They do not serve like the vertices of a 3D object when there are no contours. It is impossible to detect 3D symmetry in this dot pattern.

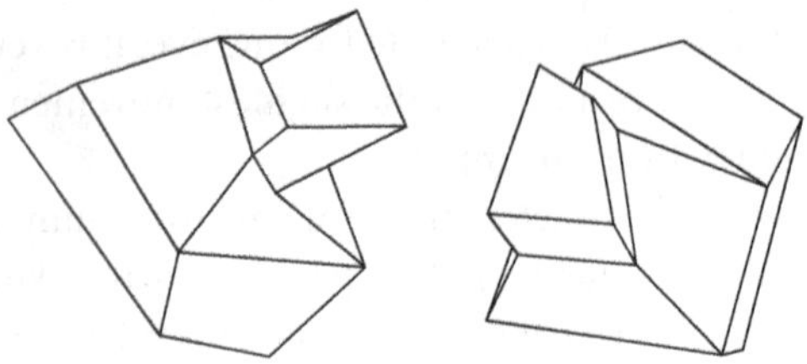

FIGURE 3.6. Two examples of stimuli representing the 3D asymmetrical shapes used by Sawada (2010) in his experiment. (With permission of the Association for Research in Vision and Ophthalmology).

The fact that subjects can perform this kind of symmetry discrimination came as no surprise because we already knew that symmetry, compactness and planarity *a priori* constraints can be used to recover a 3D symmetrical shape from a single 2D image. In two of the three stimulus conditions, used by Sawada, the 3D symmetry discrimination could be accomplished simply by verifying whether there were pairs of points in the 2D image that formed parallel symmetry line segments. Such pairs exist in the 2D image shown in Figure 3.5b, but not in either of the images shown in Figure 3.6.

Recall that if a 3D object is mirror-symmetrical, the line segments connecting pairs of symmetrical points are parallel both in the 3D object and in any 2D orthographic image. This means that the subject would be able to report that the 3D shape was *symmetrical* if he saw that all visible pairs of points in the 2D image formed parallel line segments. If at least two pairs of points formed non-parallel line segments, the subject could report that the 3D shape was *asymmetrical*. Recall that we humans can never see our retinal image so there is no basis for assuming that our subjects could have made this discrimination by using 2D features in their retinal image. They surely saw all of the stimuli as three-dimensional and judged their symmetry by using the stimulus's 3D shape, not by using its 2D features. It is important to appreciate the fact that our model must operate on the 3D recovered shape, the way our subjects operated and not on features of the 2D image, if it is going to be able to account for our subjects' performance. The model operates by first recovering a 3D shape and only then evaluating whether this 3D shape is symmetrical. Both our subjects and our model *saw* a 3D symmetrical shape when the 2D image allowed a 3D symmetrical shape to be recovered, and they *saw* a 3D asymmetrical shape when the 2D image did not allow this kind of recovery. What was surprising was that reliable performance was observed in a condition that seemed to be geometrically impossible. This condition can be called "impossible" because both the 3D symmetrical and the 3D asymmetrical shapes had 8 pairs of points forming parallel line segments. This means that the segments were also parallel in the 2D orthographic image. Once this was the case, the 2D image presented in *every trial* allowed for *both* a 3D *symmetrical* and a 3D *asymmetrical* interpretation, regardless whether the 2D image was produced by a 3D symmetrical or by a 3D asymmetrical shape. Given the fact that the symmetrical and asymmetrical interpretations of the stimuli were available on every trial, how could the observer pick the correct answer? The experimenter knew which image was which because he had made the stimuli, but, on every trial, the subject was presented with a 2D image that was completely ambiguous and uninformative. It should have been impossible for the subject to produce the correct answer reliably, but he did! How could he do this? You already know the answer to half of this question but you may not realize you do. By way of explanation: you already know that a 2D image of a 3D symmetrical shape can be interpreted as *either* 3D symmetrical or as 3D asymmetrical (think of the Ames' chair illusion). You also know that symmetry is a powerful *a priori* constraint and that a human observer has a predilection for perceiving the symmetrical interpretation whenever possible. So, *perceiving 3D symmetrical shapes as symmetrical is easy to understand.* There is nothing at all impossible here. It simply reflects a natural human tendency to perceive symmetrical shapes as symmetrical. This explains half of the trials, namely, the trials that actually had symmetrical 3D shapes. The remaining half of the trials with 3D *asymmetrical* shapes must still be explained. There is an inherent difficulty in this experimental condition—3D *asymmetrical* shapes had to be perceived as *asymmetrical* despite the fact that a 3D *symmetrical* interpretation was geometrically possible and despite the human beings' strong predilection for perceiving *symmetry* whenever possible. This predilection had to be overcome. If the subject could not overcome this predilection, he would have said that all of the stimuli were symmetrical. This would have resulted in chance performance. Performance was nowhere near chance. The subjects actually discriminated these stimuli quite reliably with their proportion correct as high as 80%. How did they manage to do this?

The *only* way to explain such reliable discriminations in this geometrically impossible condition is to realize that the 2D retinal image is not the only information the observer is able to use. The percept is not the same as the 2D image. We have known, and accepted this important fact, for more than 100 years, ever since the Gestalt Revolution. This is what was meant when the Gestalt psychologists emphasized that the percept is different from the elements from which it is made, and summarized this claim by saying that "the whole is different from the sum of its parts." Today, we can incorporate this important fact into our study of visual perception by saying that the observer's percept results from a combination of information from the 2D retinal image with the *a priori* constraints responsible for the observer's perception of 3D shape. These *a priori* constraints are at least as important as a source of information as the 2D retinal image. Once this is appreciated it becomes possible, actually, important to update a concept called the "ideal observer" that has received considerable attention since Horace Barlow introduced it into visual science about 50 years ago (see Geisler, 1989, and Geisler & Perry, 2011, for more recent applications of the ideal observer). Barlow (1962) introduced this concept when he tried to measure the *upper bound* of the human's, and subsequently, the cat's sensory coding. The concept of the ideal observer represents a hypothetical information processing system that is designed to perform some discrimination task in an optimal way. If there is uncertainty in the task, as there always is when psychophysical measurements are made, performance cannot be perfect. The ideal observer also makes some errors, but "ideal performance" is an estimate of the theoretical upper limit of a machine's or of a human's performance. A real system cannot perform better than this ideal. Barlow, in his seminal studies of visual thresholds for light, used the ideal observer analysis to determine the information available for perception in the 2D retinal image. It did not occur to him, and to many who have used this concept since, that the human observer has additional and very important sources of information that can be used to create his perceptions of the world. The human observer is not limited to the information contained in the 2D retinal image. Human observers can outperform any 2D ideal observer in a 3D shape discrimination task simply by using our 3D *a priori* constraints. It seems natural to update the concept of the ideal observer to bring it in line with the upper limit of our human observers when they solve inverse problems and no longer confine the ideal observer concept to the limits observed in experiments studying sensory capacities. This can be done by training the ideal observer to make optimal inferences much like those performed in a conventional regression analysis (a statistical technique for estimating the relationships among variables). In the Machine Learning Community this method is called a "support vector machine" (SVM) (Cortes & Vapnik, 1995; Bishop, 2006). It is worth noting that the use of an SVM to solve an inverse classification problem by using *a priori* knowledge derived from learning is analogous to, but different from, using a regularization method to solve an inverse 3D recovery problem by imposing *a priori* constraints on the family of possible 3D interpretations.

Look at Figure 3.7a. You see a number of randomly-mixed filled and unfilled disks. Imagine that the filled disks represent 3D symmetrical shapes and the unfilled disks represent 3D asymmetrical shapes. In a typical discrimination task, when a signal must be discriminated from noise, the observer is faced with the challenge of saying "yes" when a signal is presented and to say "no" when no signal is presented. This is not particularly complicated because the signal usually has a higher intensity than the noise (Green & Swets, 1966). Discriminating 3D symmetrical and asymmetrical shapes based on the information present in a 2D retinal image is much more difficult. There is no single feature in a 2D image that can do the trick. Performing a symmetry discrimination task optimally may be as difficult as separating the two clusters of filled and unfilled disks shown in Figure 3.7a. It turns out that there is always a

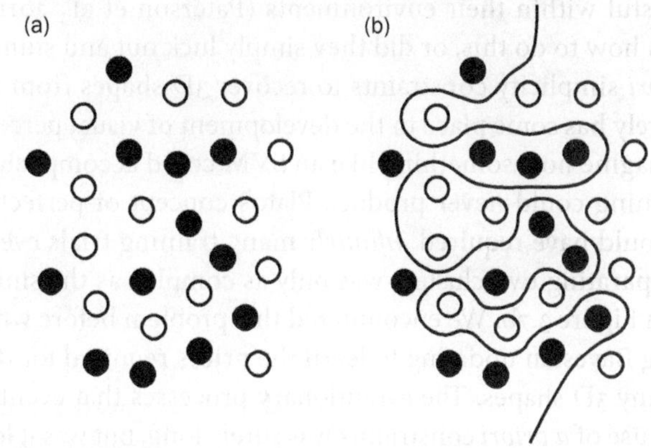

FIGURE 3.7. Discriminating filled and unfilled clusters of disks.

boundary that can separate them no matter how much the two clusters overlap. One such boundary is shown in Figure 3.7b. An SVM can find such a boundary by using some number of learning trials if it is provided with feedback. The fact that an SVM (or its Bayesian counterpart) can learn to discriminate between 3D symmetrical and 3D asymmetrical shapes based on a single 2D image does not mean that this is how a human observer performs this kind of discrimination. The human visual system uses *abstract a priori* constraints such as 3D symmetry and 3D compactness to recover 3D shapes. The SVM is not performing a 3D recovery. It learns how to classify stimuli on the basis of *experience* with *concrete* examples. The performance of the machine's learning algorithm may, occasionally, be better than the performance a human subject, but this information is likely to be useless because of the fundamental difference between the two systems. This difference encourages us to conclude that the ideal observer, despite the promise we said it might have just above, is *not* a useful concept for research on 3D visual perception. It simply cannot be extended in any meaningful way beyond the simple cases of signal detectability where it has been used so far. Machine learning algorithms are likely to be useful elsewhere in research on human vision, because they can provide a new and principled way of evaluating the amount and the nature of the information contained in a set of trials with diverse visual stimuli.

These recent advances in machine learning have raised a new, interesting question, a question for which we can offer at least a tentative answer. Namely, can an SVM *infer* the concept of 3D symmetry? The answer is probably "no," at least with the SVMs available for use today, but one must wonder whether such a machine could be developed, a machine that could represent evolutionary learning effectively. Early symmetrical animals, our earliest ancestors, going back as far as 500 million years, had visual systems not very different from ours. They would have had to use these systems to *infer* the concept of 3D symmetry from 2D asymmetrical images if they were going to be successful within their environments (Paterson et al., 2011). Did they have to learn how to do this, or did they simply luck out and stumble on how to use *a priori* simplicity constraints to recover 3D shapes from 2D images? Learning surely has some place in the development of visual perception but it is hard to imagine how something like an SVM could accomplish this if only because learning could never produce Plato's concept of perfect symmetry. *Perfection* would have required *infinitely* many training trials even when the boundary separating two clusters was only as complex as the simple boundary shown in Figure 3.7b. We encountered this problem before when we considered using Bayesian updating to learn the priors required for dealing with infinitely many 3D shapes. The evolutionary processes that eventually led to our effective use of *a priori* constraints was surely long, but was it long enough to be anything like an *infinity* of trials? This is a good question, but without good evidence for the effectiveness of learning in visual perception now, we will put all of our chips on the side claiming that the *a priori* constraints that have worked so well for us were not learned and need not be updated. Put succinctly, we believe that one or more mutations in our genetic code is responsible for the concept we call "symmetry." This does not seem farfetched because our DNA is, to say the least, symmetrical. Could it be that the secret of life resides not in the chemical composition of amino acids, but in their symmetry? Plato surely would have loved this possibility, as much as we do, despite its far out implications.

Now that you know how symmetrical, asymmetrical, and skew-symmetrical shapes are related to each other and why discriminating them may be difficult, we will provide a brief technical segue that describes the model Sawada (2010) used to explain how human beings discriminate 3D symmetry. He did not use a machine learning algorithm. Instead, he used a regularization approach. His computational model searches for a 3D shape X that maximizes the following cost function:

$$E(X) = \text{Symmetry}(X) + \text{Compactness}(X) + \text{Planarity}(X) + \text{Surface}(X)$$

This cost function consists of four *a priori* constraints. "Symmetry" evaluates the similarity of corresponding angles in the 3D shape. "Compactness" is simply a 3D compactness of X. "Planarity" evaluates the degree of planarity of the faces of X. Finally, the "Surface" constraint is the ratio between the surface area of the 2D retinal image and the surface area of the 3D recovered shape. As a result, the "Surface" constraint favors 3D shapes that have a small range in depth. After the shape X, which maximizes the cost function E(X), is recovered, its 3D mirror-symmetry is evaluated using the "Symmetry" component from this cost function. If the 2D image was actually produced by a 3D symmetrical shape, the recovered shape X that maximizes E(X) is usually very close to a *mirror-symmetrical* shape, but if the 2D image was produced by a 3D *asymmetrical* shape, the recovered shape X that maximizes

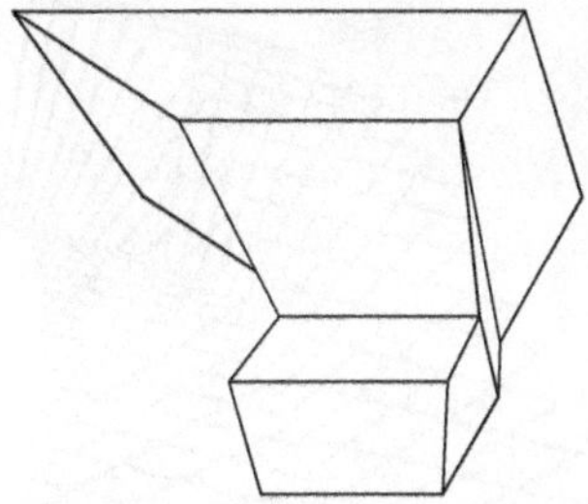

FIGURE 3.8. This 3D shape looks asymmetrical despite the fact that there is a 3D symmetrical interpretation of this 2D image. This unexpected 3D symmetrical interpretation can be seen in the DEMO 3.3.[8] (From Sawada, 2010 -with permission of the Association for Research in Vision and Ophthalmology).

E(X) is usually quite asymmetrical, despite that fact that there is another 3D symmetrical shape that can produce the 2D retinal image (see Figure 3.8 and DEMO 3.3[8] for an example). Put differently, if the 3D shapes were recovered by the human visual system using only the "Symmetry" component of our cost function, all 3D shapes in the geometrically-impossible condition of Sawada's experiment would have been perceived as symmetrical and the discrimination performance would have been at chance level. The *only* way to perceive a 3D *asymmetrical* shape as *asymmetrical* is to recover 3D shapes by using several constraints. It so happens that 2D images of 3D asymmetrical shapes viewed from most viewing directions lead to 3D asymmetrical recoveries when the recovery is done by using our cost function. Put succinctly, and somewhat cryptically, the 3D symmetry percept goes beyond 3D symmetry, itself. It must, if a 3D asymmetrical shape is to be perceived as asymmetrical and if an asymmetrical posture of an animal body is to be perceived veridically. More will be said about this in the next chapter.

3.5 Important Role of Generalized Cones in 3D Shape Perception: How Human Beings Perceive 3D Translational-Symmetry From Perspective Images

As you know from our treatment of symmetry in the first chapter, mirror-symmetry is arguably the most ubiquitous symmetry in our natural environment, but it is not the only type of symmetry that is needed to describe real objects in our natural environment. Translational-symmetry is probably the second most important kind of symmetry that permeates nature. You have seen that it can be used to describe parts of complex objects very well. Translational-symmetry, like all symmetries, refers to the

[8]http://shapebook.psych.purdue.edu/3.3

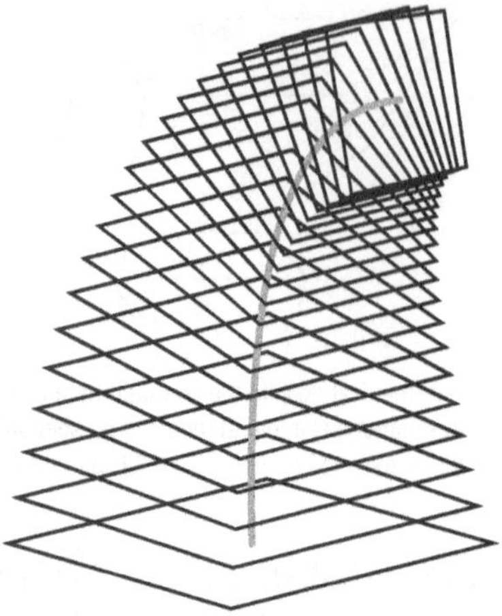

FIGURE 3.9. An illustration of how a generalized cone (GC) is generated (same as Figure 1.4).

self-similarity, inherent in the object itself, but unlike mirror-symmetry, translational-symmetry refers to the fact that the entire shape is made up of identical cross sections like those shown in Figure 3.9. In this example, the cross section is a square and this square is copied, translated, and then pasted many times along the axis of the object that has translational-symmetry. If the axis is a 3D curve like the one in Figure 3.9, the cross section has not only been translated, it has also been rotated. The size of the cross section of objects said to have translational-symmetry is also usually allowed to vary, as well. Technically, objects that possess translational-symmetry are called *generalized cones* or *generalized cylinders*. The term *generalized cone* will be used henceforth this book. A number of examples of such cones are provided in Figure 3.10.

Translational-symmetry was introduced into the study of shape rather recently, which is not surprising once one remembers that symmetry, in general, was ignored by the vision community until recently. Mach (1906) discussed 2D translational-symmetry briefly, when he contrasted it with 2D mirror- and rotational-symmetries (see Figure 3.11). But Mach's discussion of translational-symmetry was confined to discrete elements, like the texture on wallpaper. Such discrete translational-symmetry has nothing to do with

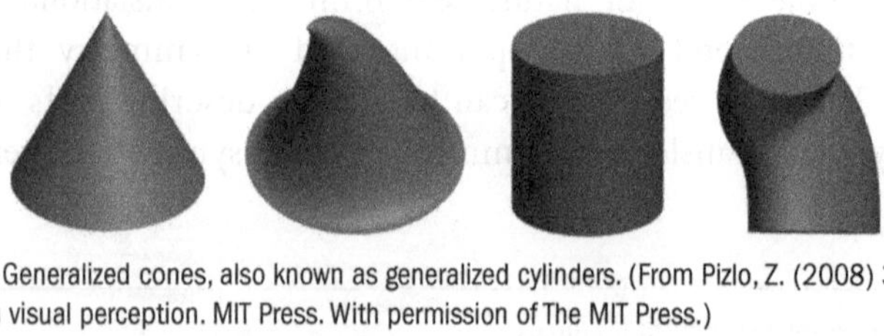

FIGURE 3.10. Generalized cones, also known as generalized cylinders. (From Pizlo, Z. (2008) 3D shape: its unique place in visual perception. MIT Press. With permission of The MIT Press.)

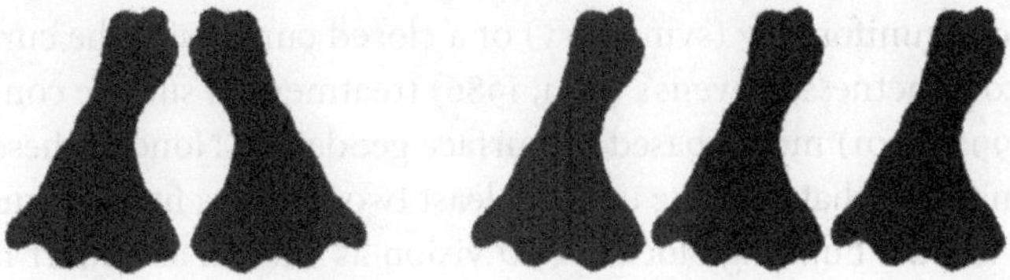

FIGURE 3.11. 2D mirror-symmetry (left) and translational-symmetry (right) (Mach, 1906). (From Sawada, T. (2010). Visual detection of symmetry in 3D shapes. Journal of Vision, 10(6), 4, 1–22, with permission of the Association for Research in Vision and Ophthalmology.)

3D shapes. It is only relevant to the perception of 3D surfaces, a fact treated extensively by Gibson (1950). Figure 3.12 shows two examples analogous to those in Gibson's (1950) book. Each of these images is a perspective projection of a planar surface represented by a repetitive (translationally symmetrical) pattern. The 2D perspective image of a translationally symmetrical pattern is, itself, not translationally symmetrical. The size, elongation, and density of the texture elements are not uniform in such 2D perspective images. Usually, this non-uniformity (skew-symmetry) is sufficient to allow the reconstruction of the 3D orientation of a surface. Gibson called this kind of non-uniformity a texture gradient. He believed that the texture gradient conveyed 3D information about the surface's orientation directly to the observer. We now know that there is nothing direct about using symmetry as an *a priori* constraint to solve this inverse problem in vision. No magic is buried in Gibson's suggested terminology, but recognizing that his texture gradient refers to translational skew-symmetry provides a common denominator for understanding how the machine vision community tried to develop their methods for the reconstruction of 3D surfaces. This includes Witkin's (1981) elaboration of Gibson's concept of the texture gradient, Brady & Yuille's (1983) proof of the equivalence of

FIGURE 3.12. Two examples of translational-symmetry.

orientational uniformity (symmetry) of a closed curve with the curve's maximal 2D compactness, Stevens's (1981, 1986) treatment of surface contours, and Knill's (1992, 2001) model based on surface geodesics. None of these attempts led to a machine that sees like us for at least two reasons: first, because 3D surfaces are not the building blocks of 3D vision as Gibson and Marr had hoped and, second, because the translational-symmetry of discrete elements is never sufficiently reliable to work well in the natural world. A continuous version of translational-symmetry, the kind represented by generalized cones, seem to better capture useful regularities of the natural world.

A first step towards making the connection between continuous translational-symmetry and shape can be found in Blum's (1967, 1973) medial axis transform, often referred to as his *grassfire model.* Blum's main motivation was to provide a simple representation of natural biological shapes. Blum, like most, perhaps even all, computer scientists studying shape, confined his analysis to 2D shapes, despite the fact that he surely knew well that all natural biological shapes had three dimensions. He did, however, provide a useful tool for representing 2D images of 3D biological shapes despite this obvious gaffe. There is no reason to believe that he actually intended to handle real 3D shapes, but the *skeleton* he introduced into the study of 2D shapes is a valuable tool for studying important natural 3D objects. Blum produced his 2D skeletons by inscribing circles into his 2D shapes and using the largest disks that touched the contour of the 2D shape in at least two points. The centers of these maximal circles were then connected to generate a line representing the 2D object's skeleton (Figure 3.13). Blum's skeleton is also called the object's symmetry axis or medial axis because it represents the spatially local symmetry of the 2D figure. The operation that produces a skeleton from the contour by inscribing circles is called the medial axis transform.

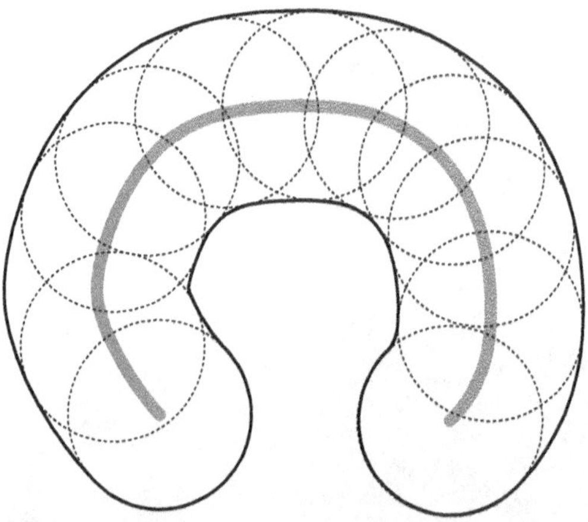

FIGURE 3.13. Blum's skeleton of a "biological" shape. The internal thick gray line line shows its "skeleton" (symmetry axis).

We will begin to explain why Blum's contribution proved to be important for our work by examining the symmetry of a closed planar (flat) figure that is represented by its skeleton (its symmetry axis). This will prove to be very useful when we analyze 3D translational-symmetry because the skeleton of a 3D generalized cone is the key concept used to represent the 3D symmetry of a generalized cone. The main change needed to transition from a 2D stimulus to a 3D stimulus is simply to move the skeleton off the plane of the 2D curve. This is not how generalized cones are usually characterized, but we will do this because it is the best way to retain all the advantages of Blum's theory of 2D shapes when we apply them to 3D shapes. When we do this, Blum's approach is simplified by eliminating one of its main operations, namely, we need not use the inscribed circles in his medial axis transform (or the inscribed spheres in Binford's [1971] 3D generalization). This simplification provides us with a much richer tool. Keeping Blum's medial axis transform for describing 3D generalized cones had proven to be a big obstacle in prior shape research. The main reason this has been a problem arises from the fact that the medial axis of a 3D object is a combination of curves and surface patches. While it is possible to extract a curve from a 2D image, it is not obvious at all how a 3D surface patch can be extracted from a 2D image. This makes the 3D shape recovery impossible to solve. We got around this problem by always using curves in our skeletons. Put simply, we kept Blum's skeleton, but ignored his medial axis transform. This was done because, despite the mathematical elegance of the medial axis transform with a 2D stimulus, this transform is neither elegant nor simple when 3D stimuli are used. With 3D stimuli, the medial axis transform is simply not very useful for describing 3D objects, and it has no value for characterizing the symmetries of 3D shapes despite the fact that it is both simple and useful elsewhere.

The difficulty with generalizing Blum's 2D medial axis transform to 3D objects is not its only weakness. Blum's skeleton only captures the spatially local symmetry of a 2D curve, not its global symmetry. This pretty much precludes using his transform to represent 3D shapes that require spatially global symmetries. This comes about because of the way the inscribed circles are used to produce the skeleton. Each point on the 2D skeleton is equidistant from two boundaries of the 2D shape. It follows that *locally*, the skeleton is a line of mirror-symmetry between the two boundaries, but *globally*, the skeleton is not an axis of mirror-symmetry simply because the skeleton is, more often than not, a curve, rather than a straight line. So, even though Blum's skeleton can be used to represent the *shape* of a 2D closed curve, it cannot be used to represent the 2D shape's symmetries. If the 2D shape is mirror-symmetrical, its skeleton will also be mirror-symmetrical, but producing the skeleton does not tell you whether symmetry is present in the 2D shape. So, what, if anything, are 2D skeletons good for? They can, actually, be very useful. A good example of this is in their use for *character recognition* when alpha-numerical symbols are

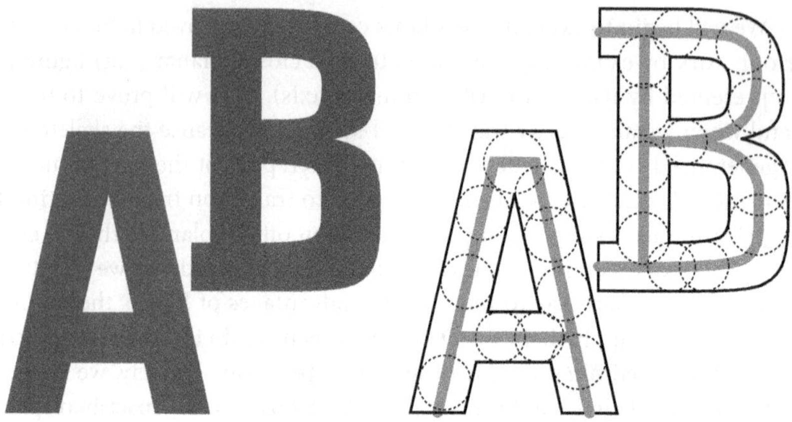

FIGURE 3.14. Capital letters A and B on left and their skeletons are shown in thick gray lines on the right.

read by machines. It is much easier to analyze the skeletons of these symbols than the symbols themselves. A simple example of letters and their skeletons is shown in Figure 3.14.

Now that you know how Blum came up with the idea of using a 2D skeleton, and why a 3D skeleton is not simply an elaboration of a 2D skeleton, we will explain how the translational-symmetry of a generalized cone can be used to recover the 3D shape of a cone. The general approach is identical to the one we used earlier when we explained what is meant by mirror-symmetry. You should recall that translational-symmetry refers to the self-similarity of a shape and that this property provides a sufficient degree of redundancy for the veridical recovery of the 3D shape from a 2D image. The computational model we developed for performing this kind of recovery will be described intuitively next. We will then describe psychophysical results showing that human observers recover generalized cones in the same way.

The 3D shape shown in Figure 3.15a was produced by using a concave quadrilateral as a cross-section and sweeping it along a planar curve, the cone's axis. The size of the cross-section was changed as the cross-section was swept along the axis (it shrank as it went up). The cross-section was always orthogonal (at a right angle) to the axis. We start by assuming that we (and the model) know the 2D projection of the 3D axis that was used to produce this kind of 3D shape. An example of such a shape and the projection of its axis is shown in Figure 3.15b. A human subject can estimate the 2D image of the 3D axis quite well. It seems likely, or at least plausible, that the subject does this by using a mechanism similar to Blum's 2D medial axis transform (Feldman & Singh, 2006).

The model begins by recovering the 2D shape of the polygonal cross-section. Recall that the cross section represents the essence of the 3D symmetry of a generalized cone. The generalized cone has two end cross-sections.

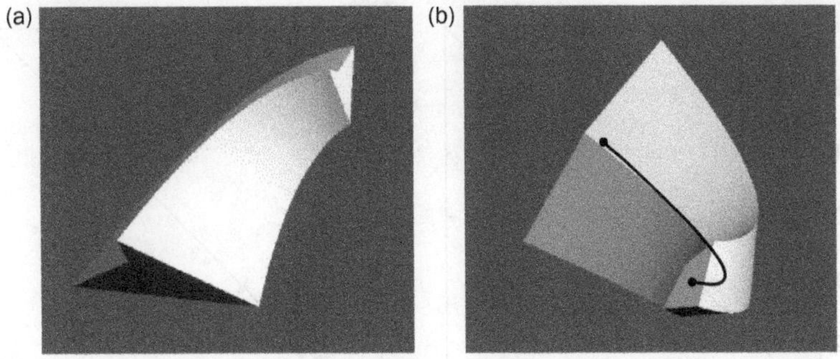

FIGURE 3.15. (a) Shows a 2D orthographic image of a generalized cone with concave cross-section. (b) Shows in black a 2D image of the axis of a different 3D generalized cone with a convex cross-section, superimposed on the image of this cone.

If at least 4 vertices of each cross-section are visible in a 2D perspective image, the shape of the cross-section can be recovered uniquely.[9] If an orthographic, rather than perspective, projection is used, the recovery is never unique; it is characterized by two degrees of freedom, the tilt of each end's cross-sections. These tilts can be estimated quite reliably from the edges of the generalized cone. Once the two tilts are estimated, the recovery of the shape of the cross section is unique. In the presence of noise and uncertainty in the 2D retinal image, the recovery must be aided by an *a priori* constraint. We discovered that 3D compactness, the constraint found to be essential for recovering 3D mirror-symmetrical shapes, is also indispensable for recovering 3D translationally symmetrical shapes. Once the shape of the cross section is recovered, the 3D recovery of the generalized cone is almost finished. The plane containing the axis of the cone can be recovered from the planes containing the two end cross-sections and the 3D axis can be now computed as a back projection of the 2D axis. Once the axis is known, the cross section can be swept along the axis adjusting the size so that the recovered 3D shape matches the 2D image.

Now that we know how a 3D generalized cone can be recovered from a single 2D orthographic image, we will compare our model's performance to our human subjects' (see Shi, 2012, for details). The subjects (YS and TK), who were shown a single 2D image of a 3D Generalized Cone like the one in Figure 3.15a, were instructed to recover the 3D shape by adjusting the aspect ratio of the planar (flat) cross section and the shape of the axis. These adjustments were made with a rotating stimulus to make sure that the subject saw the 3D shape from many viewing directions while the recovery was made. Figure 3.16 shows one subject's (YS) adjustments of the aspect ratio and of the shape of the axis as a function of the actual aspect ratio and the axis. Several dozen trials were run with randomly generated 3D shapes. The model's performance for the same

[9] Except for very rare cases in which there are two possible solutions—Longuet-Higgins (1986).

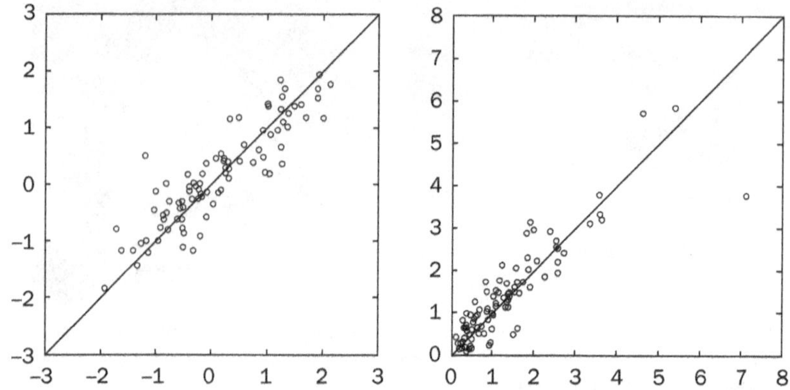

FIGURE 3.16. Subject YS's adjustments (vertical axis) vs. the true parameters of the 3D shape (left: the aspect ratio of the cross section; right: the shape of the axis of the 3D shape).

2D images is shown in Figure 3.17. Clearly, the model's and the subject's recoveries are quite similar. The correlation coefficients between the model and the subject for both the aspect ratio and the shape of the axes were high, 0.79 and 0.89, respectively.

This experiment showed that 3D translational-symmetry can be used to recover 3D shapes quite well. The algorithm that was used to do this is similar to the one used for recovering mirror-symmetrical shapes. In both cases, the recovery was based on the redundant information that was present in the 2D image, the information that inheres to the self-similarity of the 3D object. In both cases, 3D symmetry alone was not sufficient for a veridical recovery. A successful recovery required using 3D compactness, as well as symmetry constraints. Once both constraints were used, the model could produce a unique and stable 3D recovery based on a 2D image. The models' performance

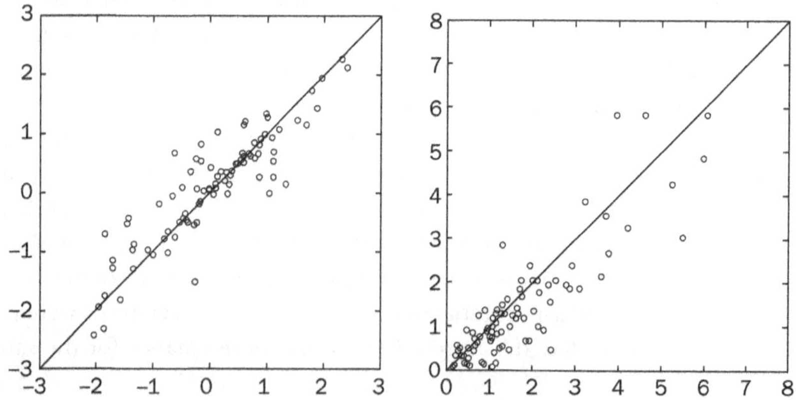

FIGURE 3.17. The model's adjustments (vertical axis) vs. the true parameters of the 3D shape (left: the aspect ratio of the cross section; right: the shape of the axis of the 3D shape).

was as good as our subjects' and both performances were close to veridical. Here, the reader should recall that our model can recover the back invisible parts of a mirror-symmetrical shape as well as its visible parts in front. We now know that this is true with translationally symmetrical shapes, too. It is also important to remember that the recovery of the *invisible* parts of a 3D object was completely overlooked in all prior research. Prior theories and their derivative experiments only addressed the perception of the *visible* parts at the front of objects. All of these experiments used stimuli and conditions that guaranteed large departures from veridicality. Our model and our experimental results on shape are completely different from all done previously. Ours clearly show that a machine with general purpose vision, capable of veridical perception, is both possible, and currently feasible, one can even say practical today, a claim that no one has had the temerity to make since 1982.

The critical aspect of our successful approach is our commitment to the importance and operation of a few *a priori* simplicity constraints. Symmetry is by far the most important of these constraints, but 3D symmetry, by itself, cannot serve as a visual stimulus because it can never actually be present in a 2D retinal image. All prior research, which concentrated exclusively on studying properties of the 2D retinal image, completely neglected 3D symmetry, the perceptual property that we now know is so critical for understanding visual shape perception. This fixation on the out-dated empiristic, Fechnerian way thinking that permeated modern visual science for more than a century allowed researchers to ignore symmetry completely. It is an intriguing, but until now unpopular, fact that the veridical perception of 3D objects and scenes depends *primarily* on abstract, universal *a priori* characteristics such as symmetry and compactness rather than on hard, concrete visual data such as the intensity of light, motion, and texture. This simple fact makes it clear that there is no role for learning and familiarity in visual perception because we get direct, sensory experience only of concrete things, never of abstract universal concepts. Abstract universal concepts are always known *a priori*, they are hard-wired into our nervous systems. It also follows from this simple fact that all non-perceptual factors such as our needs and desires cannot affect our perception of the shapes of 3D objects in 3D scenes. It is hard to imagine why one might even think that 3D symmetry could be affected by such pressures. It is scary to think of what our world would be like if they did. If abstract *a priori* concepts were sensitive to such personal pressures, our Greek forebears might never have discovered geometry, and today's physicists would not be modeling universes with eleven dimensions. If the abstract properties that permeate our world were subject to such pressures, we probably would never have developed either science or engineering. Accepting the simple fact, as we believe one must, that *simplicity constraints play the central role in visual perception, changes everything. It changes the way experiments are designed, the kinds of research questions asked and how a seeing machine will be built.*

We are not the first to make claims about the importance of built-in, abstract visual properties. Descartes, Reid, and Kant, as well as the Gestalt psychologists believed that such innate ideas, intuitions, and autochthonous grouping processes contributed a lot to our visual world but, until now, this could not be supported empirically. Computational modeling provided a way to do this. How long it takes the visual science community to accept these changes is hard to predict.

3.6 Michael Layton's Contribution to Symmetry in Shape Perception

By now, some readers, particularly those specialized in machine and human vision, may be wondering about the relationship between our work and Leyton's (1992, 2001, 2006). Leyton also concerned himself with symmetry. Leyton was perhaps the first scientist who realized that symmetry is a central concept in vision. Layton's theory of shape perception assumes that we perceive shape by reconstructing its chronology. Suppose we start with a parallelogram and ask how it came to have its shape. A parallelogram is a distorted rectangle and a rectangle is a distorted square. We can recover what happened to a given object in the past by ascertaining which symmetries have been removed. In essence, Leyton claimed that the shape of a given object *remembers* what happened to it. The history is stored in the symmetries that have been removed, or broken. In Leyton's (1992) words:

> *An asymmetry in the present is understood as having originated from a past symmetry. (p. 9)*
>
> *Increased asymmetry over time can occur in a system only if the system has a causal interaction with a second system (p. 13).*

Leyton coined this principle an "Asymmetry Principle" and claimed priority for formulating it. He also claimed priority for being the first to apply it to the shapes of objects, both animate and inanimate, including crystals, polyhedral objects studied in a field called "crystallography."

One of us[10] has been intrigued for years by the similarity of Leyton's "Asymmetry Principle" to Curie's "Symmetry Principle" (1894) that has been known in physics for more than a hundred years. It has not only been known for a long time; it has played a very prominent role in describing and explaining a wide variety of physical phenomena. Pierre Curie is credited by physicists for being the first to have formulated the "Symmetry Principle," and even Curie had a few predecessors in the 19th Century for developing this fundamental principle as modern physics changed our understanding of the physical world

[10] Pizlo.

at the beginning of the 20th Century (see Shubnikov & Koptsik, 1974, for a lucid review of the role of symmetry in physics).

In Pierre Curie's words (translated into English by Rosen, 1982, p. 20):

> *When certain causes produce certain effects, the symmetry elements of the causes must be found in their effects. When certain effects show a certain asymmetry, this asymmetry must be found in the causes which gave rise to them.*

And on the same page:

> *Asymmetry is what creates a phenomenon.*

Curie's (1894) paper, which begins with an overview of symmetry groups, includes examples of 3D shapes that illustrate these groups. It should not come as a surprise to our readers that this list contains all five Platonic solids. Curie's rather brief introduction is devoted to symmetrical 3D shapes. It sets the stage for the application of his Symmetry Principle to crystallography. After all, crystals are symmetrical polyhedral shapes. Said in less technical language:

> *a crystal under an external influence will exhibit only those symmetry elements that are common to the crystal without the influence and the influence without the crystal* (Newnham, 2005. p. 5).

So, it is clear that the Symmetry Principle was not first formulated by Leyton. Curie introduced it into science long before Leyton claimed priority. Furthermore, the observation that a Symmetry Principle can be applied to all 3D shapes, including crystals, was known 100 years before Leyton published his first book. Leyton's contribution lies, exclusively, in bringing Curie's principle to the attention of the human and machine vision communities. It is less obvious how the other elaborations that can be found in Leyton's writings contribute to our understanding of shape, and we hope that it may be easier to understand Leyton's theory now that we have placed his theory in the proper historical perspective.

Now that you know where Leyton's work fits into science, we can examine the relationship between Leyton's approach to symmetry and ours: Leyton claimed that a shape description must be based on the recovery of the history of how the object's symmetries have been removed or distorted. We only partially agree. We do agree that a chair with a broken leg should be described as just that, rather than as something like an unusual chair. The same would be true with an empty pack of cigarettes that was crumpled, but the shape of a normal chair does not lend itself to this kind of description. A symmetrical chair can be built out of asymmetrical parts, but this is not our only objection to Leyton's approach. We also object to the fact that Leyton managed to dissociate symmetry from shape. By emphasizing the process of removing symmetries from shape Leyton (2006) was led to claim that the most interesting shapes are those that do not have any symmetries (see Figures 1.7, 2.28–2.31 in his 2006 book). We disagree completely: there is *no* shape without symmetry. But there is even a more important objection, namely, a theory of shape perception should explain how we actually see shapes in everyday life. Leyton's theory says nothing about this. Our theory does. Simply put, Leyton's work has no place in our discussion because he did not address our problem. The same objection applies to another contemporary champion of symmetry in vision. His contribution will be described next.

3.7 Leeuwenberg's Attempt to Develop a "Structural" Explanation of Gestalt Phenomena

By now, some readers, particularly those specialized in mathematical psychology, may be wondering about the relationship between our work and Leeuwenberg's (1971). Leeuwenberg's theory, which is called "Structural Information Theory" (SIT), is based on the observation that symmetry is a form of redundancy, and if this redundancy is removed, a description of a curve or of an object will become shorter and thus, simpler (see Leeuwenberg & van der Helm [2013] for a recent presentation of this theory). In this theory, the shortest description, which is also the simplest, provides the basis for the human visual system to interpret both 2D and 3D shapes. It is important to note that the *only* evidence supporting this theory comes from the authors' examination of artificial and ambiguous, as well as illusory, line-drawings, the kind of highly-simplified 2D stimuli used by Wertheimer (1923) and Koffka (1935) in their studies of perceptual organization: an example is shown in Figure 3.18. Leeuwenberg's theory says nothing, whatsoever, about the veridical recovery of 3D shapes from 2D images, or about achieving shape constancy with 3D real objects in our natural environment. It should, then, come as no surprise that he is trying to solve quite different problems despite some superficial similarities in our terminology derived from our shared interest in symmetry and simplicity. Leeuwenberg's theory has been around for more than 40 years, and once we realize that it is not concerned with 3D shape perception, it is hard to understand what the specific problem needing a solution actually is. Whatever it is, we are certain that it is not the same as our problem, the perception of 3D shape. This claim is not the only difficulty we have with Leeuwenberg's theory. There are other troubling aspects in this work. They will be described next.

The authors of this theory credit Attneave's (1954, 1959) and Hochberg & McAlister's (1953) use of information theory in shape perception as the main inspiration and motivation behind SIT. Technically, unlike Shannon's

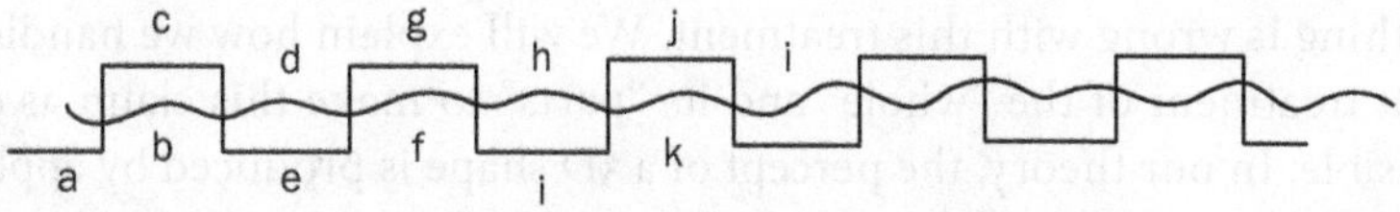

FIGURE 3.18. The simplest interpretation of this figure is that it is a sine-wave (parts b-d-f-h-k) superimposed on square-wave (parts c-e-g-i-j) (from Wertheimer, 1923). Human observers never perceive curves consisting of parts b-e-f-i-k and c-d-g-h-j. This example is often used to demonstrate the power of the Gestalt grouping principle called "good continuation."

information theory, Leeuwenberg's theory claims that the visual system uses specific elementary building blocks, such as straight line-segments and angles, to describe 2D curves and 3D objects. But note that by using a set of predefined building blocks, SIT ends up representing shapes symbolically, rather than geometrically. Shapes, as shapes, in this theory are less important than the symbols that are assigned to represent their parts. In SIT, the percept of shape is described by determining the simplicity of a string of symbols such as letters, words and even sentences in ordinary language. In this approach, the geometrical aspects of shapes take a back seat even when they are not removed entirely. It should be obvious from what we have just said that this approach violates the Gestalt's assumption of an isomorphism (sameness of form) between (1) the shapes out there, (2) the brain's representation of these shapes, and (3) the perception of them. This violation is not a superficial problem and it cannot simply be ignored. Furthermore, this violation, which is deeply rooted in the main assumptions of SIT, conflicts with the fundamental Gestalt assumptions about the basic nature of shape perception. Consider how Leeuwenberg & van der Helm (2013) summarized the relation between SIT and Gestalt theory recently:

> "According to the classical Gestalt motto, the whole is something else than the sum of its parts (Koffka, 1935: 176). Building on this motto, SIT assumes that wholes result from (non-linear) interactions between parts. To be more precise, we assume that perceived wholes (i.e., objects as we perceive them) result from interactions between the mental representations of parts. These interactions are assumed to be driven by similarities and differences between parts that may be anything in between perceived wholes and retinal receptive fields." (p. 85)

If you read this paragraph, as well as all of the authors' publications, carefully, you will discover that these authors contradict themselves and violate Gestalt assumptions. This claim is easy to support. For example, they say that the whole results from putting parts together and, at the same time, they say that the whole is completely different from the parts used to put it together.

Something is wrong with this treatment. We will explain how we handle the Gestalt treatment of the "whole" and its "parts" to make this claim as clear as possible. In our theory, the percept of a 3D shape is produced by applying four simplicity constraints to a single 2D retinal image. The resulting percept (the "whole") is different from the incoming 2D retinal image (the "parts") on five counts (1) the percept is 3D while the retinal image is 2D, (2) the percept is symmetrical but the retinal image is not, (3) the percept is always a veridical representation of the 3D shape out there but the retinal image is never veridical, (4) the percept *never depends* on the viewing direction (it exhibits shape constancy) while the retinal image *always depends* on the viewing direction and never exhibits constancy, and (5) the 3D shape determines the 3D percept of the parts of the 2D retinal image, not the other way around as implied in the quote just above. This last point will be elaborated because it may come as a surprise to many, perhaps even to most of our readers. Look again at Figure 3.5, discussed earlier. The vertices of the 3D polyhedral object in Figure 3.5b are perceived in 3D only *because* they are part of the 3D shape. When these vertices (points) are shown in isolation (Figure 3.5a), there is no three-dimensionality in your percept. The same is true with the edges of this polyhedral object. Each edge is perceived as slanted in 3D only *because* it is an edge of a 3D shape. If any of the edges (line-segments) is shown in isolation, it is perceived as a 2D edge on the surface of the line-drawing, not in three dimensions. Clearly, the 3D shape (the Gestalt "whole") determines the perceived 3D orientation of the edges and the perceived 3D positions of the vertices (the "parts"). The converse is never true because the parts, here the points and line segments, reside in the 2D retinal image, and none of the parts has 3D characteristics. The distinction between 2D parts and the 3D whole in our theory is even more dramatic when you realize that when you look at Figure 3.5b you see a 3D *opaque* object whose back, invisible vertices, edges, and surfaces are filled-in (predicted) by your visual system as well as by our machine. The concept of opaqueness does not even exist when 2D parts are not perceived as a 3D shape (see Figure 3.5a), so there is no reason to fill-in (predict) anything about its back. There is no "back" when there are only 2D parts without a 3D whole.

Now that you know what and how Leeuwenberg et al. got things wrong, what did they get right? They knew what had to be done and deserve credit for this because they were the only theoreticians during the last 40 years that made a serious attempt to put information theory, symmetry, and simplicity into a single package with relevance for the concept called shape. When the SIT was introduced in 1971, it looked like it might even help explain how human beings perceive 3D shape. It could not do this and, standing where we are now, it is not hard to see why. Three critical things were missing, (1) it was not based on projective geometry, (2) it did not use the formalism called Inverse Problems Theory, and (3) it did not make an effort to model real objects in their natural environment. They do deserve credit, however, because few others appreciated that some new way of using the Gestalt contributions to perception were essential for making progress. They deserve credit for trying to do this even if their theory contributed little to this goal. They knew what had to be done, and tried to do it, while most other theorists were locked into a pre-Gestalt 19th Century way of thinking.

4

Using Symmetry is Not Simple

This chapter begins with a brief summary of the most important landmarks reached as we advanced toward our goal of explaining how we made the machine that sees like us. In the first two chapters, we explained how the 3D symmetrical shape of an object can be recovered correctly simply by applying 3D symmetry and 3D compactness *a priori* constraints if: (1) we have a 2D image of a 3D mirror-symmetrical object and (2) we know the correspondence of the points in the 2D image that represent pairs of mirror-symmetrical points in 3D. In the third chapter, we added to our understanding of the kind of 3D shapes that can be recovered from their 2D image. Specifically, we showed that 3D *approximately* symmetrical shapes can be recovered by applying all four of our *a priori* constraints: the 3D symmetry, the 3D compactness, the planarity, and the minimum surface area constraints. New questions came up once this new knowledge was in hand (1) what happens if the correspondence of the points in the 2D image is not known and (2) what can be done if we do not know whether the 2D image represents a 3D mirror-*symmetrical* or a 3D *asymmetrical* shape? We hoped when we undertook this work that the symmetry *a priori* constraint could be used not only to produce a veridical recovery of a 3D symmetrical shape, but that it could also be used to solve the two additional problems listed just above. Only partial answers to these two questions could be provided in Chapter 3, specifically, we showed that when the correspondence of the points in the 2D image *is known*, applying all four of our *a priori* constraints allows us to decide whether the 3D shape is symmetrical. But, as we will show next, if the correspondence in the 2D image *is not known*, our symmetry constraint becomes useless, or nearly so. It cannot tell us whether the 2D image represents a 3D mirror-*symmetrical* or a 3D *asymmetrical* shape.

It is striking that a 3D mirror-symmetrical interpretation can be produced simply by applying a 3D symmetry constraint to a drawing of two completely arbitrary curves like those in Figure 4.1, and that this can be done even if the correspondences of points along these curves is chosen arbitrarily

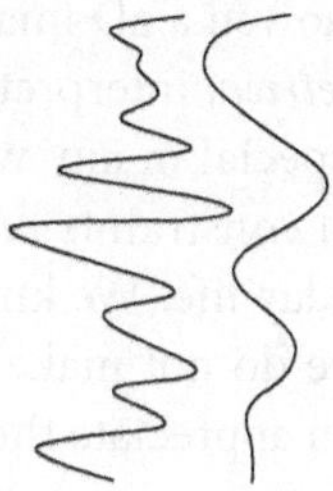

FIGURE 4.1. A pair of apparently unrelated arbitrary curves that actually is the image of a pair of 3D symmetrical curves. You cannot see the 3D symmetrical interpretation when you look at this 2D image (see text for an explanation).

(see DEMO 4.1).[1] For many examples like this, the spurious 3D symmetrical interpretation that results will be quite complex. Their 3D curves will have many twists and turns and all of the 3D symmetry will be hidden in the depth direction. Furthermore, all of these curves will be highly non-planar (they will not be flat). We will now show that such spurious, unlikely, and unwanted 3D symmetrical interpretations that are caused by arbitrary 2D curves with arbitrary and incorrect correspondences can be prevented from being selected by our visual system simply by imposing additional constraints. These incorrect 3D interpretations can be excluded if the view is not degenerate, and if the 3D curves are kept relatively simple and approximately flat (planar). Technically, we will be able to show that these additional constraints can be expressed by approximate invariants of 3D symmetry under both orthographic and perspective projection. In plain English, what we mean is that there actually are some reliable cues in the 2D image that, if understood properly, will allow us to detect the real 3D symmetry of real objects in their 2D images, despite the fact that this problem seems to be mathematically insoluble.

We already know from Chapter 3 that a symmetry constraint can produce a veridical recovery of a 3D *symmetrical* shape from its 2D retinal image. This is extremely important, as well as useful, because we know that a 2D retinal image of a 3D symmetrical object could have been produced by infinitely many 3D *asymmetrical* shapes. Similarly, if a particular 2D retinal image was produced by a 3D *asymmetrical* shape, we would want a machine, or an observer, to see the *veridical asymmetrical* shape, rather than any of the many other possible *asymmetrical* non-veridical interpretations. But, if the visual system was only able to apply a symmetry constraint to the 2D retinal image of an *asymmetrical* 3D shape, it could recover a 3D *symmetrical* shape by mistake. Examples of this kind of mistake were provided in Chapter 3 (see

[1] http://shapebook.psych.purdue.edu/4.1

Figure 3.8). In this figure, we showed a 2D image of a 3D *asymmetrical* shape that could produce a 3D *symmetrical* interpretation. Note that the particular 2D retinal image need not be special in any way to make it possible for this mistake to be made. Additional constraints *must* be available if this mistake is going to be avoided in everyday life. We know that such constraints must actually be available because we do not make such mistakes as we go about our daily business. Now that you appreciate the significance of this important fact look at DEMO 4.2.[2]

Look at the pair of curves for a few seconds before doing anything and then use your mouse to rotate it. This allows you to see it from different viewing directions. Before you fiddled with it, the two curves shown in this demo did not look symmetrical. Furthermore, they did not convey even the slightest hint of the presence of 3D symmetry. Clearly, there is a very obvious 3D symmetrical interpretation, but it was impossible to see the 3D symmetry in the original image. The original image showed a *degenerate view* of this stimulus. This example is particularly striking because of how we made it. We made the 2D image first and then computed the 3D symmetrical interpretation used to make this demo. This demo and its significance came as a great surprise. One of us[3] stumbled on this example when we showed our first demonstration at the Vision Sciences Society Meeting in May 2008, shortly after the publication of the book on the uniqueness of 3D shape. All of us ignored the importance of this discovery because we were completely occupied demonstrating our veridical 3D shape recovery from a single 2D image by application of our *a priori* symmetry and compactness constraints. It took at least a year before we realized what we had in hand. We only came to understand and appreciate its significance fully during one of our irregular brainstorming sessions. As soon as we fully appreciated what it meant, we wrote a paper describing a novel theorem stating that "any 2D image has 3D symmetrical interpretations" (Sawada et al., 2011). We knew that we were going to be able to prove this theorem, but one aspect of the proof proved to be quite tricky. We knew how to produce 3D symmetrical interpretations from any 2D image, working on pairs of points at a time (see Section 2.3), but it was not clear whether the 3D interpretation would be a 3D curve or a set of unconnected points. The latter would have been better from the point of view of a vision system. Namely, if a spurious 3D symmetrical interpretation were always a set of unconnected points, such interpretations would have been easy to detect and discard. The former, however, was more interesting intellectually and we were pleased to discover that it actually was geometrically possible. We proved that if we start with a single 2D curve, we will end up with a single 3D curve. This obviously meant that detecting *spurious* 3D

[2] http://shapebook.psych.purdue.edu/4.2

[3] Yunfeng Li.

symmetrical interpretations will be difficult. Working this complication out required more than one head. The proof we produced is an example of one of our collaborative efforts. We had to jump across several areas of mathematics to work it out.

Returning from this segue, describing what was going on behind the scenes, to our explanation of DEMO 4.2[4], we made the 2D image first and then computed the 3D symmetrical interpretation used in this demo. It is more difficult to produce such a vivid effect if you start with 3D symmetrical curves and then find the 3D viewing direction from which the 2D image has so little symmetry. Once the significance of this result was appreciated, we went on to prove several general theorems stating that *3D symmetrical interpretations are always possible*, regardless of the character of the 2D retinal image. This previously overlooked property of 3D shape recovery, which is shocking perceptually, is actually trivial geometrically. Why it is trivial will be explained later when we show that human beings almost never make mistakes about 3D symmetry. We see symmetry only when it is actually present in the stimulus, never when it is not. The key to understanding why and how this works resides in the nature of degenerate views and the fact that they are almost non-existent outside of the laboratory. It seems likely that our visual system avoids mistakes about symmetry simply because degenerate views are so unlikely in the natural world. There is almost no pressure on working out effective ways of dealing with them. All the visual system has to do is to assume that degenerate views *never* present themselves in every day life. This simplifying assumption makes a lot of sense because whenever an observer is not restrained and keeps both eyes open, it is impossible to produce two or more degenerate views that can be maintained for more than a second or two. But, note that once degenerate views are allowed in experiments supposedly on shape perception, *illusions,* like the one you saw in our demo, can find their way into the shape literature where they have no place. They cannot play any role in everyday life so they should not play any role in research on shape perception. They can tell us nothing, whatsoever, about how shape is actually perceived. They can only serve as a control condition in the laboratory to demonstrate the operational limits of the shape perception mechanisms. They have no other legitimate use. We will also show in the present chapter that an *a priori planarity* constraint is the key to the successful operation of the *symmetry* constraint and we will also provide a justification for the use of the planarity constraint in modeling. This constraint provides a way of avoiding symmetrical, non-veridical interpretations of a 2D stimulus. Finally, note that the *planarity constraint is particularly useful because it eliminates spurious 3D interpretations, not because planar curves are common in the natural world.*

---

[4]http://shapebook.psych.purdue.edu/4.2

4.1 What is Really Going On? Examining the Relationship Between Simplicity and Likelihood

In Sections 1.9 and 3.4, we discussed the relationship between built-in abstract simplicity constraints on one hand, and Bayesian priors established through experience with particular objects on the other. At that time we indicated that, despite mathematical similarities, one had good reason to assume that our shape perception is based on the operation of the simplicity constraints rather than on Bayesian priors. We will examine the relationship between simplicity and likelihood again because their relationship will prove to be particularly useful in explaining how the visual system avoids spurious 3D symmetrical interpretations. We begin with an example described by Ernst Mach just over 100 years ago. He pointed out that when a straight line-segment is projected on the retina, the observer will always see a straight line-segment, rather than a circle, despite the fact that a circle can produce a straight line-segment on the retina when it is viewed from a degenerate viewing direction. Mach went on to point out that there are two ways of explaining what was perceived with this kind of stimulation. One of his explanations was based on his *simplicity principle*. Specifically, if two or more 3D interpretations are possible, the visual system will use the simplest possible interpretation. The reader will surely agree with Mach that a straight line-segment is geometrically simpler than a circle. The straight line-segment can be represented in a single dimension but the circle requires a two-dimensional representation. It is obvious that a two-dimensional representation is more complex than a one-dimensional representation. Mach's second explanation was probabilistic (the "likelihood" of an outcome). Specifically, a straight line-segment out there produces a straight line-segment on the retina for almost all viewing directions. This is obviously not the case with a circle, which produces a straight line-segment for only the very limited number of viewing directions called *degenerate views*. For all other viewing directions, a circle produces an ellipse on the retina. Recall that these viewing directions are degenerate in that the plane on which the circle resides goes through the center of the perspective projection. We have discussed problems inherent in degenerate views in some depth already, but we will explore this concept more thoroughly here because understanding all of their implications can help us explain the perception of 3D symmetry.

Mach's example and explanation should give you at least some inkling about what the term degenerate view refers to, as well as to the fact that an explanation based on a *simplicity* principle can be related to an explanation based on a *likelihood* principle. It is probably less clear how Mach's reasoning relates to the veridical perception of 3D symmetrical shapes. We will begin to explain this relationship with a simple geometrical construction. Consider Figure 4.2, which illustrates a single point of light on the retina. The observer's visual system is faced with the question of whether a 3D mirror-symmetrical

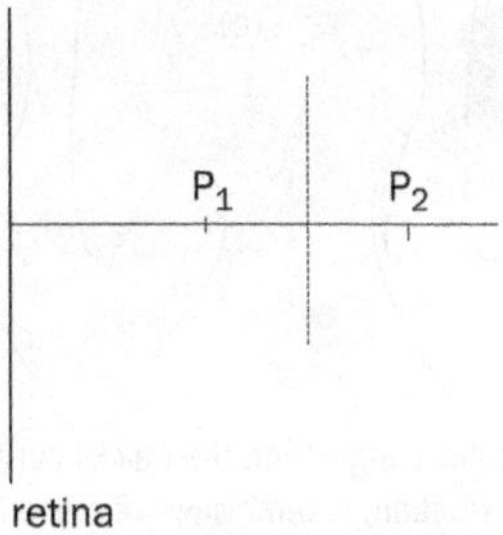

FIGURE 4.2. Two points, P_1 and P_2, fall on a line that projects to the same point on the retina.

interpretation of this retinal image can exist. The answer is "yes"—one such interpretation is shown in Figure 4.2. It shows a pair of points, P_1, P_2, residing on the line that projects to the point on the retina. Now you should be able to recognize how this figure relates to Mach, namely, the view (the direction of the view that includes P_1 and P_2) shown in Figure 4.2 is degenerate because the two points out there project to a single retinal point. If there is a single point on your retina, you will see a single point, rather than a pair of points simply because seeing a single point is *simpler* than seeing two points and seeing a single point is also *more likely* than seeing two points just as Mach claimed. The key to understanding this example is that any pair of points on a projecting line satisfy the definition of mirror-symmetry because we can always find a plane orthogonal to the line-segment connecting the two points and bisecting it. Technically, let the depth of P_1 be z_1 and the depth of P_2 be z_2. The two points are mirror-symmetrical with respect to the plane bisecting the line-segment P_1P_2. The depth at which the symmetry plane bisects the line-segment P_1P_2 is $(z_1 + z_2)/2$. So, simply by allowing a degenerate view, we were able to sneak in mirror-symmetry. The remainder of this section will describe more elaborate and more realistic examples of the construction shown in Figure 4.2. These examples will be followed by a formulation of new invariants of 3D symmetry.

One cannot overemphasize the importance of this material for understanding how a machine that sees like us was built. In a sense, veridical shape perception is like walking a fine line between *overlooking* the symmetries of all natural objects and *seeing* symmetries among objects where there actually are none. Note that such questions are completely new because the importance of *a priori* constraints in general, and the role of a symmetry constraint in particular, are quite new.

We can now move from the recovery of a pair of points to the recovery of curves. Look at Figure 4.3. This image was used in DEMO 4.2[5] you just saw. The two curves in (a) do not look like a pair of 3D mirror-symmetrical curves

[5]http://shapebook.psych.purdue.edu/4.2

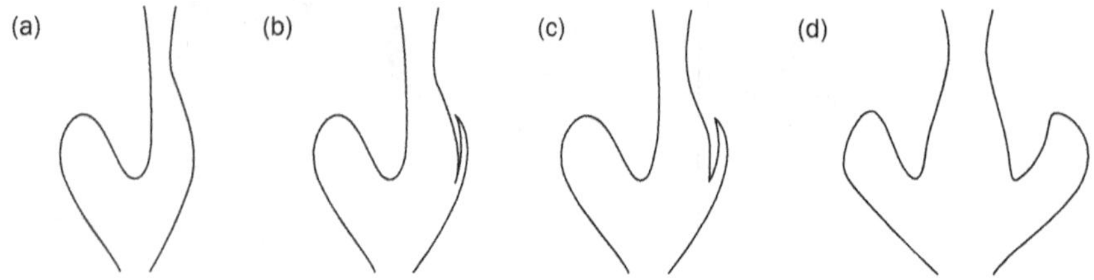

FIGURE 4.3. Examining Mach's probabilistic argument: the pair of curves in (a), which do not look mirror-symmetrical, have such an interpretation; several views of one such interpretation are shown in pairs (b–d).

despite the fact that such an interpretation is possible. Several views of one such interpretation are shown in (b-d). We are using this figure and the demo to show that it is easy to apply Mach's probabilistic arguments about degenerate views that were just described. If the 3D curves are like those shown in Figures 4.3 b-d (as well as in the demo), the image in (a) is obviously degenerate. You can clearly see that a large section of one curve is hidden along the depth direction, the *lip* shown on the right in (b) and (c). Even a smallest change in the 3D viewing direction produced by rotating the curves in this demo reveals this hidden lip. It should be obvious that the chance (likelihood) you will ever encounter a degenerate view on your retina like the one in Figure 4.3a in everyday life is virtually nil. Geometrically, if we assume that all 3D viewing directions are equally likely, the probability of actually ever looking at a 3D object from a degenerate view is *zero.* Practically, however, as we know from material in Section 3.1, the probability can never be *exactly* zero because there is a finite number of receptors on the retina, but it will be very close to zero.

It is also possible to use Mach's simplicity argument with the contours shown in Figure 4.3. The rightmost 2D curve in (a), which is not too far from a straight line, is obviously *simpler* than the rightmost 2D curves shown in (b–d).[6] Each of these 3 curves has two very curved segments. Now, we must compare the simplicity of 2D curves to the simplicity of 3D curves. First, recall that a 2D curve may reside within a 3D space. We made use of this fact at the beginning of this section when we said that Mach pointed out how a circle in a 3D space can produce a line-segment on the 2D surface of the retina. The comparison of the simplicity of a 2D curve to the simplicity of a 3D curve is not trivial mathematically because describing a 3D curve

[6]Following the intuition behind Attneave's (1954) argument, more bits of information are needed to describe a curve which contains high curvature parts than are needed for a curve that is approximately straight. High curvature parts are simply more *surprising* so they will have a longer (more complex) description (see Feldman & Singh, 2005, for an example of how the complexity of a description can be computed and its length estimated).

requires measuring the information about two curvatures at each point (the curvature and torsion). Describing a 2D curve only requires measuring information about one curvature at each point because the torsion is zero along the entire length of the 2D curve. To get an intuitive appreciation of the difference between *curvature* and *torsion* imagine comparing a circle to a spiral. A single turn of a spiral is produced by cutting a circle and stretching the two ends in opposite directions. The resulting difference between the original circle and the spiral is the fact that a torsion (twist) of a spiral is not zero. The problem of comparing a 2D retinal curve to a 3D curve can be reduced, or even eliminated entirely, if a planarity constraint can be applied to the 3D recovery. It can be applied in Figure 4.3 because the 3D curves shown in (b–c) are not far from planar (flat) (see DEMO 4.2[7]). The simplicity of the 3D interpretation can be compared directly to the simplicity of the 2D images in (b–c) when the torsion of the 3D curves is close to zero at every point. The 3D symmetrical interpretation shown in (b–c) is simpler than the 2D asymmetrical retinal images (b–c) by a factor of about 2 because the 3D symmetrical interpretation consists of two identical curves, whereas the 2D asymmetrical images in (b–c) consist of two different curves.[8] This is not the case with the image shown in (d). Here, the 2D image, itself, is symmetrical, which makes it somewhat simpler than the 3D symmetrical interpretation. Note, however, that the difference in simplicity between the 2D and 3D interpretation is not large, so one may wonder why we *never* see the 3D symmetrical interpretation. The answer is not based on the simplicity of curves. It is simply based on the fact that a 3D symmetry constraint is not effective in 3D shape recovery when the 2D retinal image *actually is symmetrical*. This brings us back to the concept of degenerate views because the figure in (d) represents a degenerate view, but here the view is called "degenerate," not because several points or several contours overlap in the image, but because this view is both unlikely and useless for making a 3D recovery. A 2D image of a 3D mirror-symmetrical shape is itself symmetrical only for a very small set of viewing directions and, here, even a very small change of the viewing angle makes the 2D image asymmetrical. The fact that a symmetrical 2D image can prevent a symmetry constraint from being useful was discussed in previous chapters.

The next example provides additional arguments for the usefulness of the planarity constraint. Look at Figure 4.4a. This figure looks like a pair of

---

[7]http://shapebook.psych.purdue.edu/4.2

[8] The number of bits of information needed to describe two identical curves is obviously twice the number of bits needed to describe one of them. But, if the second curve is described as a copy of the first curve, the resulting description of the two curves will be only slightly more complex (longer) than a description of only one of them. It will be *more* complex because of the extra information needed to describe the copy and paste operations.

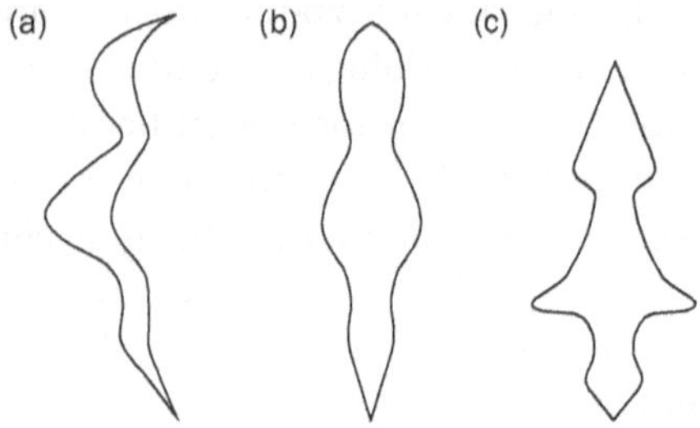

FIGURE 4.4. How a planarity constraint can eliminate degenerate views (see text for the explanation).

symmetrical curves residing on a 3D wavy surface. The view in (b), in which the 2D image is symmetrical, confirms that the curves shown in (a) actually are symmetrical. The interactive DEMO 4.3[9] allows you to view such 3D symmetrical curves from many different viewing directions. The view in Figure 4.4c will surely be as surprising to you, as it was to us, when we tell you that this view (c) shows a different 3D interpretation of the image in (a). Now that you know this, look at the interactive DEMO 4.3[9] again where you can see many views of this surprising 3D symmetrical interpretation. There are in fact infinitely many pairs of 3D symmetrical curves that can be produced (recovered) from the 2D image shown in (a) and none of them looks like the curves you see when you look at (a). The choice of the interpretation produced depends on the choice made about the correspondence of the features in this 2D image. There are infinitely many different possible correspondences, so there are infinitely many different 3D symmetrical interpretations. What on earth is going on? What is the difference among these figures? The main difference between the 3D interpretation in (b) that you (and everyone else) will perceive and the surprising interpretation in (c) that you cannot perceive when you look at (a) is that (b), but not (c) consists of two planar (flat) curves. *Planarity serves to eliminate degenerate views by making it trivial to detect them.* When both curves out there, which form a mirror-symmetrical pair are planar (flat), a degenerate view is produced when (1) the image of at least one of them is a perfectly straight line-segment or (2) when the 2D image, itself, is mirror-symmetrical. Clearly, these two cases can always be verified. Additional computational benefits accrue when the curves are planar (flat). These cases will be discussed later in this chapter.

---

[9] http://shapebook.psych.purdue.edu/4.3

4.2 Clearly, Simplicity Is Better Than Likelihood—Excluding Degenerate Views Does Not Eliminate Spurious 3D Symmetrical Interpretations

Up to this point, it seemed that spurious 3D interpretations could always be excluded simply by excluding degenerate views, but we will now see that this is not always the case. The next example shows that the 3D percept can be explained by a simplicity principle, whose likelihood counterpart is *not* related to degenerate views. This is illustrated in Fig. 4.5.

Look at Figure 4.5a. This pair of polygonal lines does not look mirror-symmetrical, but a 3D mirror-symmetrical interpretation of this pair actually does exist. This is illustrated in Figures 4.5 b-c and in DEMO 4.4.[10] Here, nothing is hidden in depth. All line-segments of the 3D interpretation are visible in the 2D image. Also, all corners in the 3D interpretation are visible in the 2D image. Still, it is impossible to see the 3D symmetrical interpretation from the 2D image in (a), as well as from most images that can be produced in the demo. So, degenerate views, the views that are almost never experienced in real life, cannot be the entire story because here the 3D symmetry cannot be seen from most views. It seems that the 3D symmetrical interpretation is simply much too complex. The close relationship between simplicity and likelihood, described by Mach, does not work in this case. This implies that the likelihood of the 3D interpretation must be derived from its simplicity and not from the likelihood of the 3D viewing direction. Here, it seems that the human visual system uses the following qualitative, yet powerful criterion, for deciding whether a pair of curves in the retinal image represents a pair of mirror-symmetrical curves in 3D space: *the local sign of curvature (the sign of the angle) must be the same or opposite for all*

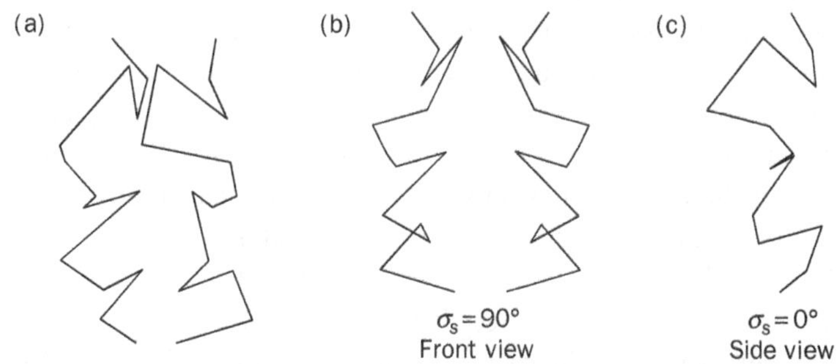

FIGURE 4.5. (a) Nothing is hidden in depth so this view is not degenerate but these two curves are not seen as mirror-symmetrical. The front and side views in (b–c) show that these 3D curves actually are mirror-symmetrical.

[10] http://shapebook.psych.purdue.edu/4.4

pairs of corresponding points in 2D retinal contours. This criterion is always satisfied if the two curves in the 3D symmetrical interpretation are planar (flat). This was the case in Figure 4.4a and b (more examples will be shown and discussed in Figure 4.10). This criterion actually makes a lot of sense because it is an approximate invariant of a pair of 3D symmetrical curves under both orthographic and perspective projections, as long as the 3D symmetrical curves are simple. By "simple," we mean "approximately planar (flat)." Using this invariant will allow the visual system to decide whether the mirror symmetry constraint should be applied in the 3D recovery of a given pair of curves. The recovery is guaranteed to be simple when this criterion is satisfied. For this approach to work, the visual system must begin by detecting higher level features in the 2D mages, such as corners and curvatures. How this can be done will be discussed next.

4.3 What Goes With What? A New Kind of Correspondence Problem

At this point you should have noticed that we have used several related concepts when we discussed the veridical recovery of both symmetrical and asymmetrical shapes. All of the concepts used so far are important because they serve as additional constraints that can be used to make our symmetry constraint effective. We used the concept called a degenerate view in this way when we showed that you can never see multiple points or curves that project to the same part of the retina. When this is the case, the visual system *should* assume that the 2D retinal image was obtained from a non-degenerate view simply because degenerate views almost never occur in everyday life. We also showed that the simplicity inherent in a 2D or a 3D curve is similar conceptually because simple curves are less likely to produce degenerate views than more complex curves. It follows from both of these examples that the visual system should, and does, prefer to favor simple interpretations. The planarity constraint can also be put on this list. Planar (flat) curves are usually simpler than non-planar (non-flat) curves primarily because non-planar curves require two types of curvatures to describe them (torsion as well as curvature). It follows that the visual system should favor planar (flat) interpretations over interpretations that are not flat. Once we note that all of these three types of constraints are closely related to each other, could it be that they are simply different names for the same underlying principle? Our *theory of vision* would be simpler were this to be the case, but simplicity, is not *always* the best thing to have. It might be better for the visual system to treat these three similar concepts as three separate tools for the recovery of 3D shape because, depending on the particular 2D retinal image, one tool might be much easier to apply computationally than another. This computational advantage might be more important than any slight loss of accuracy that might result from its use. Issues like this might operate in 3D shape recovery just as they do when speed and accuracy are traded-off elsewhere in human behavior.

At this point we realized that what we call the *symmetry correspondence problem* is both important for our work and very difficult to solve. In visual science, this problem falls under a broad conceptual umbrella called the *correspondence problem*. There are numerous correspondence problems in diverse areas within our field. All of them are computationally difficult as well as important. All correspondence problems boil down to "what goes with what." Variants within this rubric are identified and labeled by what goes with what under a particular stimulating condition. Note that similar concerns are found elsewhere in perception where the problem under study is called a *Perceptual Constancy*. There are many kinds of perceptual constancy, including size and speed as well as shape. There also are many kinds of correspondence problems. The binocular (Stereo) correspondence problem has received the most attention to date. Our visual system, by having two eyes, receives two slightly different views of the 3D scene in front of us because this kind of parallax: (1) helps us break camouflage, (2) provides a useful cue to depth, and (3) allows us to see 3D shapes veridically (see Chapter 5 for an explanation of (3)). The visual system must figure out which point in the left eye goes with which point in the right eye, which point *corresponds* with the other, to fuse these two different views so you will only see a single 3D scene. This will also make it possible to use binocular information to compute the relative depth of objects in the fused 3D scene. When there are a large number of points in the visual scene, as there usually are, achieving binocular correspondence may require an exhaustive search in which each point in the left eye is compared with each point in the right eye. Such an exhaustive search could never work (recall the computational explosions described in Section 3.1), so the visual system must, and does, simplify the problem by imposing some constraints on the search. It solves the problem by knowing that it is *not* necessary to compare *all* possible points. This does not seem to be farfetched because corresponding points in the two eyes will usually have rather similar coordinates. They will be similar because the distance between the eyes is fairly small (only 5 to 7 centimeters) when compared to the smallest viewing distance likely to be encountered frequently, namely, our normal reading distance, which is about 35 centimeters. In succinct technical language, *binocular disparities* are usually quite small. This means that the visual system actually only has to perform a local search to establish correspondence. The search may even be simplified further if higher order features, such as edges, rather than points, are matched. As noted before, simpler stimuli often present more difficult computational problems than more complex, more natural, visual stimuli. Thanks to work of Julesz (1971), Marr (1982), and others substantial progress has been made toward understanding how the human visual system solves the binocular correspondence problem. We made good use of their contributions to develop our machine.

Motion correspondence is a closely related concept. Consider a sequence of images in one eye in the presence of motion of the observer, or of the object out there, or both. If I walk around a chair while looking at it, and perceive the chair as one and the same object, my visual system must be able to establish which points in the retinal image *now* correspond to which points a fraction of a second *later.* If the motion is smooth and slow, motion correspondence will only require a local search. One might suppose that it could be easier to cope with the motion correspondence problem than with binocular correspondence problem. It is not because having to deal with the time dimension introduces complications. Namely, when the object is not perfectly rigid, like a walking person, a running dog or a flower bending in the wind, motion correspondence is substantially more difficult. This difficulty does not arise in binocular correspondence. This difference probably accounts for why fewer successful methods have been developed for solving the motion correspondence problem than for solving the binocular correspondence problem (see Hildreth, 1984, for one solution).

A correspondence problem also has to be solved whenever we must recognize an object. This problem is studied experimentally by presenting you with two objects and asking you to decide whether the two objects are the same or different. It is obvious that you must figure out which points in one object should be matched with points in the other before the two objects can be matched. This correspondence problem is similar to both the binocular and motion correspondence problems. There is, however, an additional difficulty because if the 3D orientation of the object is free to vary, a more or less global search may be required. As you already know, global searches should be avoided whenever possible and this can be done if the shape of the object is represented by its symmetries. We pointed out this possibility in Section 1.3 and more will be said about it in Chapter 7.

Now, consider the task called *Contour Interpolation*. This is our 4th example of a correspondence problem. Look at the Figure 4.6. The object in this figure is represented by an incomplete contour hidden among many other irrelevant contours. The visual system must figure out which piece of contour should be connected to which other piece before you can see the hidden object. Ideally, spatially-local information, such as proximity and smoothness, will make such correspondence and interpolation problems easy. This is easier said than done. To date, efforts to solve this problem have concentrated on deciding whether two isolated pieces of contour should be connected and *how* they should be connected, namely, should they be connected by a straight line-segment, or by a curve. Kellman & Shipley (1991) formulated a well-known criterion for doing this that they called *relatability*,

FIGURE 4.6. There is a hidden object in this figure. Can you see it?

but it is not this simple. The example in Figure 4.6, which is more realistic than the stimuli Kellman & Shipley used, shows that contour interpolation is a spatially-global combinatorial problem in which multiple pieces of contour, not just two, have to be considered at the same time to produce a closed curve needed to find the hidden contour. No spatially-local rule can be used to solve the contour interpolation problem in such cases. Figure 4.7

FIGURE 4.7. The solution of the contour correspondence problem introduced in Figure 4.6. The hidden "cup" is outlined with a continuous line.

shows the correct interpolation produced by the algorithm we developed to solve this kind of problem (see Gupte et al., 2012). The problem is solved by finding the Shortest Path in the representation of the retinal image that is available in the primary visual (V1) area in the visual cortex of the brain. The retinal image is transformed when it is projected to the visual cortex. Technically, this transformation is called "log polar" (Schwartz, 1980). Intuitively, this transformation can be described as follows: when the center of a circle coincides with the center of the retina, the circle is transformed into a straight line in the brain. It follows that straight-line interpolations in the brain correspond to circular arcs on the retina. The fact that a circle on the retina maps to a straight line in the brain implies that a shortest path in the brain always corresponds to a closed curve on the retina that is not very different from a circle. This is a straightforward implementation of two important features of the Gestalt Theory of Perceptual Organization, called *closure* and *simplicity*. Finding closed curves representing objects in retinal or camera images has been an open problem for a long time in computational vision. The problem remained unsolved because it is computationally *intractable*. Even when there are no irrelevant pieces of contour in the image, determining the order in which a set of N pieces of contours should be connected may require trying all possible orders. This cannot be done because the number of different orders is prohibitively large. Formally, this is equivalent to what is called the traveling salesman problem (TSP), a well-known intractable problem in applied mathematics in which the task is to find the shortest tour among a number of cities (Lawler et al., 1985; Pizlo et al., 2006; Pizlo & Stefanov, 2013). The problem of finding a closed contour in the retinal image, after the image is transformed to the log-polar map known to exist in the visual cortex, can be solved by finding the shortest path. This observation is critical from a computational point of view because very efficient algorithms for finding the shortest path are available now. These efficient algorithms determine a globally optimal solution to the shortest path problem by using spatially local operations. So, a difficult problem in retinal representation becomes easy in its cortical representation. The Gestalt psychologists pointed out about 100 years ago that changing the representation of a difficult problem requiring insight for its solution is essential for solving problems like this (Duncker, 1945; Wertheimer, 1945). One has to abandon "mental sets" (*Einstellung*) brought to the problem to solve it. One of their examples of such a problem was asking a subject to construct 4 identical triangles by using only 6 wooden matches. This problem cannot be solved on a flat (planar) surface. Everyone tries this first and fails. The solution is actually quite easy once the problem is visualized in a 3D representation. So, simply changing the representation from 2D to 3D is all that was needed to solve what seemed to be an impossible problem. The Gestalt psychologists never applied the methods they developed to study problem solving to explain visual mechanisms. We were probably the first to do this when we used the algorithm for determining the Shortest Path in the cortical representation of the retinal image to solve the difficult problem of determining which closed contours represented objects in a retinal image. This is not the first, nor will it be the last, time that we will show you how the Gestalt approach can be used to explain Gestalt phenomena and how our appreciation of their approach contributed to the progress we made.

The symmetry correspondence problem is similar to the four correspondence problems just described. In all of them, "what goes with what" is the question at issue. The only difference among them is the input and the characteristics being evaluated. All correspondence problems are *combinatorial optimization problems* in which one is *never* able to try *all* possible correspondences. For mirror-symmetrical objects, the correspondence in 3D is established by the plane of symmetry. The plane of symmetry is implicit (abstract) in the sense that this plane is not part of the object. Once the plane of symmetry is specified, all pairs of symmetry corresponding points and features are easy to find because they are equally distant from the plane of symmetry and the lines connecting them are orthogonal (at 90°) to this plane. The observer is, however, faced with a different problem, namely, detecting the 3D symmetry correspondence in a 2D orthographic or perspective image. A 2D image of a 3D symmetrical object is, itself, almost never symmetrical (see the introduction section in Chapter 3), so the search for 3D symmetry correspondence in a 2D skew-symmetrical image is a very difficult problem. The symmetry correspondence problem may actually be more difficult than any of the other correspondence problems. The two main reasons for this are (1) the feature of interest (the 3D symmetry) does not exist in the 2D image, and (2) symmetry, by definition, is spatially-global.

To summarize our brief review of correspondence problems, we can say that solving any one of them represents a substantial contribution to visual perception. As we write, these problems have not received the attention they deserve in the human vision literature. Human vision research has always focused more on sensory coding and cue integration than on correspondence problems. This is not surprising because vision has been dominated by the Fechnerian way of thinking in which perception is treated as a Forward Problem. As you know from Chapter 1 the choice of research questions and their relative importance changes completely once the paradigm is shifted to viewing perception as an Inverse Problem. Here, symmetry, which had been almost completely ignored before our work, starts playing a major role, illusions become *completely* irrelevant, and combinatorial optimization problems start closing the gap between perception and problem-solving research.

4.4 Everything Becomes Easier Once Symmetry Is Viewed as Self-similarity: The First Working Solution of the Symmetry Correspondence Problem

We will continue our discussion of symmetry by describing the first realistic solution of what we will call the symmetry correspondence problem now that you know how this problem fits into the big picture. We are calling it realistic because it really works. We needed to solve this problem if we were going to make an autonomous machine that could see like us. Solving it remained elusive for several years. Recall that we started building our machine by explaining how a 3D shape can be recovered from the 2D contours present in a single retinal image. We and everyone we knew considered this to be *the* most difficult problem in vision. Those who were skeptical pointed out that our work had not really solved this problem because our machine could not, on its own, extract the 2D contours needed as input for the 3D recovery. We had to extract this input for the machine before it could make the 3D recovery. They were, of course, referring to the two important steps we listed in Section 2.5 where we described what had to be done before the machine could take care of the recovery. Namely, figure-ground organization had to be accomplished and symmetry correspondence had to be established in what always is a 2D *asymmetrical* retinal image. We suspect that there was an additional reason for their skepticism. Using *symmetry* as an *a priori* constraint was a direct assault on all *empiristic* models of vision. It was obvious that symmetry, which is a spatially-global characteristic, probably cannot be learned from examples and almost all computationally-inclined vision scientists are strongly committed to a critical role for learning in vision. Recall the role of learning in the Bayesian models of vision described in Sections 1.3, 1.9, and 3.3 where we pointed out that if we were right about the role of symmetry, then these models are clearly wrong, and it is not only these models that are wrong: this way of thinking about visual perception is wrong. So we, and now you, should not be surprised to hear that our initial 3D recovery from a 2D retinal image did not receive favorable attention. Acceptance would have to wait until the machine could prepare the input on its own.

The first of the two missing steps, figure-ground organization, was solved first. Solving figure-ground organization, which was accomplished in December 2010, refers to finding objects in the 3D scene and in the 2D perspective images. We demonstrated the ability of our seeing machine to do this on its own at Visual Sciences Society Conference in May 2011. The solution will be presented in Chapter 6. Solving the second of the two missing steps, the symmetry correspondence problem, proved to be quite difficult and it took much longer, as one might expect. It was not solved convincingly until October 2012. Why was it so difficult? It probably was difficult because one has to overcome conventional ways of thinking about the problem to solve it. One has to think outside of the box in contemporary jargon. The natural tendency when taking on a problem like this is to try to simplify it. Two quite different types of simplifications are available. The intuitively more obvious type of simplification is to use simpler stimuli. Here, this would mean using synthetic images of toy examples, but this would obviously be the wrong way to go. Recall that visual perception is a difficult inverse problem whose solution depends on the application of effective *a priori* constraints. From this perspective, *simpler means closer to reality not less complex*. We explained the importance of doing this in Section 1.6 when we described Egon Brunswik's commitment to ecological validity. We adopted his approach and were able to provide the first working algorithm that solves the symmetry correspondence problem by using realistic stimuli. The following 5 characteristics of reality proved to be essential for the solution. We, and our model, needed to have the following knowledge about the world (1) the direction of gravity, (2) that objects tend to stand on a relatively large planar (flat) surface (a "floor") that is often orthogonal (at 90°) to the direction of gravity, (3) that objects are symmetrical, (4) that their plane of symmetry is parallel to gravity, and (5) that objects have approximately vertical legs and/or surfaces.

Using these 5 characteristics (constraints) we are able to: (a) detect the ground plane and vertical walls and also to ignore them in the analysis of objects, (b) compute the horizon on which the vanishing points of all objects reside, (c) identify the vanishing point that specifies the 3D orientation of the symmetry plane of a 3D object: this can be estimated from the three-dimensional figure-ground organization, (d) estimate the 3D position of the symmetry plane of an object on the floor from the figure-ground organization, (e) establish a possible symmetry correspondence between points of a 3D object in its 2D image by using lines emanating from a vanishing point of this object, (f) identify near parallelism of pairs of mirror-symmetrical edges of a 3D object in its 2D image, (g) identify the translation-invariance of edges in the 2D image of the left half of a mirror-symmetrical object with respect to the corresponding edges of the right half of the object (the translation-invariance in the image is along the direction determined by the vanishing point), (h) establish the overlap of important pairs of edges in the 2D image of a 3D object, when viewed from the vanishing point, and (i) verify that a 3D recovery of a pair of 2D corresponding edges of a 3D object resides inside the 3D convex hull of this object estimated by figure-ground organization.

Figure 4.8 shows a representative 2D camera image of a real 3D object (a stand). Pairs of corresponding edges are labeled by letters. These correspondences, which are nearly perfect, are sufficient for a good 3D recovery from

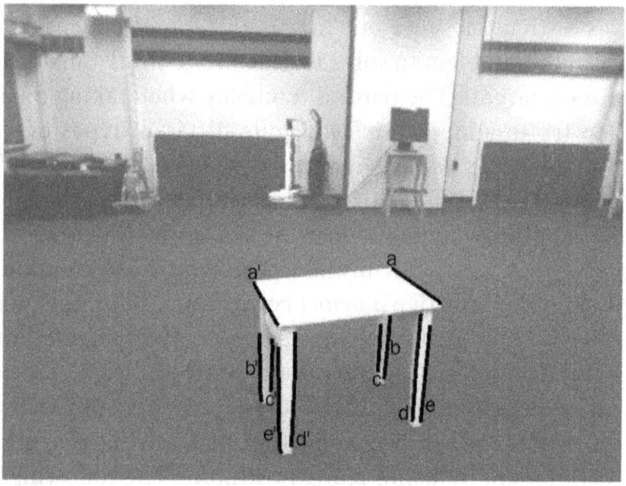

FIGURE 4.8. An illustration of the symmetry-correspondence established in a 2D camera image of a real object in a natural scene. Correspondences are identified by lines labeled a to e. Look at DEMO 4.5[11] to see this 3D recovery.

this 2D image. Additional examples showing how well our model can solve the symmetry correspondence problem will be provided in Chapter 6 after the solution of the figure-ground organization problem has been described. Here, we confine our explanation to the computational aspects of the symmetry correspondence problem that are based on the planarity constraint. You will see how this constraint allows us to apply the same formalism to two rather different aspects of our problem (1) describing the object's symmetries and (2) characterizing the relationship between the 3D shape and its 2D retinal image. It is possible to apply the same formalism to both problems because they share the concept of invariance, which is the central concept of *Group Theory*, the theory that provided the foundation for classifying geometries, referred to in Section 1.6 (Klein, 1939).

Look at Figure 4.9. The 2D curve on the left was produced by making a haphazard scribble. The pair of curves on the right are exact copies of the curve shown on the left. The single 2D curve on left does not look 3D, probably because there are no effective *a priori* constraints that could guarantee a *unique* 3D interpretation that is the best, the simplest, and the most likely interpretation. Your percept is quite different when you look at the pair of curves on the right. These two curves are interpreted as a skew-symmetrical image produced by a pair of 3D mirror-symmetrical curves. The skew-symmetrical nature of this 2D image results from the fact that one of these curves is a translation of the other. Furthermore, each of these curves is planar (flat) in 3D and the

---

[11] http://shapebook.psych.purdue.edu/4.5

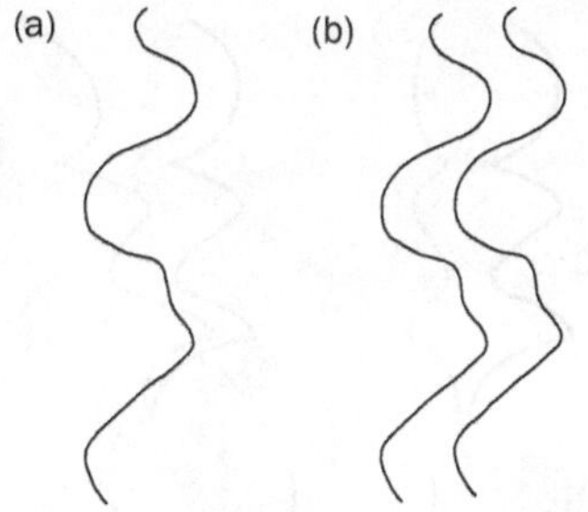

FIGURE 4.9. The curve on the left (a) was produced by making a haphazard scribble. This curve does not allow any vivid 3D interpretation. The pair of curves on the right (b) is an exact copy of the one on the left. This pair, which represents a translational symmetry in the 2D image, allows a vivid 3D mirror-, and translationally symmetrical interpretation.

planes on which these two curves reside are parallel in 3D. This example is similar to the one shown in Figure 2.9 in Chapter 2. The difference is that the example in Figure 2.10 was produced by arranging parallel line-segments representing symmetry lines. The example shown here was produced by using 2D translational symmetry. Note that in both cases, we are dealing with "parallel" lines. In the example in Figure 2.10 we had parallel straight line-segments in the 2D image. In the example here, we have "parallel" curves in the 2D image. The word "parallel" was put in quotes because, geometrically, the concept "parallel lines" is reserved for straight lines. We are calling the lines in Figure 4.9b "parallel" because one curve was produced by translating the other in the 2D image. If we divided each line into large number of short line-segments, the pairs of these segments would actually be parallel.

Note that the 3D mirror-symmetrical interpretation of the lines in Figure 4.9b is also a pair of lines representing 3D translational-symmetry. In other words, these two pairs of 3D curves are characterized by both kinds of symmetries. In this case, it seems that your 3D percept is produced by a *mirror*-symmetry constraint, rather than by a *translational*-symmetry constraint. One reason for this claim is that the application of a translational symmetry constraint could also produce a 2D percept that is *identical* to the 2D image in Figure 4.9b, which is *not* mirror-symmetrical. In fact, there are many 3D interpretations of this image that are translationally, but not mirror-symmetrical. The fact that you perceive a 3D mirror-symmetrical interpretation, rather than any of the other interpretations, indicates that a mirror-symmetry constraint is operating. It is responsible for what you are seeing. Whether a mirror- or translational-symmetry constraint is actually applied to the 2D image of a particular 3D shape will depend on which constraint leads to a simpler 3D interpretation, that is, the interpretation which has the higher "shape measure" (see Section 1.3 and Li et al., 2013).

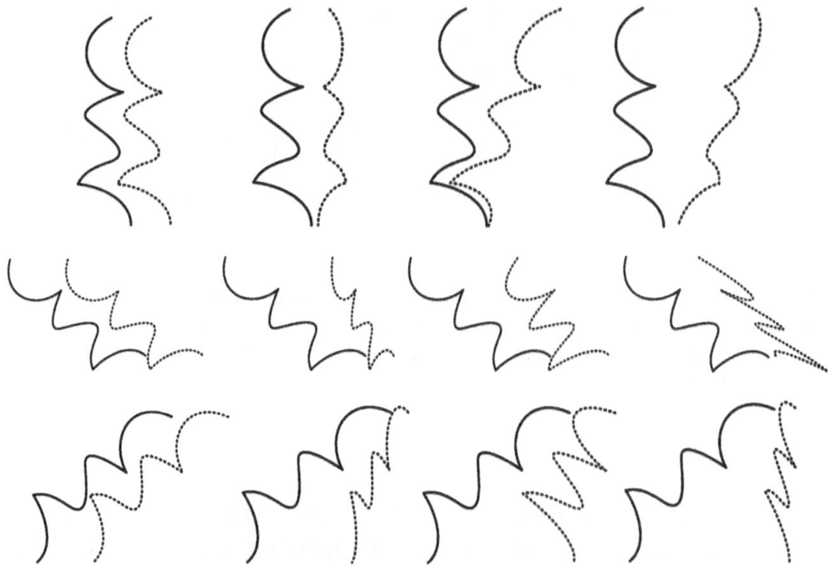

FIGURE 4.10. Twelve pairs of 2D curves. These represent all possible types of 2D transformations that conform to 3D symmetry and planarity constraints.

Observers often report that they see the 3D curves residing on a common undulating surface. In such cases, the curves *could be* interpreted as geodesic lines. Stevens (1981) and Knill (2001) did, in fact, propose that the 3D percept is produced by applying a geodesic constraint to the curves on the common surface. We do not accept this interpretation. We believe that the human visual system applies the symmetry constraint to the curves regardless of where the curves reside, a common surface or not. Our theory gives a better account of the available results where violations of the geodesic constraint did not prevent the observers from seeing 3D interpretations (Knill, 1992).

Now look at Figure 4.10. There are 12 pairs of 2D curves. They show how the planarity and symmetry constraints operate in producing a 3D percept. The left member of each pair, shown by a solid line is the same, except for a different 2D orientation across the three rows. The member of each pair shown by a dotted line was produced by translating the solid curve along the horizontal direction (first column on left), by translating and stretching along the horizontal direction (second column from left)[12], by translating and shearing (third column from left), and by translating, stretching, and shearing along he horizontal direction (right column). Note that these three transformations, translation, stretch, and shear, must be applied along the same direction in the image. If they are not, the 3D symmetrical interpretation will not be simple,

[12] Note that reflection is equivalent to stretching by -1.

that is, a pair of planar mirror-symmetrical curves in 3D will not be a possible interpretation of the stimulus. In all 12 cases shown in Figure 4.10, you see a pair of 3D mirror-symmetrical flat (planar) curves. You can *always* see all of these 3D interpretations *because* they are all flat (planar) and simple. They almost never produce degenerate views. Their 3D *shape*, however, is different across the 12 pairs as predicted by our model. The curves in each pair reside on two planes whose relative 3D orientation changes from pair to pair because each pair in the 2D image was produced by a different 2D transformation consisting of translation, stretch, and shear. Technically, these three types of transformations represent a 4-parameter subset of a 6-parameter 2D affine group (see Sawada et al., 2013, for technical details). The affine group is relevant here because it is the appropriate description of an orthographic projection of a planar figure to the 2D retinal image. We need not deal with a full 2D affine group characterized by 6 independent parameters, simply because the mirror symmetry in a 3D representation does not allow 2 of the 6 parameters to vary. Put differently, when we start with an arbitrary pair of mirror-symmetrical planar curves in a 3D space and produce a 2D orthographic image of this pair, the 3D reflection that describes the symmetry of these curves in 3D is represented by a 2D affine transformation between the images of these two curves. This 2D affine relationship was called a skew-symmetry in Section 3.1. It is being used the same way here because the term "skew-symmetry" refers to the fact that the 3D symmetry has been distorted, but not completely lost in the 2D retinal image. The present discussion adds to what was said about skew-symmetry in Section 3.1, by adding the qualitative invariant introduced in Section 4.2, namely, the sign of curvature is the same or opposite for all pairs of corresponding points in a pair of curves that are images of planar (flat) mirror-symmetrical curves. In plain English, whether a human observer will actually see a 3D symmetrical shape when presented with a pair of curves on his retina depends on whether the retinal curves satisfy one of the following criteria (1) hills and valleys of one curve face in the same direction as the hills and valleys of the other curve, or (2) hills and valleys of one curve face in the opposite direction than the hills and valleys of the other curve. In both of these cases, the 3D symmetrical interpretation will be seen by a human observer because the interpretation is simpler.

Some readers might have realized that the examples in Figure 4.10 assumed an *orthographic* projection from a 3D scene to a 2D image. Be assured that all of the claims made about them remain true even when a *perspective* projection is applied. Remember that we are always interested in both an orthographic and perspective projection because a perspective projection provides the correct description of the image formation in the eye, and an orthographic projection is a very useful approximation that is used by the visual system. Most of the observations we made about Figure 4.10 remain true when a perspective, rather than an orthographic, projection is used because differences in the type of projection lead only to *quantitative* differences in the skew-symmetry in the retinal image. *Qualitatively*, the skew-symmetry is the same in both types of projections. This should not be surprising because you saw a demo in Section 3.1 that had a chair whose projections could be manipulated. This demo showed how a perspective projection can be reduced to an orthographic projection by simply moving the center of projection farther and farther from the image plane. Returning to technical language, the skew-symmetry in a *perspective* image of a pair of planar mirror-symmetrical curves is characterized by a 5-parameter subset of a 2D *projective* transformation. So, the number of parameters needed to describe skew-symmetry in the retinal image is similar in both types of projections. The 5th parameter in the case of a perspective image represents the distance of the vanishing point from the center of the image (more precisely, from what is called the principal point). Note that the intuitive explanation provided at the end of the previous paragraph applies here, too.

At this point you might be wondering about the severe criticisms we made of using affine and projective models of the human visual space in Section 1.6. Was this criticism justified now that we are using affine and projective groups to explain your visual percepts? It was because our predecessors used affine and projective groups to "explain" distortions of visual perceptions, but we are using affine and projective groups to explain the mechanisms the visual system uses to produce veridical perceptions. Specifically, we are using affine and projective transformations to explain how the symmetry correspondence problem is solved in 2D skew-symmetrical images. We are not using them to explain the perception of 3D space.

We conclude this chapter by pointing out that establishing symmetry correspondence in the 2D image is essentially a 3D operation. The same is true of our solution of the figure-ground organization problem that will be described in Chapter 6. The visual system "represents" vision problems in 3D and it also solves these problems as 3D. There is not a single visual operation whose output makes reference to a 2D characteristic. Treating the early stages of vision, as almost everyone else has, as 2D operations, has been a major millstone on the road to developing a theory of vision. Studying and using 2D images makes no sense because we cannot, and do not, see our retinal images. All permanent characteristics of objects and scenes are 3D, not 2D, because the world around us is 3D. So, the visual system, if it is going to perform veridically, must "think" in 3D. So, J. J. Gibson (1979) was on the right track when he insisted that we should think about our percepts as residing in the 3D world, but it is critical to remember that they actually do not reside in this world; they reside in our minds as 3D models of the world. Also, contrary to what Gibson claimed, there is nothing *direct* in our perceptions. The computations underlying them are fast and accurate but the problems in vision are *inverse* so computations are essential. Finally, our percepts are veridical because many effective constraints are available, not because there is an abundance of visual cues or because we see by using "affordances" (action possibilities). One can only wonder on which side of this argument Gibson would be today.

5

A Second View Makes 3D Shape Perception Perfect

There were several theoretical breakthroughs between 2006 and 2008 while the 3D shape recovery model was being developed. These breakthroughs allowed us to claim that virtually everything interesting and important about 3D shape can be done on the basis of the properties of only a single 2D image (Pizlo, Li & Steinman, 2008). At the time, there was not the slightest intention of studying 3D shape either binocularly or monocularly as an observer moved. But one of us[1], who was finishing up his dissertation, insisted that we do. His advisor's[2] reluctance was not entirely sensible because some 10-year-old, preliminary results suggested that binocular viewing, but not monocular, allowed an observer to recover the shape of a slanted planar (flat) figure almost perfectly (Pizlo & Scheessele, 1998). As soon as we started collecting data with both eyes viewing, we were amazed by how much having two images contributed to the accuracy of the perception of 3D shape. Our observers achieved virtually perfect shape veridicality for a wide range of viewing directions (15° to 75° relative to the symmetry plane) and distances (50 centimeters to 3 meters). These data presented us with a huge theoretical problem, namely, what mechanism is responsible for this remarkable enhancement? The answer turned out to be reassuring, rather than disturbing, considering that voluminous literature had proven that binocular space perception is *never* veridical. We knew of only one binocular mechanism that was sufficiently effective to pull this kind of thing off. It is called "stereoacuity" and it is demonstrated by judging the depth-order of two points or features in a visual scene. The human beings' ability to do this is remarkable. Thresholds for such judgments are on the order of seconds of arc (the size of visual objects are described as the angles they subtend at the observer's eye). When we took this problem

[1] Yunfeng Li

[2] Zygmunt Pizlo

on, it was not at all obvious how stereoacuity could contribute to the accuracy of the perception of 3D shape. The depth-order of features, in itself, does not seem to be very informative. But, when depth-order is combined with our *a priori* symmetry constraint, it becomes clear that stereoacuity can make a major contribution to the veridicality of the recovered shape. How does it do this? Stereoacuity works because when a 3D symmetrical object is viewed from a non-degenerate viewing direction, that is, whenever the right stimulus is presented under the right viewing conditions, the depth-order of its features determines its 3D symmetrical shape almost uniquely. This insight, which popped up during one of our[3] brainstorming sessions, made it possible for us to model how stereoacuity could enhance 3D shape perception. With this model in hand we had no difficulty convincing ourselves that stereoacuity played an important role in 3D shape perception. It had proven to be as effective as one might expect. Note that our work with stereoacuity accomplished two things. First, we found out that once we have two images of a 3D shape, the depth-order of these images allows an observer to achieve shape constancy from any viewing direction. We also discovered a new and novel purpose for stereoacuity. Until we made this discovery, we, and everyone else we knew, taught that stereoacuity is used to thread needles, an activity appearing rather late in our evolutionary history. Those of us who wanted to extend this teleology farther back in time taught that it could be used to locate tiny fleas in our family members' furs. Having perfect shape constancy from virtually any viewing direction, seems to be a more important purpose for stereoacuity than sewing or grooming members of our group.

5.1 What We Know About Binocular Vision and How We Came To Know It

The fact that the retinal images in the two eyes are different because they are obtained by viewing the 3D scene from different viewing positions was already known to Leonardo Da Vinci (1452–1519), but an adequate description of the geometry of binocular vision was not presented until the 19th century. Wheatstone (1838) did for binocular vision what Brunelleschi had done with monocular vision 400 years before (you read about him in Section 3.1 when we talked about a perspective projection). Both Brunelleschi and Wheatstone viewed visual perception as an interpretation of the image of the world out there on the surface of the retina. Others in Brunelleschi's day and beyond viewed perception as a step in a causal chain of events (Fechner (1860)). Both

---

[3]Li, Pizlo and Sawada.

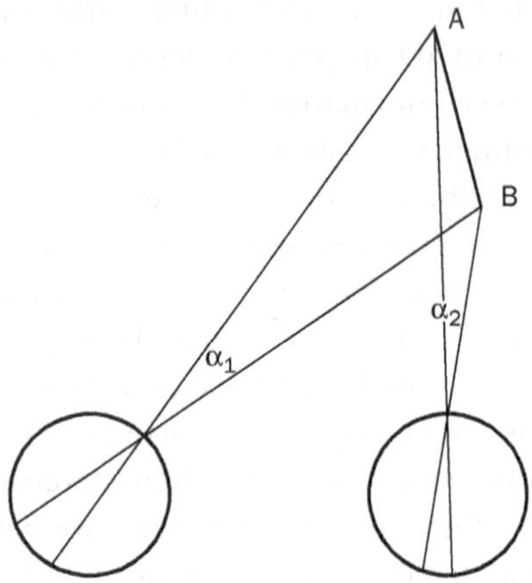

FIGURE 5.1. Binocular disparity of point A relative to point B is the difference between the viewing angles α_1 and α_2.

of these pioneers produced demonstrations of this claim by determining the minimal stimulus that would be sufficient for a veridical 3D perception. How they did this will be explained by Figure 5.1. The field had to wait another 100 years before an analogous demonstration was created by Hans Wallach to explain what is called "motion parallax," that is, obtaining a second view with a single eye when the observer or the object of interest moves (see Wallach & O'Connell, 1953). Look at Figure 5.1.

When a line-segment AB is viewed by two eyes, or by one eye that has moved relative to the segment AB, the visual angles produced in the two eyes are different. This difference is called "binocular disparity," or more precisely, "horizontal binocular disparity." Wheatstone, by using the Rules of Perspective Projection described by Brunelleschi, drew perspective images that represented the retinal image in the left and in the right eye. He then presented these two images to both eyes in such a way that the left eye could see the left image, but not the right image, and the right eye could see the right image, but not the left image. He used mirrors to accomplish this in what is now called a *mirror-stereoscope*, which was not very different from the way Brunelleschi used a mirror in his demonstration. The resulting percept was very vivid and veridical. By veridical here, as elsewhere, we simply mean that the percept agreed with the 3D object depicted by the pair of images. Many, perhaps even most, of our colleagues would call this an "illusion" because the percept was a 3D object, while the physical stimulus was a pair of line-drawings. Employing this kind of logic, as is done often in our field, may be intriguing when teaching undergraduates, but it always leads to a dead end once this road is taken. Because, once you realize that the visual system is actually solving a difficult inverse problem when it produces a unique 3D interpretation of a pair of two 2D retinal images, it becomes obvious that viewing stereograms is analogous to viewing a 3D real scene binocularly. It is analogous because in both cases (1) the input to the visual system consists of two 2D images, (2) this input is identical, (3) the visual mechanism underlying its operation is identical, (4) the *a priori* constraints used by this mechanism are identical, and (5) the resulting percepts are identical.[4] So, on what possible basis might anyone want to call one percept veridical and the other illusory? Doing this makes no sense, whatsoever. In fairness to our numerous illusion aficionados, comparing and contrasting stereograms to a real 3D scene does make sense but only if you are trying to find out what property of the distal stimulus (the object out there) is essential for veridical perception. If you do not know what this might be, comparing the veridicality of perception with stereograms depicting 3D objects to the veridicality of perception with 3D objects, themselves, can be useful. Thanks to our new definition of *shape*, however, this issue has been resolved, hopefully, once and for all. If the 3D object, which is used to produce the 2D retinal images, actually has shape (as we define shape: the object has one or more symmetries), then the percept produced by this stimulus *must* be veridical. The issue of whether the subject's retinal images were produced by a real 3D shape or by a stereogram representing the 3D shape is completely without content now that we have a useful analytical definition of shape.

Note that there still is another problem here. Namely, the visual system must figure out which point in the left retina goes with which point in the right retina before binocular disparity can be computed and used for the reconstruction of depth. This must be worked out before we can proceed. In Section 4.3, this came up when we discussed the binocular correspondence problem. Here, we will continue this discussion by assuming that you remember what this problem is and how it can be solved. Recall that the solution of the binocular correspondence problem is not trivial because even when the 2D images are only moderately complex, there are many possible correspondences, most of which are wrong. The fact that the visual system actually can solve the binocular correspondence problem in the absence of any higher-order visual features, such as contours (lines), was demonstrated by Julesz (1960, 1971) when he popularized random dot stereograms (RDS) as stimuli for binocular vision research (see Figure 5.2). Julesz's work, which was picked up by Marr (1982) and his team, encouraged the computer vision community to produce better and better algorithms for solving the binocular correspondence problem and, in time, their efforts paid off handsomely. Currently, readily-available tools can solve this problem reasonably well. The solution is never perfect, but it is good

---

[4]There is a phenomenological difference in the perception of depth with stereograms and with natural binocular vision, namely, with a stereogram all depths can be perceived in sharp focus simultaneously, while only a narrow range of depths is in sharp focus when viewing a real 3D scene. To the best of our knowledge this difference in the perception of depth has no effect on the perception of 3D shape.

FIGURE 5.2. Random dot stereogram. See Wikipedia for an explanation: http://en.wikipedia.org/wiki/Random_dot_stereogram

enough to use it for at least one critically important stage of visual processing, namely, figure-ground organization. Originally, the computer vision community hoped that understanding binocular vision would solve all of the problems inherent in 3D vision. It did not. But, now that we know that stereoacuity can provide a mechanism for making 3D shape perception veridical, one may say that Julesz was on the right track when he emphasized the role of binocular vision in breaking camouflage. Figure-ground organization is all about breaking camouflage and having more than a single image provides the most effective way of breaking it. The importance of stereovision for breaking camouflage is hardly new. It was used in WWI and played a critical role in WWII when camouflage and aerial stereo-photography came into widespread use.

Unfortunately, the success of Julesz's work and the compelling examples he showed at meetings and used in teaching blinded the machine and human visual science community to the important problems that remained in binocular vision. They made little progress after they made Julesz's RDS the stimulus of choice for studying *all* aspects of binocular vision. We now know that RDS are useful only for studying figure-ground organization and for nothing else. The fact that an observer can see a square floating in front of a background (the favorite stimulus in these studies) does not imply that this is how we see 3D shapes in everyday life. A square floating in front of a background lacks the three critical characteristics needed before we can accept any visual stimulus as ecologically-valid: (1) the stimulus must have contours in each retinal image, (2) the symmetrical object must have volume, and (3) the view must not be degenerate, because degenerate views produce symmetrical, rather than the skew-symmetrical retinal images of real objects. Perhaps, Julesz and his followers made this mistake because they thought that 3D vision consists of only one step, figure-ground organization. They assumed that 3D perceptual processing ends once the visual system knows which points belong to an object and which points belong to its background. This assumption was made explicit by Rock (1983) who said that the binocular perception of a 3D shape is simply a matter of description, much like the monocular perception of a 2D shape in the frontal plane. In Rock's words:

> "what has been said about two dimensions can easily be extended to the third. Thus it seems probable that few if any entirely new principles need be invoked to deal with object-form perception in daily life. Presumably the shape of each face of an object is described as a two-dimensional structure and depth relations are incorporated into the overall description insofar as they yield spatial relationships about the structure of the object." (p. 87)

Accepting this assumption made it reasonable to concentrate on using RDS of geometrically simple figures, as well as completely unstructured objects that lacked volume and symmetry, in almost all research on binocular vision for decades. It made it easy to accept the inevitable large failures of veridicality and the complete failures of shape constancy that would fill many journal pages with results explaining nothing relevant to vision in the real world. The human vision community, almost without exception, was quite happy with such results. This approach it not entirely without merit, at least sociologically, because it is much easier to generate interest in undergraduate students in the Sensation & Perception class with vivid visual illusions than with explanations of veridical perceptions. There is even a better professional reason for favoring research on illusions because it is well-known that "publish or perish" drives activities much more in the academy than teaching. It is much easier to come up with a computational model that *cannot* discriminate between two very different stimuli, than with one that can. Formulating a model that produces chance performance in a shape constancy, or in any experiment, is not challenging. Formulating a model that predicts a veridical percept is much harder.

This ends our brief summary of the state of binocular research when we took it on as part of our work on the perception of 3D shape. When we started, it was commonly assumed that solving the binocular correspondence problem was the only difficult problem in binocular vision and that, once this correspondence problem had been solved, all that remained to be done was to measure binocular disparities. What would this entail? Specifically, what is the relationship between disparities measured on the retina and the perception of metric depth and the perception of 3D shape? There are two types of binocular disparity: horizontal and vertical. Both are relevant to the geometry of binocular vision, but throughout its history, horizontal disparity has been considered much more important than vertical disparity in human vision. For years, all books on human binocular vision relied on the following equation for providing an approximate relationship between horizontal disparity and depth:

$$d \approx \frac{\delta D^2}{I}.$$

where δ is binocular horizontal disparity, d is the relative depth between two points, I is the interocular distance and *D* is the viewing distance.

The viewing distance *D* seemed to be the key to 3D vision. The other two variables on the right-hand side of the equation can be assumed to be known to the visual system: the interocular distance *I* is pretty much constant during the adult life of the observer, and the disparity *δ* is measured on the basis of the two retinal images. So, the reconstruction of relative depth *d* is directly related to the ability to reconstruct the viewing distance *D*. The general agreement was that human observers are *not* very good at reconstructing *D*. Specifically, *D* is often underestimated for larger values of *D*, and overestimated for smaller values of *D*. The error can be as large as by a factor of 2, 3, or even 5. Once the viewing distance *D* is misperceived, the relative distance *d* for any pairs of points on a 3D object will also be misperceived. Consequently, if all relative depths within an object are misperceived, the 3D shape, itself, must also be misperceived. Right? No. The reader already knows this from the first four chapters of this book. He will know that 3D shape can be recovered very well without reconstructing depth. But the reader also already knows that this possibility did not occur to many since binocular vision came under study 200 years ago, and when it did occur to some individuals, it was not taken seriously by others. Even we failed to study binocular shape perception when we began because our observers and our model did so well when they perceived 3D shape with only one eye (monocularly). We persisted in thinking that we need not worry about binocular vision for quite a while. We preferred to think that the only role the second eye served was to provide a spare and to provide a larger field-of-view which allowed us to keep our head and eye movements modest. Why on earth were we comfortable with holding what we now know was a completely ridiculous opinion about the importance of having two eyes, rather than only one? We will start explaining this embarrassing state of affairs by reviewing the evidence that allowed us to believe that binocular vision does not offer much for the veridical perception of 3D shape.

Consider the following set of psychophysical results. They were collected between 2003 and 2005 and published in two papers, one in 2005 and the other in 2011 (Pizlo et al., 2005; Li & Pizlo, 2011). In the experiment published in 2011, which served as part of the master's thesis of one of us,[5] we examined the role of *a priori* constraints in both monocular and binocular shape constancy.

[5]Yunfeng Li.

Six types of stimuli were used. They differed from one another by the degree of regularity they contained. Regularity as measured by symmetry, volume, and planarity. Our "truck," a symmetrical polyhedron, was the most regular stimulus used. The least regular stimulus was an unstructured 3D polygonal line. The remaining stimuli had intermediate levels of regularity. The subject viewed each stimulus with one eye or with both eyes. This was a shape constancy experiment so the subject was shown two stimuli, one after another, and had to decide whether the shapes of both stimuli were identical. The second stimulus was rotated by about 90° around the vertical axis when the same stimulus was shown twice. The subject was told that the two 3D objects should be considered as having the same shape if they were identical except for their 3D orientation and size. We found that performance with our most regular stimulus was quite reliable. The proportion correct was 75%, and performance with our least regular stimulus was at chance-level. We expected, and were pleased with these results, and we were not surprised by the fact that binocular performance was very similar to monocular performance. Technically, the linear correlation coefficient between monocular and binocular viewing was 0.94. For our other readers, when binocular performance with a given stimulus was reliable, monocular performance with that stimulus was also reliable, and conversely, when monocular performance with a given stimulus was not reliable, binocular performance with that stimulus was almost surely not reliable, too. This result allowed us to believe that binocular and monocular shape perception were likely to share the same mechanisms. With these results, and with this indisputable logic, we were not surprised that binocular performance was always better than monocular performance. After all, having a second image should not be able to hurt the percept. Having more than one view could only help.

We drew similar conclusions from the second shape constancy experiment performed in the 2011 study. Here, we only used "truck" stimuli and tested the effect of adding several conventional depth cues—shading, texture, binocular disparity, and internal contours. These stimuli are shown in Figure 5.3. Again, the subject viewed these stimuli with one or with two eyes. Why did we test so many cues? We tested so many simply because they had all been used extensively by others previously. Binocular disparity had to be included because it was often considered to be the *most* effective depth and shape cue, and texture was included because it had figured prominently in the theories and speculations of such luminaries as Gibson (1950, 1979), Julesz (1971), Stevens (1981, 1986), and Marr (1982). Shading was known to be less effective than binocular disparity or texture, but it had *always* been included in any discussion of the reconstruction of 3D surfaces (e.g., Koenderink et al., 1995). Finally, internal contours were included because they had been analyzed by a number of computer vision pioneers, such as Roberts (1965), Guzman (1968), Waltz (1975), and Sugihara (1986), as well as by Biederman (1987), one

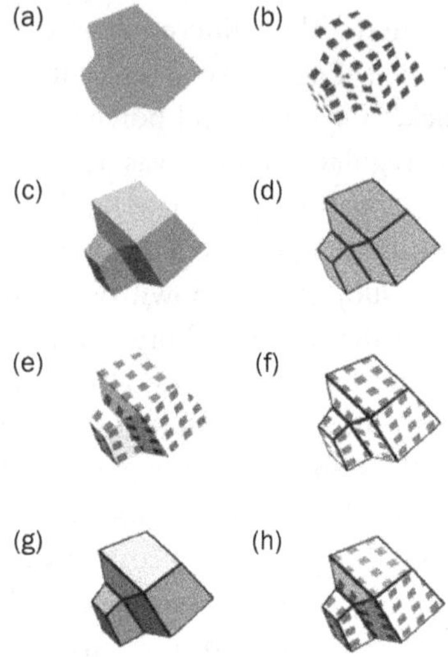

FIGURE 5.3. Stimuli in Li & Pizlo's (2011) experiment. (a) occluding contour. (b) texture. (c) shading. (d) internal contours. (e) texture and shading. (f) texture and internal contours. (g) shading and internal contours. (h) texture, shading, and internal contours. (From Li & Pizlo, 2011).

of the most influential psychologists working in shape perception. The main result in this experiment was similar to the first. Monocular and binocular performance were highly correlated (r = 0.92) across the 8 stimuli types shown in Figure 5.3. The effect of texture was quite small, and the effect of shading was non-existent. The effect of edges was large and binocular performance was always slightly better than monocular performance. Surely, you will agree that these two experiments did little to encourage us to assign any special role to binocular vision in 3D shape perception. This attitude was reflected in the title chosen for a review paper we had published a few years earlier, "Binocular disparity only comes into play when everything else fails" (Pizlo et al., 2008).

As if this was not enough to discourage us from assuming that binocularity played an important role in 3D shape perception, we also discovered a new binocular phenomenon in the Fall of 2004, that clearly showed that 3D shape affected binocular vision much more than binocularity affected 3D shape perception. This discovery, which was presented as a demo at the Vision Science Society Meeting in May 2005, was published in the same year (Pizlo et al., 2005). The stimuli that produced this new phenomenon, which we will call the "shape before disparity" phenomenon, are shown in Figure 5.4. This figure shows the stimuli for two pairs of stereograms. Both stimuli on top look like cubes and both stimuli on bottom look like hexagons with dots inside. But, the stereogram pair, shown on bottom is actually almost identical to the pair shown on top. The only difference is that in the bottom pair, the Y-junction has been removed and only the vertex of this junction is shown. Clearly, the images on top look like cubes but the images on bottom do not. Our new

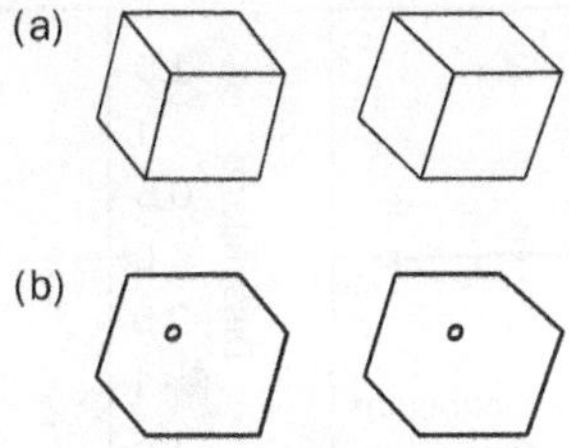

FIGURE 5.4. Stimuli used in Pizlo et al.'s (2005) paper. See DEMO 5.1[6] for the animation. (From Pizlo et al., 2005).

phenomenon was produced simply by keeping the 3D stimulus presented to the left eye stationary, while the 3D stimulus presented to the right eye made left-right oscillations in 3D. If the 3D percept were determined exclusively by binocular disparity, the subject would have perceived a non-rigid 3D configuration that is being stretched and compressed along the direction of the line-of sight emanating from the left eye. If binocular disparity was critical, its effect would have been perceived with *both* stereo-pairs shown in Figure 5.4. It should have affected the pair on top as well as the pair on bottom. The effect of binocular disparity was only manifested with the stereo-pair on bottom but not with the pair on top. On top, subjects perceived a rigid cube performing right-left oscillations with an amplitude roughly half of the amplitude of the rotating cube. This means that their visual system *first* recovered two 3D shapes, one from each eye, and then fused the disparate 3D shapes of the cubes and only then produced the percept of an oscillating cube.

This phenomenon was so convincing and so unexpected that we invited David "Martin" Regan and his wife, Marian, both experts in binocular vision to Purdue in the Fall of 2004 to confirm our observations. It took Martin less than half a minute to conclude and proclaim that "*this phenomenon invalidates all existing models of stereo-motion.*" The percept with the oscillating cubes on top (a) clearly discredited any important role for binocular disparity in 3D shape perception. The visual system produced a 3D cube interpretation from each eye and then "averaged" these two 3D percepts to form a single (cyclopean) binocular percept. This was not done with the stimulus on bottom (b) because each monocular stimulus had been impoverished so much that it could not produce a monocular 3D percept of a cube that could be fused. In other words, the visual system could solve the inverse problem of 3D shape recovery from each 2D image in (a), but not from the images in (b). So, if everything else fails, binocular disparity will determine the percept, but when a monocular 3D shape percept is possible, binocular disparity has no role in 3D shape perception.

[6] http://shapebook.psych.purdue.edu/5.1

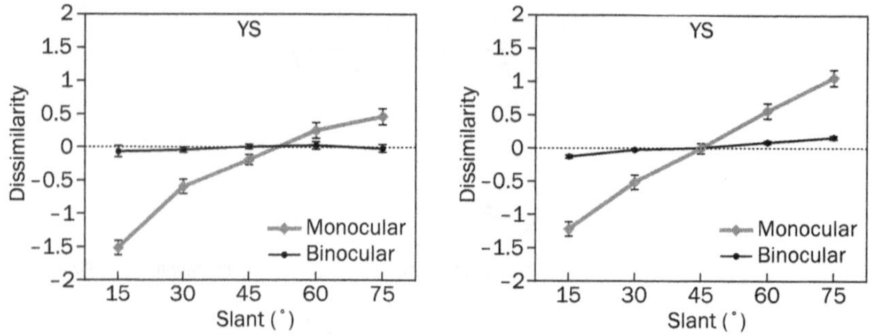

FIGURE 5.5. Results of subject YS (left) and results of our YS: Model (right) that simulated the performance of this subject. Monocular performance is shown by the thick gray lines and binocular performance is shown by the thin black lines. (From Li et al., 2011 with permission of the Association for Research in Vision and Ophthalmology).

This new phenomenon should have been enough to squelch any interest in binocular vision, but it did not squelch it because one of us[7] *insisted* that a binocular shape recovery experiment had to be included in his doctoral dissertation. Doing more, rather than less, is hard to deny in these circumstances so a binocular condition, as well as a monocular condition, were run early in the Spring of 2009. We used our truck stimulus and repeated the monocular shape recovery experiment that had been performed two years earlier (Li et al., 2009). The subject, using both eyes in the binocular session, and only one in the monocular session, viewed a stationary symmetrical 3D shape from a non-degenerate viewing direction. He was instructed to adjust the aspect ratio of a rotating 3D shape, which was viewed with a single eye, in both types of sessions. Results of one subject are shown in Figure 5.5.

The ordinate (Y-axis) shows the error of the adjustment on a logarithmic scale. Zero at the middle of this scale means that there was no error. The abscissa (X-axis) shows the orientation of the symmetry plane of the 3D object relative to the observer (YS and YS: Model). We varied the orientation of the symmetry plane because we knew from our original study that this orientation affects the accuracy of monocular 3D shape recovery and expected it to affect binocular viewing, too. We found that orientation was important, specifically, when viewing was monocular, there were appreciable errors (as much as a factor of 2) when the aspect ratio was recovered with viewing orientations close to degenerate views (15° and 75°). This is evident in both YS's and in the YS: Model's data, but it is important to realize that *aspect ratio* is only 1 of the 15 parameters that are used to characterize this 3D shape. All of the remaining 14 geometrical-characteristics of the 3D shape had no errors when viewing was monocular. Eight subjects participated in these experiments, 3 were naïve and 5 were familiar with the issues under study. The performance of the naïve and

[7] Yunfeng Li.

knowledgeable subjects was similar as were the Models based on their performance. These results allowed us to conclude that *monocular* shape perception is always *nearly veridical*, and it actually *is veridical* for 3D viewing orientations that are not close to degenerate. The completely unexpected result in light of our and others' prior work was that when viewing was *binocular*, 3D shape was perceived *veridically for all* viewing directions. Look at the curve drawn with the thin black line in Figure 5.5. It almost coincides with the X-axis perfectly. The errors are hardly noticeable. We were stunned by this result. We had had no idea that using two eyes to provide binocular vision could be so important and that shape perception could actually be *so* veridical. This surely sounds funny, here, because we have stressed the veridicality of shape perception throughout this book, and have pointed out repeatedly how well veridicality was supported by common sense. But faced with the perfection produced by viewing binocularly, we could not help but be overwhelmed when we discovered the *real* importance of both veridicality and common sense.

Let's stop and think about what we've got. Look around your office if you're at work, or around your room if you're at home. Once you have done this, ask yourself whether you are really certain that you are seeing the shapes of objects as they really are out there. If you decide that you are, you should settle back in your chair and utter a deep sigh of relief because you can now be confident that this is really true. You can be confident because your subjective impression (your phenomenology), until now supported primarily by your common sense, has been confirmed in a well-designed, well-executed laboratory experiment. Our results make it clear that veridicality, even, perfect veridicality, should be *expected* when an experiment on 3D shape perception is done properly. Note that our result cannot be a "fluke" (technically, an experimental artifact). Sloppy, ill-conceived experiments cannot produce *perfect* accuracy and *perfect* reliability, especially once we know that from a computational point of view the inverse problem that the visual system had to solve was extremely difficult. Veridicality cannot be more perfect than what you see in Figure 5.5 when the subject and our model viewed 3D shapes binocularly. Like it or not, such veridicality should be taken seriously from here on, and taking it seriously will affect what can be concluded from experiments on 3D shape. Because, henceforth, if you run an experiment on 3D shape, whose results show a departure from veridicality, or even worse, its complete failure, this result can no longer be taken as a reason for excitement about a new "effect" of some stimulus condition on perception. This mistaken claim has been made all too often in the past. Instead, your first reaction should be concern about what caused what we all now know was the *unexpected*, poor veridicality of your observers, who will be called "subjects" if your mistake finds its way into print. Less than virtually perfect veridicality in a properly performed binocular experiment on 3D shape is a sign of the experimenter's incompetence, not a justification for announcing a "discovery." We conclude this discussion by pointing out that experimental results "demonstrating" failures of perception are both misleading and uninteresting, particularly when you want to build a machine that can see 3D shapes and scenes veridically.

We were not the only ones who were startled by our binocular results. It also came as a surprise to our most fervent adversaries. To illustrate, one of these adversaries, a leading shape researcher, who was completely convinced that 3D shape was built from surfaces, accepted an invitation to visit Purdue around that time to check out our binocular shape recovery setup. We prepared a dozen shape recovery stimuli and asked him to adjust the aspect ratio of a rotating 3D shape, viewed monocularly, to the aspect ratio of the test stationary 3D shape, viewed binocularly. He stopped after the 3rd trial and announced that he did not need to run any more trials. He added that the adjustment was easy and that he was confident that all of his adjustments were very accurate. These claims are supported by his data which showed virtually perfect veridicality of shape perception. His experimental data confirmed his phenomenology. We thought, actually hoped, that this might convert him from building shapes from surfaces to recovering 3D shapes by using *a priori* constraints but we were wrong.

Our expert visitor later said that the subject should adjust the aspect ratio of the 3D object along the depth direction, rather than along the direction of the symmetry plane. Adjustments in the depth direction are known to introduce the *shape ambiguity* confound into a shape recovery experiment. Pizlo (2008) discussed the importance of avoiding this confound when studying shape in his book on the uniqueness of 3D shape in visual perception, so it seemed odd that our visitor brought this confound up. If he had actually read this book, it is hard to understand why he persisted in thinking that our experiment was confounded. The shape *ambiguity* problem comes into play whenever judging shape is impossible without judging depth. This almost never happens in everyday life and it can happen in the laboratory, *only* if the subject is asked to adjust 3D shape along the depth direction. Bringing shape *ambiguity* into a shape *constancy* or into a shape *recovery* experiment would be justified if, but only if, shape ambiguity and shape constancy were based on the same perceptual mechanisms. They are not. Solving a shape *ambiguity* problem *does* require depth perception but it *does not* require the operation of *a priori* constraints; solving shape *constancy* and shape *recovery* problems *does* require the operation of *a priori* constraints and *does not* require the perception of depth. So, there is no confound where our visitor said there was one and there is a confound where he said there was not a confound. Put simply, our visitor got this backwards. He continued making this claim about a confound until May

2012, when, without any kind of explanation, he conceded in a conversation with one of us[8] that "we had a point."

Here, we return from our segue to the sociology surrounding our research to the time we were ready to show a demo of our subjects' and models' binocular shape recovery at the Vision Science Society's conference in May 2009. This demo was a success but it was by no means easy to do. We packed a minivan with a large, heavy desktop PC, a CRT stereoscopic monitor, a projector, and all the other gadgets needed to show our demo and drove from West Lafayette, Indiana, to Naples, Florida. We were delighted to see dozens of visitors, including a large group of stereovision aficionados, at our demo and many volunteering to serve in our shape recovery experiment. We showed their aspect ratio adjustments live on a big screen as they made them, and the audience cheered them on or booed them, depending on whether they thought that each brave volunteer was doing a good job as he tried to make his recovery look as veridical as possible. Realize that this was tantamount to looking directly into a subject's mind to judge the veridicality of his perception by comparing its quality to your own. Everyone watching this performance was asking himself, "was he seeing the same thing I am"? It seems that he was more often than not. Not a single person who ran the test questioned whether his binocular shape percept could actually be veridical. It was obvious to everyone who ran and who watched that it can. Those who produced what looked like perfect recoveries were proud and showed it, and others, who had difficulty twiddling the dials, or who fell short of perfection for some other reason, felt and looked ashamed. No one argued about veridicality and no one complained about confounds. It was one big noisy happy crowd. During such sadly all too rare moments one is encouraged to think that Leibniz was correct when he claimed that ours is "*le meilleur des mondes possible*" (*the best of all possible worlds*).

Now that you know where we are and how we got here, we will explain how our binocular shape recovery actually works. You will discover that our claim that "*binocular disparity* [only] *comes into play when everything else fails*" is not in conflict with the fact that the *binocular* perception of 3D shape is *always* perfect. The next section will unscramble this conundrum.

---

[8]Z. Pizlo.

5.2 How We Worked Out the Binocular Perception of Symmetrical 3D Shapes

Once we had measured the performance of binocular observers in a 3D shape recovery experiment and found it to be perfect for all viewing directions, we were faced with the challenge of emulating it in our machine. This loomed large because the binocular vision literature is enormous, both for human and computer (machine) vision. Should we start a search in this huge literature for an explanation of our results? Could we find theories and models that could help us understand how using two eyes could explain the results of our binocular experiment? We were familiar with a large part of this literature, but an exhaustive search would have buried our noses in books and our foreheads in front of screens for months. We decided not to search but this decision was not made because of laziness. We decided to think outside of the box instead of immersing ourselves in the human literature because we knew what we would find. We knew that everyone knew that *we never see the world around us veridically.* A literature search could not help us find out how binocularity could produce perfectly veridical 3D shape perceptions. Even the computer vision literature could not help because interest in 3D machine vision had pretty much evaporated 20 years ago, when most members of the computer vision community switched to treating the world as a set of 2D images. Binocular vision, in this approach, became a special case of multi-view geometry where the emphasis is placed on acquiring more and still more visual data. *A priori* constraints were not popular in computer vision community primarily because they implied that one must agree to simplifying and restricting assumptions. A really ambitious machine vision person should be willing to deal with general cases and not feel constrained or hampered by constraints of any kind. We, on the other hand, had observed perfect binocular shape perception with symmetrical, volumetric objects, and we *knew* that the only way we could make sense of the veridical binocular perception of 3D shape would be based on our *a priori* constraints. We were stymied at this impasse for about a week.

In the Spring of 2009, we found ourselves still exploring how a 3D symmetrical shape could be recovered from a single 2D *orthographic* image. Our interest in making recoveries with 2D *perspective* images only came up a little later (see Chapter 6). *Perspective* images are more interesting than *orthographic* images because they represent the actual projection from the 3D scene to the retinal image. Furthermore, applying a mirror-symmetry constraint to a *perspective* image leads to a *unique* 3D shape recovery, whereas applying the same constraint to an *orthographic* image *only* leads *to a one-parameter family* of 3D shapes. In plain English, a perspective image provides more information than an orthographic image. Our use of orthographic, rather than perspective, images in our models was motivated by three facts. First, our results on 3D symmetry discrimination suggested that the human visual system uses invariants of an orthographic projection with both orthographic and with perspective images (see Chapter 3 and Sawada & Pizlo, 2008). Second, when monocular 3D shape recovery is tested by using perspective images produced by having large simulated objects viewed from near viewing distances, performance is not better with perspective images than it is with orthographic images. Finally, in many real life situations, an orthographic projection will be a good approximation of the actual retinal image. This last fact implies that in many real life situations the information provided by the perspective image on the retina cannot be much greater than the information provided by an orthographic image. These three reasons encouraged us to use 2D orthographic images in our computational models. The fact that a 2D orthographic image does not lead to a unique 3D interpretation was not a problem in the context of binocular vision. To the contrary, it actually encouraged us to take the contribution of the second image seriously. How could binocular vision help when it came to choosing the correct member in the one-parameter family of possible 3D mirror symmetrical shapes? Symmetrical interpretations differ from one another by their aspect ratios. BUT! When the viewing direction is not degenerate (neither orthogonal nor parallel to the plane of symmetry), *changing the aspect ratio of a 3D object will change the depth-order of its points* (see DEMO 5.2).[9] This "light-bulb" lit-up above our heads in a brainstorming session one morning in the Spring of 2009. The interaction between 3D symmetry and the depth-order of points solved our binocular recovery problem because depth-order can be discriminated extremely well. The ability to discriminate depth-order binocularly is called *stereoacuity*. Stereoacuity is probably the keenest discrimination we humans can make. This kind of acuity is so good that it is measured in seconds of visual angles (e.g., Steinman et al., 1985). Our claim that stereoacuity is responsible for the veridical binocular perception of shape is a completely new idea in vision. It was first presented publically at the Visual Sciences Society conference in May 2009 and published in 2011. By the time it was published, we had a convincing empirical verification of our theory. Our subjects' stereoacuity thresholds had been measured and their binocular shape performance could be predicted very well from their stereoacuity thresholds. Now that this has been explained, we will compare our new explanation of the role stereoacuity plays in binocular 3D shape recovery to our previous results, as well as to the results of others working on binocular vision. We are doing this to explain why our discovery had not been made by others earlier. We will also explain how our new theory of stereoacuity can explain the recent excitement surrounding what is called "3D movies."

[9] http://shapebook.psych.purdue.edu/5.2

5.3 How Our New Theory of Shape Perception, Based on Stereoacuity, Accounts for Old Results

In this section, we will explain why (1) the correlation between binocular and monocular performance in shape constancy experiments provides support for our new theory, (2) the "shape before disparity" phenomenon we published in 2005 fits into our new theory, and (3) others failed to observe veridical shape perception in binocular experiments with 3D symmetrical shapes. We begin by calling attention to the fact that in the new theory, the contribution of binocular vision comes into play rather late in visual processing. Visual processing begins with the production of a one-parameter family of mirror-symmetrical shapes and stereoacuity only kicks-in along with the operation of the 3D compactness constraint only after this has been done. There will be no benefit from using stereoacuity if the one-parameter family of symmetrical 3D shapes has not been produced. This happens when the symmetry constraint cannot be applied with unstructured objects such as a 3D polygonal line or with symmetrical objects missing many of their important contours. Stereoacuity only works through its interaction with 3D symmetry. This explains the high positive correlation between monocular and binocular shape perception observed in the two experiments by Li & Pizlo (2011) described in Section 5.1.

Now, how does the "shape before disparity" phenomenon we published in 2005 fit into our new theory of stereoacuity? This phenomenon did show that binocular disparity, as defined in Figure 5.1, makes little, if any, contribution to 3D shape perception as long as the 3D shape can be recovered by the application of symmetry and compactness constraints to a single 2D retinal image. Note that the way the stimuli used to demonstrate this phenomenon in Figure 5.4 were set up, binocular disparities of all points either increased or decreased when the 3D configuration changed over time. The binocular disparity information provided in this display, indicated that the fused 3D object was being stretched (or compressed) along a direction very close to the depth direction. This temporal manipulation of the stimulus did not produce a change in the depth-order of pairs of its points. Once the depth-order of points did not change, the changes of binocular disparities were ignored by the visual system and the shape percept was produced by the operation of the symmetry and compactness *a priori* constraints. There was a brief change in the depth-order of all of the points when the entire 3D object "flipped" over from being convex to concave. This brief change in depth-order was probably ignored by the visual system because of the operation of a well-known *a priori* constraint, according to which we tend to see objects from outside, rather than from inside (Mamassian & Landy, 1998).

Now, look at Figure 5.6. It shows a degenerate view of a pyramid with a square base. The apex of the pyramid is pointing directly towards you. When such an object is viewed with two eyes and the observer is asked to judge the ratio of the height of the pyramid to the width of its base, the observer will make large systematic errors. These errors mean that his binocular percept is far from veridical, it is illusory. Our anti-veridicality adversaries like to argue that this illusion, which is obtained with symmetrical shapes, that is, the kind of shape we insisted should be used, conflicts with our results and, therefore, discredits our models. There actually is no conflict because the individuals making this claim did not run a proper experiment. What they did do, does not test our work. First, their stimuli were viewed from a degenerate viewing direction. This meant that changing the aspect ratio of this 3D symmetrical shape was always confounded with changing its depth. It also did not change the depth-order of the pyramid's vertices. If depth-order does not change, stereoacuity cannot help in the recovery of the pyramid's 3D shape. This will be true even if the viewing direction is not *exactly* degenerate because this 3D object is rather simple: it only has 5 vertices. With so few vertices, small or even moderate changes of the object's aspect ratio will not change the depth-order of even a single pair of vertices. Second, our 3D symmetry constraint cannot be effective when its 2D retinal image is mirror-symmetrical as it is when a degenerate view is used. So by (1) confounding shape perception with depth perception, (2) making stereoacuity ineffective by using a low complexity test object, for example, a pyramid, viewed from a degenerate viewing direction, and (3) making the symmetry constraint ineffective by using a degenerate viewing direction, our anti-veridicality adversaries created a stimulus that stacks the cards entirely in their favor. Their stimulus is completely useless for studying the perception of shape in the laboratory and completely useless for studying the veridicality of shape perception in our normal visual environment.

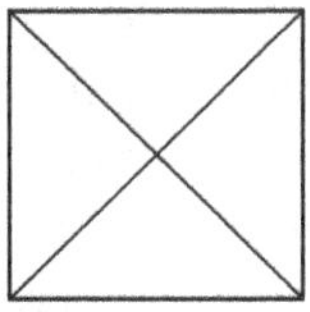

FIGURE 5.6. Degenerate view of a square pyramid.

5.4 3D Movies: What They Are, What They Want To Be, and What It Costs

Three-dimensional movies are currently at the cutting edge of home entertainment technology and are now commonly used in movie theatres. Some of the material we just described has implications for the effectiveness and, hence, the satisfaction that this technology may be able to provide. First, we must ask what we mean when we call these "3D movies." All we mean when we say that it is a 3D movie, is that it is a movie viewed with both eyes while wearing stereoscopic spectacles. But all conventional movies are 3D in the sense that all viewers see 3D objects and 3D scenes depicted in the movie as 3D even when it is not made with binocular disparity and they do not wear special spectacles. The 3D percept we all perceive is simply the result of applying *a priori* constraints to our 2D retinal images. Adding binocular disparity to these images, which is what the new technology does, enhances the experience, but this enhancement, like most things in life, comes with a cost. It is a matter of simple geometry that there is *only one correct viewing position* in a 3D public movie theatre, or at home, and only one person can sit in this special seat. So, if we want to obey the rules of geometry, we can only allow one viewer into our 3D movie theatre. So what happens if dozens of viewers are let in and seated? The geometry will be wrong for all but one viewer. In fact, there is not even a guarantee that the correct viewing position will actually be available inside the theatre. The unique, correct viewing position in the theatre is the position where the retinal images produced in the viewer's eyes when the 3D movie is viewed are *identical* to the retinal images that would have been produced in the viewer's eyes had he viewed the actual 3D scene filmed by the cameraman. In fact, even if there were to be such a position within the movie theatre, the distance between this person's eyes (his interocular distance) would have to be the same as the distance between the optical centers of the camera's lenses used to make the movie. So, we can safely claim that the viewing geometry is very likely to be wrong for all possible viewers in all possible theatres. There are two especially important sources of errors in the geometry of binocular viewing. The first is the wrong viewing distance. If the viewing distance differs from the correct viewing distance by a factor of k, then all distances reconstructed from binocular disparity (using equation on p. 150) will be different by the same factor. It follows that the perceived distance between two objects in the 3D scene will be incorrect by a factor of k. Fortunately, an incorrect viewing distance has *no* effect on the depth-order of features. This means that all 3D symmetrical shapes in the movie will be perceived veridically by the viewers and by our binocular model as we know from our research. The shapes of objects will be perceived veridically by all of the attendees, regardless of how far from the screen they are sitting (Li et al., 2011). This fact, a spill-off from our research on stereoacuity, explains why most viewers are not bothered by the fact that they cannot be, or are not, sitting in the one correct viewing distance to view a 3D movie. They do not even know, or need to know, that there is a problem with the geometry of viewing. The second source of error in viewing geometry is the viewing angle. Here, small departures from the correct viewing angle are not likely to be noticeable for the same reason such departures do not matter much in a conventional movie theatre where both eyes see the same image projected on the screen. Large departures from the correct viewing direction in both the ordinary and 3D theatre will lead to 3D projective distortions in the perceived 3D shapes and 3D scenes. These distortions may result in perceiving rigid symmetrical objects as asymmetrical and non-rigid, so finding a seat near the center of the theatre is, as your grandmother surely advised, a good reason for arriving early enough to find one.

Now that we have explained why errors in the viewing distance are not a problem in watching 3D movies, we will provide a few details about our binocular model of 3D shape recovery. These details will illustrate how the Bayesian formalism is applied to solving an inverse problem in vision and how such models can be verified in psychophysical experiments (see Sections 1.8–1.9 for background on inverse problems and Bayesian inference). As we pointed out before, the Bayesian formalism and regularization methods are mathematically equivalent. One can always express a cost function by using Bayes' formula (and vice versa) in such a way that the minimum of the cost function corresponds to the maximum of the posterior. We used the Bayesian method for the computations at this point in our project because it seemed more natural, and also because we had never used it in our prior models and thought that it would be fun to try our hands at something new.

5.5 Bayesian Model of Binocular Shape Perception

It is one thing *to say* that "stereoacuity is combined with a symmetry constraint in producing veridical 3D shape perception" and quite another *to formulate* a computational model of binocular 3D shape recovery. As we explained near the beginning of this book, a "theory" expressed in plain English is not really a proper theory. It is an "intuition" or a more or less organized set of intuitions at best. A proper theory of vision must specify (1) what the visual input is, (2) what is being computed, (3) how the veridical 3D percept is produced, (4) the degree to which the 3D interpretation is robust in the presence of visual noise and occlusions, and (5) the conditions under which the percept will *not* be veridical. Any attempt to provide more than verbal answers to such questions requires considerable elaboration of the computational details that are needed to make the model work. Here, we will only highlight the most important features of our model and explain why they are important because details of this computational model have been printed and are readily available (see Li et al., 2011, for details). The material that follows is intended to provide an overview designed to encourage our readers to delve into the details now in print.

We used a Bayesian formalism to model how stereoacuity enhancement could be used to solve the Inverse Problem of 3D shape recovery. We will use this formalism in this section, too. We are doing it this way because the Bayesian formalism seemed to be particularly appropriate. Why? We told you in Sections 1.8 that inverse problems can be handled by using either deterministic or probabilistic analyses, and the choice depended on the preference of the particular modeler. If the modeler knows the probability distributions of at least some of the underlying characteristics, a probabilistic approach using Bayes rule is both natural and convenient. If these probability distributions are not known in advance, a deterministic approach using a cost function might be more convenient. We used a deterministic approach in our monocular shape recovery models; specifically, we always used cost functions that combined the 2D retinal image with our *a priori* constraints of symmetry, planarity, compactness, and minimum surface. We did this because all of these four constraints can be treated as deterministic. We also treated the 2D retinal image as deterministic, ignoring any inherent probabilistic uncertainties. We simply assumed that these uncertainties would be small enough to ignore. But the conditions became different when we turned our attention to the binocular enhancement produced by stereoacuity. Here, the Bayesian formalism became more appropriate because the depth-order judgments, as measured by the stereoacuity threshold, are inherently probabilistic. This means that we will need to express some of our *a priori* constraints in a probabilistic, rather than in a deterministic, way.

Using the Bayesian formalism for describing our 3D shape recovery model means that we will be using a quite different technical language in which, instead of talking about a "visual image," we will talk about a "*likelihood function*" and instead of "*a priori* constraints," we will talk about the "*priors*." We will avoid all empiristic overtones of the Bayesian approach and only use their terminology. In other words, the *prior* as we use it is not derived from experience, is not updated by experience, the visual algorithms are innate, and there is no need for perceptual learning. Mathematically, the regularization method of solving inverse problems based on a cost function that we used in all of our prior work is equivalent to a Bayesian method. Choosing the Bayesian method was dictated by the fact that stereoacuity, which refers to the ability to judge which of two points is in front, is, as pointed out in the introduction to this section, inherently probabilistic. If the depth difference between two points is large, the probability of judging that the closer point is actually closer is close to one. This means that the observer can *always* be confident about the depth-order. If the depth difference is close to what we will call the "stereoacuity threshold," the observer will be correct in judging the order 84% of the time. If the depth of two points is identical, the observer will judge that one is closer than the other 50% of the time, which corresponds to complete uncertainty. The probabilistic nature of stereoacuity is related to visual uncertainty, so it makes a lot of sense to model it as such.

The first step in developing this model was to implement the observer's ability to judge the order of points in depth. The model begins by computing a *cyclopean* image, as the average of the left and right retinal images (a mythical giant member of the Cyclops clan, who was called Polyphemus, had a single eye in the middle of his forehead). The model computes the one-parameter family of 3D symmetrical shapes by assuming that the cyclopean image is a 2D orthographic image of a 3D mirror symmetrical shape. The members of this family have different aspect ratios and different slants of the symmetry plane. A 2D version of the 3D shapes is shown in Figure 5.7 to make it simpler to illustrate this fact. In this figure, 2D mirror-symmetrical polygonal shapes are used instead of 3D mirror-symmetrical polyhedral shapes. Also, to capture the fact that the projection from the shape out there to the retinal image is many-to-one, we use a 1D retina, represented by the x-axis, instead of the 2D retina. The depth direction is represented by the z-axis. This simplified illustration represents *all* important aspects of what pertains with real 3D shapes.

Three members of the one-parameter family of symmetrical shapes are shown in Figure 5.7. The shape on the left is elongated compared to the other two shapes, and the shape in the center is the roundest (most compact). The aspect ratios are related to the slant of the symmetry axis of these shapes. The slant on the left is 50°, in the center 45°, and on the right 39°. Changing the slant and the aspect ratio of the symmetrical shapes changes the depth order of some pairs of points. Two such pairs are marked on the left image and two other on the right. Take the points 3a and 4b. The point 3a is slightly in front of 4b in the shape shown on left, but 3a is much farther in depth than 4b in the shape shown on right. Our model evaluates the depth-order for all pairs of points in the shape in front of the model's eyes using a stereoacuity threshold that is equivalent to the threshold of one of our subjects, and assigns the probability that one point will be perceived in front of the other assuming that the true depth-order is represented by a shape from the one-parameter family of shapes. In the shape shown in Figure 5.7, there are 8 vertices, so there are 28 pairs. The model assigns the probability of depth-order judgment to each pair and then multiplies all of these probabilities to estimate the probability that all pairs have the particular order represented by the shape

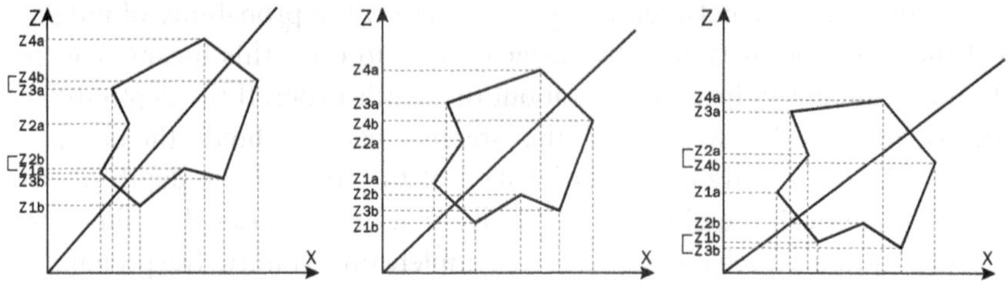

FIGURE 5.7. Consider the left and the middle panel. When the slant of the symmetry axis is changed from 45.00° to 50.19°, two pairs of points change their order in depth. The z-coordinates of these points are marked by two brackets on the z-axis of the graph on the left. Similarly, when the slant of the symmetry axis is changed from 45.00° to 38.66°, two pairs of points change their order in depth (see the graph on the right). (From Pizlo et al., 2010).

from the one parameter family of shapes. Mathematical details for doing this can be found in Li et al. (2011). This overall probability is shown in Figure 5.8 (the curve drawn with the solid line on the left). The maximum of this curve corresponds to the actual 3D shape "shown" to our binocular model. The x-axis represents the dissimilarity (ratio of aspect-ratios) between a given 3D shape from the one parameter family and the actual (true) 3D shape. Positive dissimilarities on the abscissa (x-axis) represent "taller" shapes compared to the true shape, while negative dissimilarities represent "wider" shapes. Zero dissimilarity means the shape is identical to the true shape. In Bayesian terminology, the solid curve is the "likelihood function." The likelihood function is the probability that a given pair of images in the "model's eyes" could have been produced by a 3D shape from the one parameter family of shapes. It can be seen that the likelihood function has a single maximum corresponding to the actual 3D shape presented to the model. 3D shapes whose aspect-ratios are very different from the true aspect ratio are unlikely: their probabilities are very small.[10] Despite the fact that the likelihood function is supposed to represent the information contained in the visual data, it is not uncommon for the likelihood function to also represent some priors (*a priori* constraints). In the terminology we usually use in our model, the likelihood function represents the "symmetry constraint." The fact that the symmetry constraint is "built into" our likelihood function can be seen in that the model evaluates only 3D shapes from a one-parameter family of symmetrical shapes, rather than all 3D shapes, symmetrical and asymmetrical that could produce a given cyclopean image. A Bayesian modeler would say that symmetry is an implicit constraint, or an assumption, in our model.

Next, we will explain the curve shown as dotted line in Figure 5.8. This is a Gaussian distribution (bell-shaped curve) that assigns probability densities

[10] The ordinate in Figure 5.8 represents probability density, not probability, itself.

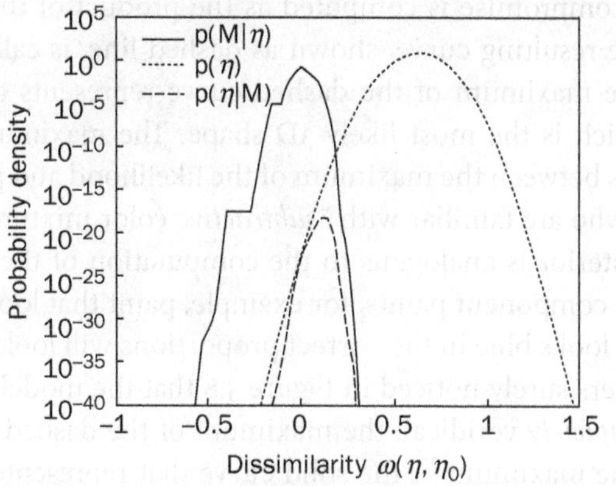

FIGURE 5.8. Graphs illustrating how the likelihood (solid line on left) and the prior (dotted line on right) are combined to compute the Bayesian posterior (dashed line in the middle). (From Li et al., 2011 with permission of the Association for Research in Vision and Ophthalmology).

to all members of the one-parameter family of 3D symmetrical shapes. Do not be alarmed by the fact that this curve does not look much like a bell-shaped curve. This is how a bell-shaped curve looks when a logarithmic scale is used on the axes. This curve represents the model's predilection for preferring compact 3D shapes. The maximum of the dotted curve represents the most compact 3D shape that could produce the given 2D cyclopean image. Using Bayesian terminology, we would say that this *most compact* 3D shape is the *most likely a priori*. By *a priori* here, we mean the state before the model's second "eye" was opened. Note that this 3D shape, which is the most likely *a priori*, is not a veridical percept of the 3D shape in front of the model's eyes. In Figure 5.8 the most compact 3D shape is 50% taller (dissimilarity = +0.6) than the shape in front of the model's eyes. The shape in front of the model's eyes is less compact and, hence, less likely—its probability is lower. We hope that this explanation is sufficient to allow the reader to understand what happened to our *a priori* compactness constraint when we switched to the Bayesian formalism. In our deterministic models, described in all of the previous chapters, we measured 3D compactness of every member of the one-parameter family of 3D mirror symmetrical shapes. Shapes with different aspect-ratios had different compactness. Now that we are using the Bayesian formalism, shapes with different aspect-ratios have different probabilities. The only critical aspect of this change from compactness to probability is that the maximally compact shape is *also* the most likely shape. If the model used only one eye, the 3D shape recovered by the model would have an aspect-ratio corresponding to the maximum of the dotted curve (the "prior's" probability distribution). However, when depth-order information becomes available, the model's binocular 3D shape percept is a compromise between the model's predilection for a compact shape and the stereoacuity information provided about the depth-order of its vertices. This compromise is computed as the product of the solid and dotted curves. The resulting curve, shown as dashed line, is called the Bayesian "posterior." The maximum of the dashed curve represents the "best bet" of the model, which is the most-likely 3D shape. The maximum of the posterior always falls between the maximum of the likelihood and prior curves. For those readers who are familiar with "*subtractive* color mixture," the computation of the posterior is analogous to the computation of the reflectance of a mixture of two component paints, for example, paint that looks yellow mixed with paint that looks blue in the correct proportions will look green.

Some readers surely noticed in Figure 5.8 that the model's binocular percept is not *completely* veridical: the maximum of the dashed curve is slightly shifted from the maximum of the solid curve that represented the actual 3D shape. It seems that combining compactness with stereoacuity was not the best idea in this case. Using stereoacuity only (the solid curve), would have produced a perfect recovery of 3D shape. Its maximum is almost dead-on zero. What is going on? At this point, we have to remind the reader about Johannes Müller's Doctrine of Specific Nerve Energies presented in 1835, which states that the visual system has access only to the activities of the "nerves" serving the retinal images. It does not have direct access to objects out there. It should also be noted that there will be cases when the likelihood function is *not* very informative. This can happen when the viewing distance is large, and the depth-order of points is very difficult, or even impossible, to judge (the viewing distance, 50 cm, used for producing Figure 5.8 was fairly small making depth-order judgments very reliable). The quality of the retinal images may also be low because they have low contrast or because one object is occluding another. In such cases, the maximum of the likelihood function will be misleading or difficult to estimate. In all such cases, using a compromise between the *likelihood* and the *prior*, following the rules of Bayesian inference, is the smart thing to do. If, on the other hand, binocular viewing conditions are very good, as they were in our experiment whose results are shown in Figure 5.5, the binocular percept was close to perfect even when the viewing directions were close to degenerate.

It is known that stereoacuity may vary substantially among observers. In fact, one of our subjects had a quite high stereoacuity threshold (recall that thresholds are inversely related to sensitivity—very sensitive subjects have low thresholds). His threshold was higher than YS's by a factor of about 4. This should lead to substantially poorer binocular shape recovery. It did, as can be seen in Figure 5.9. TK's binocular performance was not much different from his monocular performance because his likelihood function was fairly flat (uninformative). Furthermore, the visual system of this subject assigned a relatively high weight to the monocular compactness prior, as verified in another experiment. A higher weight meant that the dotted curve in Figure 5.8 was narrower for this subject. As a result of these two factors, the maximum of his posterior

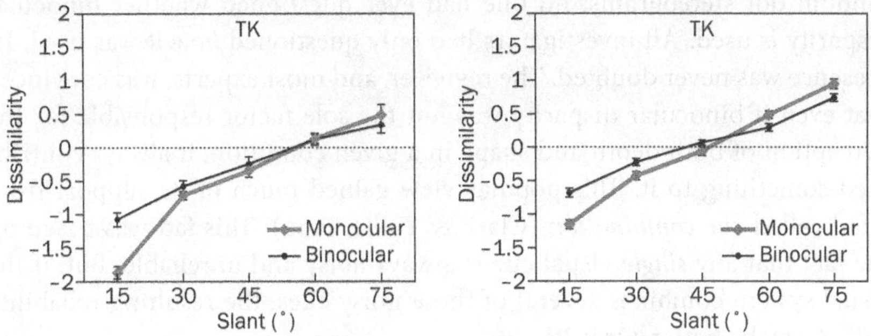

FIGURE 5.9. Monocular and binocular performance of subject TK (left) and TK: Model's performance (right). Monocular performance is shown by the thick gray lines and binocular performance is shown by the thin black lines. (From Li et al., 2011 with permission of the Association for Research in Vision and Ophthalmology).

coincided with the maximum of the compactness prior. When our model was given TK's stereoacuity threshold and TK's predilection for compactness, the model's binocular performance was very similar to TK's. Does this mean that TK would have a lot of trouble perceiving 3D shapes veridically outside of the laboratory? Not really because his poor stereoacuity will only come into play when his viewing direction is degenerate or nearly so. Outside of the laboratory, TK can compensate for his deficiency simply by moving his head. We did not allow him to do this when we measured his stereoacuity. Finally, with real objects standing on a real ground, the observer can recover a unique and veridical 3D shape by using an additional constraint that the object's plane of symmetry is orthogonal to the horizontal ground and parallel to the direction of gravity. This will be explained in Chapter 6 and the geometrical argument will be illustrated by psychophysical results showing that TK's and YS's perception of spatial relations in a 3D real room are actually very similar.

5.6 Why We Could Claim That Our Model is Complete?

This question was raised by one of the reviewers of a paper we published in the *Journal of Vision* (Li et al., 2011). This reviewer was surprised, one might even say, "shocked," that we called our model *"complete"* without making any use of binocular disparity, as defined on p. 150. His surprise is understandable because the entire 170 year history of research on the binocular perception of 3D shape and space was based on binocular disparity while stereoacuity had played only a marginal role, where it was used to explain such esoteric abilities as threading a needle or aligning two off-set bars. Using Kuhn's (1962) terminology, our claim was challenging the entrenched binocular paradigm. During the last 170 years, including the last half century of very active research that followed Julesz' (1960) seminal paper employing random dot stereograms, no one had ever questioned whether binocular disparity *is* used. All investigators had only questioned *how* it was used. Its presence was never doubted. The reviewer, and most experts, was convinced that even if binocular disparity was not the sole factor responsible for the perception of both depth and shape in a given condition, it always contributed something to it. This popular view gained much of its support from a fad called *cue combination* (Clark & Yuille, 1990). This fad was based on the fact that any *single* visual cue is always noisy and unreliable. But, if the visual system combines several of these noisy cues, the resulting reliability will *always* be better. Or is it?

Consider two visual cues, say texture and binocular disparity, that can be used to measure the same characteristic, say the slant of a surface. Now, assume that neither of these cues has *any* systematic error. In statistical parlance, this means that each cue provides an unbiased estimate of the slant. Let the reliability of each cue separately, as measured by the reciprocal of variance of random error, be $1/s_{texture}^2$ and $1/s_{binocular}^2$. If these cues are combined, the resulting reliability is better than either of the two component reliabilities. Mathematically, $1/s_{combined}^2 = 1/s_{texture}^2 + 1/s_{binocular}^2$. No matter how unreliable one cue is compared to another, it always pays to combine them. Except if one of them provides a biased estimate of the slant. In plain English, if one cue has no systematic error and the other does have a systematic error, the visual system is likely to do well, actually do optimally, by ignoring the cue that has the systematic error. This fact is obvious statistically, but it has been overlooked by many proponents of cue combination. The more cues the merrier is not a universal verity when it comes to vision, and it is certainly not true in 3D shape perception.

Going back to our reviewer's complaint, once we had formulated a model that produces a veridical 3D shape recovery without binocular disparity, why on Earth would we want to add binocular disparity, which is well-known to produce systematic errors all of the time, with all possible types of stimuli and with all types of judgments? If *cue combination* is assumed to be a fundamental Law of Vision, we must add a super-ordinate law, namely, *don't fix what ain't broke*. We do not know whether we convinced the reviewer who wanted us to add binocular disparity to drop his request, but we are sure that we convinced the editor (Michael Landy), who was handling our manuscript, because he understood the issues raised by cue combination better than most contemporary vision scientists, as can be judged by one of his important contributions to this topic (Landy, Maloney, Johnston & Young, 1995).

Our argument with this reviewer did not end here. He wanted us to put binocular disparity in conflict with symmetry to support our claim that the visual system had a predilection for symmetry. Binocular disparity can provide the visual system with metric information (albeit always biased information) about depth and this information can be put in conflict with the symmetry of a 3D shape. We agreed and ran subjects in this kind of conflict experiment. Note that this experiment, in effect, replicated the conditions found in a 3D movie theatre where viewing distance is almost always incorrect. This was done in the laboratory by having the subject view a stereoscopic monitor with the actual viewing distance from the monitor different from the viewing distance simulated by binocular disparity. Under such conditions, binocular disparity will indicate that a 3D object is stretched or compressed along the depth direction. Depth-order is not affected, but the symmetry of the object is destroyed for all, except degenerate, viewing-directions. Degenerate viewing directions were not used, so our conflict situation was a pure conflict between metric depth indicated by binocular disparity and the symmetry of the test object. The subjects reported that the 3D shapes looked symmetrical in almost all trials, and the recoveries of the 3D shapes showed very little influence of the conflict (Li et al., 2011, pp. 13–14). The visual system's predilection for 3D symmetry is very strong, indeed. Note that this experiment provides direct support for our claim that an incorrect viewing distance is of little significance in 3D movie theatres. It also provides additional support for our claim in Section 1.6 that Koenderink's experiments, in which an elliptical probe was used to "measure" the percept of 3D surfaces of mirror-symmetrical objects, such as human bodies, did not measure anything meaningful; certainly not the perception of the 3D shapes of human bodies as had been claimed. Once we appreciate that human beings have a very strong built-in predilection to perceive mirror-symmetry, human bodies will always look symmetrical, not distorted as Koenderink and his associates had concluded.

6

Figure-ground Organization, Which Breaks Camouflage in Everyday Life, Permits the Veridical Recovery of a 3D Scene

Up to this point our computational models required human intervention at the front end. Specifically, the human had to do three things: (1) locate where the objects are in the 2D image, (2) mark their contours in the 2D image, and (3) indicate their relationships. So now, as this story draws near to its conclusion, we will explain how the machine, working entirely on its own, can do all of these things. Note well, this does not mean that our work is over, but it is not far from over. This book takes us as far as providing a "proof of concept" in the form of computational models that emulate a number of critical human 3D visual capabilities (1) the recovery of a 3D shape from one or two 2D retinal images, (2) figure-ground organization based on two retinal images, and (3) the recovery of a 3D scene. These models have already been implemented in an autonomous robot and tested with real images of indoor 3D scenes. This implementation is the first working version of a machine that can see, much as we do, entirely on its own. We believe that it actually will be possible to emulate human visual performance more elaborately fairly soon, but we still have a way to go. Three necessary elaborations will be described in Chapter 7. Now we will explain how we worked out the first stage of visual processing, the stage that had proven to be by far the hardest thing we had to do.

The first operation, called figure-ground organization (FGO), must determine which regions in the 2D image represent individual objects. We started to do this several years ago by applying a variety of commonly-used local and global operations. Regions in the image representing the same object should have similar texture, so, determining the boundary of such a region should produce what is called an *occluding contour*. We hoped that approximating this contour with what is technically called an α-hull (alpha hull) would do the trick (the α-hull is a generalization of a convex hull, which can be used to describe non-convex regions). The α-hull only worked with simple cases; cases in which objects did not occlude each other and where the background had a uniform color. We demonstrated this stage of FGO development at the Vision Sciences Society Meeting in May 2010. This required covering a florid carpet on the floor of the demo room with a uniform light-blue sheet. Without this homogeneous sheet, achieving FGO would have been impossible. We simply could not do this at that time. The fact that we overcame this problem and can now handle FGO very well came as quite a surprise. This seemed to be impossible when we first took it on.

After the meeting, we set out to find an alternative to "breaking" camouflage by simply hiding it under a homogeneous sheet. We started by using 2 images for FGO instead of the single image we had used up until then. We decided to break camouflage by using an off-the-shelf stereo correspondence algorithm to obtain a 3D depth-map of the scene. This kind of map is always quite noisy so it cannot be expected to yield good results when used to recover 3D shapes and 3D scenes. We knew this but decided to give it a try because it had proven to be quite helpful in breaking camouflage during two World Wars, despite its inherent noise. We began by simply trying to identify the floor visually in the stereoscopic depth-map. Note that when you do this, the presence of texture on the floor becomes a virtue, instead of the obstacle it had been when we showed our demo based on the α-hull. Distinctive texture is great for establishing stereo correspondence. The more the merrier. You cannot have too much. This technique worked well beyond our expectations. The floor, which provided the background for everything standing on it, was easy to identify and locate, once it had been identified. It became trivial to remove the floor from the depth-map. This was all we needed to solve the figure-ground segregation part of the FGO problem. This left us the problem of finding the 3D points that represented each of the objects in the scene.

Most natural objects, including horses, humans, chairs, and tables have parts that are oriented vertically. This fact implies that the projection of our 3D depth-map vertically onto a horizontal surface will provide strong indications of the presence and positions of such objects on the surface. Technically, this means that it will be easier to distinguish signal from noise in this 2D projection than it was in the original 3D depth-map. Once this has been done, the model determines distinctive clusters of points in this 2D projection. These clusters of points represent the 3D objects. Note that it is easy to separate objects from one another in a top view because occlusions are very rare in top view images. Using top views in vision research is quite unusual. Most prior research tried to separate objects from each other in a perspective (side) views of a 3D scene. This was always difficult because, in side views, occlusions are the rule rather than the exception. Pieces of furniture were used as the objects to be separated in our work on this problem. Look at Figure 6.1.

FIGURE 6.1. A natural scene as "seen" by our machine. Top left: furniture arranged haphazardly in our laboratory. Top-right: outlines of each piece of furniture (their convex hulls) drawn by the machine. Bottom: machine's top view of the relative sizes and positions and pathways among the 3D convex hulls.

This figure shows how the positions and orientations of individual objects are estimated within the 3D scene by fitting rectangles to the objects. Five free parameters are needed to locate them within the scene—their position, their orientation, and the lengths of their two sides. The result of this operation is shown at the bottom of the figure. It shows what the machine is "seeing." It is seeing all 6 objects that were in front of it. Can you see all 6? This is not easy to do because the 6th object, the stand inscribed in dotted line in the image on the top right, is almost completely occluded by the chair in front of it (inscribed in solid line). The model is also able to estimate the height of each object from the scene's 3D depth-map. This estimate allows the model to draw 3D boxes that approximate the sizes and locations of all of the objects. The next step is to project these 3D boxes onto each of the 2D images. This locates the 2D regions associated with each object. Once this is done, FGO has been completed. The completed solution of the FGO problem is shown in the image on the top right. Note that this problem was solved in two different representations: on the scene's 2D image and also on the scene's floor. *This means that the model not only knows how many objects there are, it also knows their positions and the distances among them.* Note that this model detects all kinds of objects very well, not only the kind of furniture we used in Figure 6.1. Note also that all of this was done without familiarizing the model with any of the objects and without any laser measurements of absolute distances. Finally, note that the model can detect standing, walking, and sitting humans in a variety of natural postures as well as all the other 3D objects within all of the scenes. This is illustrated in DEMO 6.1,[1] in which a number of people are simply wandering around a room. The green curves (convex hulls) on the left show the location of individuals that were detected and on the right is a top view of them. The circles in the top view represent the center of each individual.

With this in hand, we could return to our goal of liberating our machine from all human interference. This brought us to detecting contours of the objects in the 2D image and to establishing their *relational structure*. Detecting contours now, *after* FGO was established, proved to be much easier than trying to do this before the objects had been separated from their backgrounds. You will not be surprised to discover that we did this, once again, by taking advantage of *a priori* constraints. How we did this and how it can best be explained is directed primarily towards our technical readers but we suspect that our intuitive readers will be able to follow what comes next if they give it a try. Most mirror-symmetrical objects, including animal and human bodies and many man-made objects, present themselves in most natural 3D scenes with symmetry planes that are vertical. Once the symmetry-plane is vertical, the pairs of symmetrical points and features form horizontal lines in the 3D scene. In a camera's image, these lines project to a vanishing point located on the vanishing line representing the scene's horizon. Similarly, in a camera's image, all vertical edges in the 3D scene (such as the legs of animals and chairs) project to lines that intersect at another vanishing point at the top of the retina in the eye (remember, the retinal image is upside down). The positions of these two vanishing-points are easy to determine once the direction of gravity and the horizontal orientation of the ground-plane is known. If an object has (approximately) two planes of mirror symmetry, as most of our furniture has, there will be a third vanishing-point. This point will be located on the horizon. Having and using as many as two or three vanishing points makes it possible to extract edges in the object's image and then to establish their symmetry correspondences (see Sections 4.3–4.4 for the definition and discussion of symmetry correspondence problem). An example of extracting contours and establishing symmetry correspondence is shown in Figure 4.8 in Section 4.4. More examples will be shown later in this chapter. As you will see, this kind of output is sufficient to provide our machine with *everything it needs to know to perform effectively in our environment.*

6.1 Estimating the Orientation of the Ground-plane

It is interesting, actually unfortunate, that almost all prior research on FGO used 2D images representing toy examples. Even more disturbing scientifically is the fact that all stimuli in these FGO studies were chosen to be ambiguous,

[1] http://shapebook.psych.purdue.edu/6.1

such as Rubin's famous picture of a silhouette of two faces that could also be easily seen as a vase (see Figure 6.2): the figure can be perceived either as the figure or as the ground and vice versa. This contrasts drastically with what pertains in our everyday life where we *never* experience figure ground reversal. A chair in front of me never looks like its background no matter how long I stare at it or no matter how hard I try to make the chair's background look like an object of any kind. The chair always looks like an object (a figure) and the floor upon which the chair stands and the wall behind the chair always look like the background (ground) for the chair. It is hard to understand how studying *2D ambiguous stimuli* would be a good, much less the best, way to understand the *unambiguous perception of 3D objects and the surfaces around and behind them*? The only possible justification for doing this is the, now commonly and fortunately rejected, assumption that the brain is a "linear system." A linear system allows one to predict the system's responses to arbitrarily complex visual stimuli by studying its responses to much simpler stimuli. This is not possible in nonlinear systems. A linear system is easy to model so it is not surprising that it engendered a lot of excitement when Campbell & Robson (1968) introduced their Theory of Spatial Frequency Channels. Their theory assumes linearity in brain function. It took the vision community about 15 years to loose interest in it. If the visual system were linear, and it is not, the percept of a real 3D scene could be explained simply by a superposition of percepts of 2D stimuli like those used in the faces-vase illusion.[2] The mind and the brain are more complex and much more interesting than can be modeled with a linear system. The willingness to assume that a system as complicated as the human brain, as well as its mental output, could actually be *linear* probably derives from the persistent influence of Structural Psychology in which elementary sensations were used to build complex percepts by means of associative learning. You already know that we subscribe to a quite different view, a view that emphasizes that "the whole is different from the sum of its parts," so we will move on to considering *real* 3D scenes without first decomposing them into *unreal* simple elements.[3] We will treat a 3D scene as a *whole* and we will use *a priori* visual constraints, such as the symmetry of objects,

---

[2] Note that 3D, not only 2D, visual illusions, can be setup in the laboratory (see Hochberg, 1987, for some examples) but the fact that 3D, as well as 2D, stimuli can produce illusions does not make illusions more important than they actually are outside of the laboratory. Recall that prior to Biederman's work on shape, it was almost universally accepted that our perceptions in everyday life are never veridical. This unfortunate assumption encouraged perceptionists to go out of their way to avoid studying veridical perceptions in the laboratory. This was a huge mistake. If illusions ruled in everyday life, one *should* concentrate on studying them. The more illusions, the merrier. But, now that we all know that veridical perceptions is the rule in everyday life, one *should* study them. Studying veridical perceptions must take precedence over studying illusions if progress is going to be made.

[3] An excellent summary of what was accomplished by working with 2D stimuli in the area called "figure-ground organization" during the 100 years following the Gestalt Revolution can be found in Wagemans et al. (2012a, b).

FIGURE 6.2. Rubin's faces-vase illusion.

the three-dimensionality of space, and the horizontal ground, and non-visual constraints, such as gravity to construct our *whole,* that is, the real 3D scene as it is out there. We begin by explaining how we made use of gravity and the horizontal ground in our search for an effective solution to the figure-ground problem.

We started by installing an inclinometer on our robot. This inclinometer measures the direction of gravity, providing our machine with the kind of information primates get from the vestibular system in their inner ear. We know that human beings can sense vertical and horizontal directions without systematic errors and with random errors less than 1°. We bought an inclinometer with similar performance characteristics. The orientation and position of the horizontal floor can be estimated by sensing the direction of gravity and assuming that the floor is orthogonal (90°) to it. The vertical distance between your eyes and the floor beneath you corresponds to your *visual* height. So, a human observer and our machine, fitted with its inclinometer, have a good expectation (*a priori* information) about where the floor is located. Both now need some kind of visual information to confirm their expectation about the floor's location. We found that the easiest way to provide this confirmation was to use a stereoscopic system (two cameras) to solve the stereo correspondence problem and then compute the 3D depth-map (using triangulation) for all visible surfaces and to identify points that lie on the plane of the floor.[4] Is this an easy thing to do? We knew that the stereo correspondence problem is computationally difficult and there is no algorithm that guarantees a correct solution all the time, but we are not

[4]"Motion parallax," that is, using only one camera and a horizontal displacement emulating a head translation would work as well.

looking for a perfect solution. The presence of some noise, uncertainty and a few errors will eliminate only a handful of points from the correct selection for our floor. We did not need to identify all of the points so we used an off-the-shelf algorithm for stereo correspondence and found that it worked well enough to satisfy our needs (Li et al., 2012). Note that clearly visible, even florid, texture is not a problem here. In fact, it helps, but not having a lot of obvious texture is also fine. Even when a floor has a completely uniform color, it is never entirely devoid of texture.

But, as soon as we had worked this out, one of us[5] realized that the floor can be detected *without using* an inclinometer, *without knowing* the robot's height and *without assuming* that the floor is orthogonal (90°) to the direction of gravity. In all of the furniture arrangements we tested, 3D points lying on the floor represented more than 50% of all visible points, and often as much as 80% of all visible points. One can identify the floor simply by estimating a 3D plane that fits *most* of the 3D visible points entirely on the basis of the number of points. This visual method is as good as the "vestibular" method, which uses an inclinometer's reading and knowledge of the body's height to determine the position of the floor. This fact caused one of us[6] to have a fit. He was upset because he was proud of the fact that had convinced some skeptics about the merits of our work at the 2011 Vision Sciences Society meeting by resting his arguments primarily on the important role that gravity played in our solution of the FGO problem in everyday life. Gravity, for him, was obviously the *sine qua non* of FGO and this very reassuring snug rug had just been pulled out from under his feet. This caused him a few days with nearly sleepless nights trying to find a way to live with the fact that our machine did not have to make use of gravity to function effectively in our visual world. It obviously did not need gravity so why and how was it made to work without it? He credits a dream as the source of his current equanimity now that he knows that he is living in this dual-FGO-solution world. He dreamt that he was a marine animal contemplating life on land and woke with the realization that FGO started in the oceans, where only visual information was available, and only added gravity when he moved up to live on land. This realization instigated a series of emails in which he apologized for the disruption in our work that his unseemly fit had caused. He also explained what he thought the *deep meaning* of this dual FGO was. A few highlights of this exchange:

> "TO PIZLO: I have found a way of living with the new solution of our FGO problem. Realized why our FGO works well without gravity. Our marine animals must see the 3D world and navigate as we

---

[5] Y. Li.

[6] Steinman.

do so it is not surprising that gravitational information is not essential.

FROM PIZLO: Are you saying that animals do not sense gravity in the water?

TO PIZLO: You cannot know up from down under water if you do not watch the bubbles from your respirator and divers wearing bubble-free respirators can mistake one for the other if they do not watch their depth gauges. The buoyancy felt underwater overwhelms all gravitational signals.

FROM PIZLO: Are you sure that the vestibular system is ineffective in the water?

TO PIZLO: Gravity has little influence on buoyant objects like animals. That's why they train astronauts under water. Fish often have bladders that allow them to have neutral buoyancy and they are influenced little by gravity. Visual cues will be much more prominent than gravity under water.

AGAIN TO PIZLO: Fish and marine mammals live in visual environments at least as rich as ours. Many are like dense jungles. Sea otters live and function in dense beds of seaweed and most fish live on coral reefs around wrecks and in other areas that provide shelter so your gravity-free FGO probably came first with gravity only coming into play when marine life came up on land. So, both ways of handling FGO are important and my concerns about needing to emphasize gravity was not part of the true story. We discovered how gravity can help FGO first but the true order in nature was surely different."

At least among the four of us, we now agree unanimously that our machine, like us, has two ways of estimating where the ground surface is located: one is visual and the other is not. The visual way of estimating the ground surface will surely be the more reliable of the two because it does not rely on the assumption that the ground is orthogonal to the direction of gravity, as must be done when the ground surface is estimated from the direction of gravity.

6.2 How a Coarse Analysis of the Positions and Sizes of Objects Can Be Made

Once the 3D points representing the floor are identified, they can be ignored; that is, they simply can be treated as background. The same can be done with the 3D points representing vertical walls when walls are present. The remaining 3D points represent the objects, which are often called "figures" in visual science. One could claim that the main step in solving FGO has been

FIGURE 6.3. A 2D gray-scale image of a 3D indoor scene. There are 11 pieces of furniture in the center of this dance floor. The floor is highly-textured. It also contains shadows and specular (mirror-like) reflections. As you can see, solving FGO is not a very different task than breaking camouflage.

accomplished at this point and one should note that this step is far from trivial considering the complexities inherent in analyzing and interpreting real 2D images. Look at Figure 6.3, which shows an indoor 3D scene containing more objects than were present in Figure 6.1. This dance floor is highly-textured. It also contains both shadows and specular (mirror-like) reflections. This figure makes it very clear that when Bela Julesz argued that FGO is the same as breaking camouflage, he was probably right, and when he claimed that binocular vision plays an important role in this process, he was probably right, too.

You already know from our previous discussions of combinatorial explosions that solving the stereo correspondence problem will be manageable if the images do not contain too many pixels (see Section 5.1). The image in Figure 6.3 has 800 by 600 pixels and its horizontal field of view is 90°. This means that there are only 9 pixels per degree. You surely agree that this resolution is relatively coarse so one might be inclined to ask whether is it sufficient to analyze the 3D objects and their shapes shown in this photo? This is an important question because the highest resolution, which is found at the center of the human retina, is higher by an order of magnitude. There are 180 cones per degree at the center of your retina, which is 20 times more than are present on this camera's photosensitive surface. Looking at the photo in Figure 6.3 suggests that there is no problem with the sampling rate we used, only 9 pixels per degree of visual angle. The photo suggests that there is no problem because you can see all of the 3D shapes fairly well in this photo, but once you ignore your phenomenology and turn to science, you will discover that effective processing at this low level of sampling will be surprising to many vision scientists. It certainly was to us. The sampling rate used to make this photo is actually equivalent to the sampling rate on the part of the retina that is 11° away from its center. We only began to wonder about how our model's vision could be so effective with such a low sampling rate after we had actually solved the FGO problem. Fortunately, we did not let it slow us down. We probably would not have even tried to solve the FGO problem had we paid more attention to the resolution we were working with. Now that you know about the relatively coarse tool we used to analyze our 3D shapes, we will return to how we used it.

After the 3D points representing the ground have been ignored, the remaining 3D points represent the visible surfaces of the objects in the scene. Remember, our ultimate goal is to recover 3D shapes based on the 3D symmetry constraint applied to 2D contours in the camera's image. So, we are actually after contours, not surfaces, and contours are tricky to work with because contours, unlike surfaces, are abstractions; they are not physical characteristics. A surface is a physical characteristic because we can touch it.[7] Contours are actually intangible. Consider a human face. When an artist produces a line-drawing of a face, the nose is likely to be represented by a curve in the artist's 2D image. But this curve is not an image of any physical curve that is actually present on the nose, itself. Noses can usually be well-represented by surfaces that, locally, have a high degree of curvature. This means that the 2D contour, representing the nose, corresponds to the narrow region on the surface of the nose that has a high curvature. But, if you are asked to draw this contour on the actual nose of a person sitting in front of you, you will be uncertain about where this line should actually be drawn. So, a contour made to represent a 3D nose is an "abstraction" because it cannot actually be found on the nose being drawn. Many man-made objects, such as chairs, have fairly sharp edges, so one might hope that these sharp edges are physical, tangible contours. They are not. The actual edges of all chairs, tables, as well as of grand pianos are *always* round so, there will always be some uncertainty about which points on the edge represent *the* contour. A *perfect* real edge would have to be *perfectly* sharp, that is, it would have to be a geometrical line with zero thickness. But zero thickness is obviously an abstraction, too. It follows that a camera can never provide a direct measurement of edges regardless of its sampling rate, so edges must always be inferred from texture information. Such problems do not come up when surfaces are being sensed and measured. Surfaces always have colors and textures and these properties always provide rich data for visual measurement. The relationship between surfaces and contours is, therefore, very interesting and any machine that wants to see like us must address the computational aspects of this relationship directly. The task

---

[7]See Section 1.7 for the Bishop Berkeley's claim that touching is more certain than seeing.

confronting the machine is to find ways of capitalizing on the strengths of surfaces and edges, while at the same time avoiding the weaknesses of each. In our computational model we use surfaces to solve the FGO problem and to produce a coarse description of the 3D scene. Specifically, our model solves the stereo correspondence problem for texture, but not for edges. The recovery of 3D shape is done for contours, but not for surfaces and our model solves the symmetry correspondence problem for edges, but not for texture. At some point the model's visual analysis must transition from texture to edges and the ultimate success of its visual analysis will depend critically on how well it makes this transition. The next two steps for locating objects in the 3D scene and in the 2D images, which will be described in the next two subsections, rely on texture information. The following three steps for extracting 2D edges, establishing 3D symmetry correspondence, and recovering 3D shapes rely on edges. These analyses represent the gradual transition from the physical world of surfaces to the ideal world containing the abstraction called shape.

6.3 How a Useful Top View Representation was Produced

Once the background is removed, the 3D points that remain represent the objects in the scene, but these objects are expressed in the camera's coordinate system. This is not ideal because it means that the representation of the objects, both their positions and their orientations, will change whenever the camera's orientation relative to the room changes. This is undesirable for several reasons. First, if the object in the room is stationary it should be perceived as stationary regardless of any movements that the camera makes. If the object is always represented in the coordinate system of the machine's camera, every movement of the camera would have to be estimated and then "subtracted" from the 3D motion of each object relative to the camera. One would have to do these computations almost perfectly, and make them as accurate as possible, because failures to do so would result in "visual" hallucinations of stationary objects wandering around in the 3D space in front of the machine. The more objects, the more computations with more and more hallucinations. It is much simpler to express the 3D objects in the coordinate system of the 3D scene, rather than in the camera's coordinate system, as soon as possible and proceed directly to the next stages of FGO and 3D recovery problems in this new representation. We are convinced that using the environmental coordinate system (technically, the *allocentric* frame of reference) is as important in human vision as it is in machine vision. How else would we be able to see a stable world in the variety of real life situations, such as when we drive a car or watch a movie? It is possible, perhaps even likely, that switching from the camera to the environmental coordinate system to see the 3D scene veridically as we move around is what is meant when investigators work on what is called *optic flow* in the conventional psychophysical and computer vision literature. The main difference between us and those who work on optic flow seems to be that we recognize that a 3D visual interpretation of a scene is an inverse problem and we solve it as such, whereas those working with the optic flow method try to deal with it as a forward problem based on cue combination. Those working on 3D scenes by using optic flow handle it as a forward problem. They analyze the pattern of 2D retinal stimulation to determine the direction of the observer's self-motion. This interest in using optic flow to study 3D scenes was started by J. J. ("Jimmy") Gibson (1950), who adopted a quite extreme version of the forward problem approach to vision, by claiming in his theory of *Direct Perception* that the visual system simply picks up the necessary information from the retina and/or from the visual field. He actually proposed that neither computations nor *a priori* constraints are needed to recover a 3D scene; some indescribable, built-in mechanism simply pulled this off. The second reason for using the coordinate system of the 3D scene, rather than the camera's, derives from the fact that the agent (human or machine) usually walks on the "ground," the surface upon which most other objects reside. From our point of view, what really counts are the positions of the objects relative to the 3D scene and the distances among them as measured, horizontally, along the ground; not along the direction of the observer's or the camera's line-of-sight. This distinction becomes very important when the machine becomes free-ranging and must plan optimal paths or tours within its environment.[8] The third reason for representing objects in the coordinate system of the 3D scene is that the symmetry planes of mirror-symmetrical objects are typically parallel to the direction of gravity and orthogonal (90°) to the floor. This is what takes place when you stand or sit upright. The relationship between the symmetry plane of a 3D shape and the orientation of the ground surface provides a very powerful *a priori* constraint that can be used in the recovery of a 3D shape. So, once one realizes that the vertical orientation of the symmetry planes of humans, animals, and many man-made objects is important, the observer (man or machine) should, and so probably does, represent objects in the coordinate system of the 3D scene. This coordinate system is defined by the horizontal floor and the direction of gravity.

Changing the reference frame from the camera to the frame of the 3D scene is geometrically easy to do as long as the camera "knows" its orientation and position relative to the room. The relationship between the camera and the scene, which is called the *extrinsic camera calibration*, is accomplished by estimating the orientation and position of the floor. How this is done was described in the previous section. After changing the frame of reference, we

[8]Here, the machine, like us, will be faced with solving the Shortest Path and Traveling Salesman Problems both of which are solved on the plane of the floor.

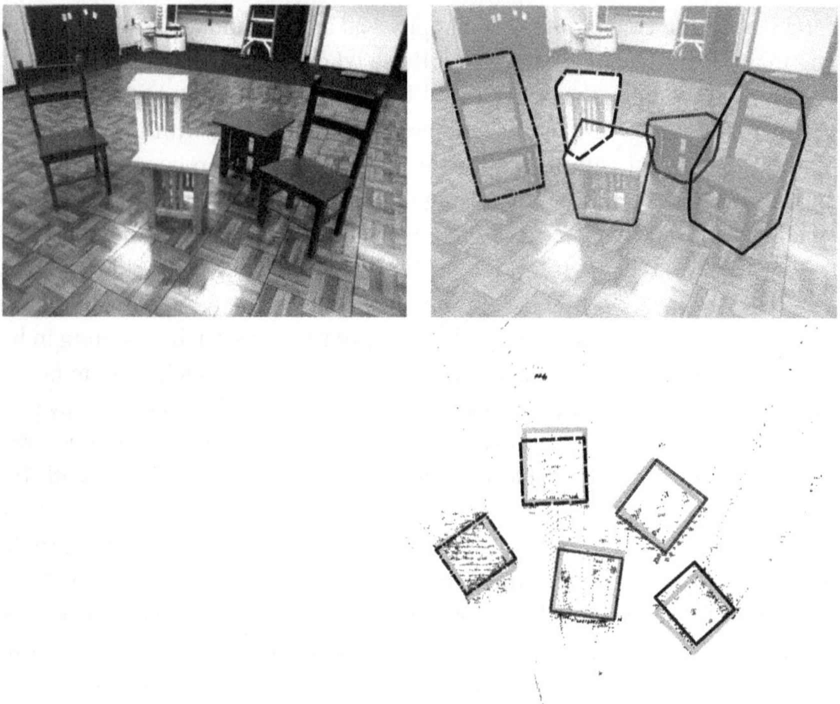

FIGURE 6.4. Top-left: five pieces of furniture in the center of the dance floor. Bottom-right: a top view of the 3D scene. This top view is the solution of the 3D FGO problem. Gray rectangles represent the true positions, sizes, and orientations of the objects. Black rectangles represent the recovery made by our machine. Dots are the projections of the 3D points. The solution of the 2D FGO problem is shown on the top-right.

project the 3D points representing visible surfaces of the objects onto the floor. The result of doing this is shown in Figure 6.4, where a simple 3D scene, along with a top view of it, is shown. The next step is to identify clusters of dots in this 2D map of the floor. Ideally, each cluster will represent only a single object. Identifying and separating individual objects, what is being done here, is usually called "figure-ground organization," but a better name would be "figure-figure organization" because the ground was removed earlier. Note that separating one object from another in the top view representation, shown Figure 6.4, is considerably easier than it is in the original perspective (side) view. As mentioned earlier, perspective (side) images usually contain a substantial degree of occlusion because objects closer to the camera often partially occlude objects that are farther away. Occlusions are not present in the top view representation. This is what makes this kind of representation so remarkable. This advantage comes about simply because the machine's camera and the human eye is higher than the objects in this scene, so at least one surface of each object is likely to be visible in the perspective (side) image. This surface allows the object to be included in the top view representation.

How the positions, sizes, and orientations of individual objects were estimated is also shown in Figure 6.4. This was done by fitting black rectangles to individual clusters of dots. Rectangles are the perfect choice for representing our furniture because all of our pieces actually were rectangular, but a rectangular representation is a good choice for any mirror-symmetrical object for three related reasons. First, pairs of mirror-symmetrical points form line-segments that are orthogonal (at 90°) to the symmetry plane. So, even with biological objects like the bodies of animals, which do not have sharp rectangular corners, rectangularity is present, implicitly, in the relationship between the symmetry line-segments and the symmetry-plane. Second, once a rectangle is fitted to the top view, one of the rectangle's sides has the direction of the symmetry-*plane* and the other side has the direction of the symmetry-*lines*. Finally, if a mirror-symmetrical object is elongated in one direction (if its aspect ratio is other than one), the elongation is either along the symmetry-plane or orthogonal (at 90°) to it. No other direction is possible. Fitting a rectangle is based on estimating 5 parameters—the position (x and y coordinates of its center), the orientation, and the lengths of its sides. We provided our machine with some information about the approximate size of the objects in front of it. This was done to improve the reliability of its ability to identify the individual clusters representing individual objects. Without such information, objects that are close to one another might be interpreted as a single object, or a single object might be interpreted as two separate objects. Such errors can be corrected at a later stage in the recovery of the 3D shape. Note that unless objects are carefully positioned, two or more symmetrical objects are unlikely to form a symmetrical configuration. It is not easy to put 4 chairs around a table in a perfectly symmetrical configuration to say nothing of the pains required to prepare proper settings on a banquet table set for a Queen. Individual objects almost always have more symmetries than configurations of multiple objects. This fact often provides a very good criterion for identifying individual objects even when we do not have any information about their sizes. Put succinctly, symmetries within objects are more likely than symmetries among them. The gray rectangles drawn in Figure 6.4 represent the *ground truth*, the "exact" positions of the four corners of each object present in this particular 3D scene. Before we go on to explain how the ground truth is established in our laboratory, we would like to point out that what started with the relatively modest single goal of solving the FGO problem, actually succeeded in accomplishing a second, more ambitious goal. We figured out how 3D scenes can be recovered. This goal is usually considered to be the final step in visual processing. In effect, we killed two birds with one stone. Our computational model shows that the perception of 3D space is to a large extent independent from the perception of the 3D shapes located within it. This will not be news in the vision literature because it has been accepted for 30 years that the *where* and *what* systems use different parts of the brain

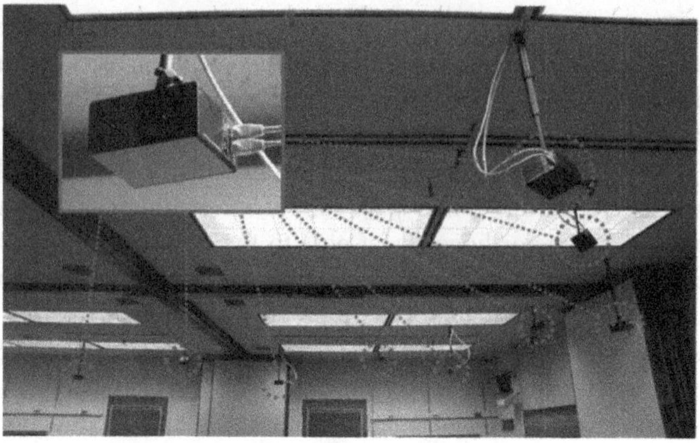

FIGURE 6.5. The locations of the cameras of the Phasespace System.

(Mishkin et al., 1983). Our computational models show these different systems cooperating actively.

Coming back to ground truth after a segue to the brain, how was it established? Our robot, Čapek, resides and can move about within a 7 meter by 8 meter (23 foot by 26 foot) room. An optical measuring system (Phasespace System) was used to calibrate a region 5 meters long by 5 meters wide by 1 meter high within this room. This system uses 16 pairs of one-dimensional digital cameras, each camera providing information with 10-bit precision (1 part in 1024). These cameras are mounted on rods at two different levels on the ceiling (see Figure 6.5). The central portion of the room, which serves as the 3D calibrated working space, is calibrated by locating the positions of LEDs, identified by their flicker rates, which have been placed in a large number of positions within the room. The locations of these LEDs were measured by triangulation (technically and more precisely, by estimating the intersection of 32 planes). The 3D positions obtained this way are relatively accurate, specifically, the position *accuracy* is better than 2 centimeters along all three directions (about 3/4 inches) and the *precision* (reliability) of these measurements is 2 millimeters. The update frequency rate of the system is 30 Hz, a bandwidth sufficiently high to cope with the range of all natural movements made by our human subjects and by our robot. Čapek and our human subjects can work within a well-understood and well-calibrated space. This calibrated space has been used to find out how well human beings can locate objects and pathways within it, as well as for Čapek to "see" scenes and navigate among objects. By making similar measurements within the calibrated region, we were able to determine how well Čapek could emulate a human being's performance when asked to view similar 3D scenes and to navigate within them.

At this point it seems both timely and worthwhile to call attention to the fact that there are some unforeseen aspects to what has been accomplished so far. It is not all weights and measures. Having and using a top view opens up new ways for explaining human 3D vision and for making a machine to emulate it. The top view is special because it allows the use of a new *a priori* constraint. We found that despite the fact that we can only see the front surfaces of objects in a 3D scene directly, a top view has information about where the backs of objects are located even when their backs are hidden when the scene is seen from the front. The fact that this is possible is not news. In Section 2.3, we explained how the back, invisible parts of a 3D shape can be recovered by the application of *a priori* symmetry, compactness, and planarity constraints. Here, we have been able to produce a very similar result by applying only two *a priori* constraints: symmetry, which we knew already, and ground surface, which was new. Furthermore, the top view contains important additional information about the invisible *spaces behind* the objects, namely, the sizes and locations of the *pathways* among them. This means that once the top view of the 3D scene has been made, the observer (machine or human) has a spatially-global map of the 3D scene produced from a single vantage point. No running around the room is required to determine where things are or how to navigate among them. Furthermore, our spatially-global map can be produced within fractions of a second with MatLab software. Such almost instantaneous, essentially biologically-real time, recovery of 3D visual scenes is essential for successful interactions within dynamical environments like ours. Our approach to this problem is completely different from the current state-of-the-art in robotics. Currently, in robotics, methods such as SLAM (Simultaneous Localization and Mapping) are used to navigate within 3D scenes containing objects. SLAM uses laser sensors to measure distances between the current position of the robot and the visible surfaces of the nearest objects in the 3D scene. These laser sensors cannot see objects behind objects that are nearby because the lasers are mounted just above the floor, probably for safety reasons. If the sensors were mounted at the eye level of a human observer, the robot could see farther, but the "laser's gaze" would pose a danger if it fell into a human's eye. This is yet another reason why robots with laser sensors are not likely to have a bright future in our daily life. This instrumentation is not only potentially dangerous, it has other quite serious limitations. Most of us would find it very hard to perform a task requiring coordination with a robotic agent when its eyes are near the floor and yours are a meter or more above. Getting down and crawling about might help coordinate our efforts, but this would surely not be ideal either. Furthermore, robots using SLAM, or something like it, can only form a spatially-local map of its immediate neighborhood because their laser sensors only see nearby objects. To map any but the simplest 3D scene, a SLAM-fitted robot must move around the scene for several minutes before it can "know" what is present in the scene and where it is relative to other objects. It must "look" behind all of the objects present to find out what, if anything, is there and can only then measure pathways among them. The situation is even worse if any objects can move. By the time a SLAM-fitted robot has looked behind the nth object, the 1st may be in a new position, and the robot may be "dead" if it is performing in the kind of simulated shooting game that has been popular since computer-based games came into use. It is important to note that a dynamical environment is not a problem with our approach because a spatially-global map of a 3D scene is produced instantaneously from a single vantage point and it is updated several times each second, so if any object moves, this will be detected and the spatial map will be updated right away.

Now, recall from Section 1.6 how much fuss was made in prior studies about the huge distortions of binocular visual space that human subjects have shown in laboratory experiments on space perception. Common sense tells us, and we are convinced tells you, too, that this cannot be what is going on in our everyday life. We all see things as they are out there. When we start navigations within rooms containing many objects, such as chairs, a table, a fireplace in one wall, and a fish tank near another, we are never surprised by visual errors of any kind. The room does not seem to change its size or shape. The chairs always have vertical legs and a horizontal seat, so we never have to wonder whether it is safe to sit upon them. The surface of the table always looks horizontal when it is, so we never fear that it cannot support our cup of coffee, and the fish stay out of the fireplace no matter where we look, nor how often we look around. Seeing the 3D environment veridically is the necessary, as well as the sufficient, condition for the successful cooperation and interaction of human beings with each other and with their environment now, as well as back in the day when they were hunting and looking for food on the African plains. Imagine how long it would take to build one's house if what had been constructed so far looked completely different to each and every member of the construction crew. There is obviously something wrong with the existing literature on the human being's binocular perception of the 3D space that surrounds them.

This obvious problem encouraged us to repeat Foley's triangle construction task (Kwon, 2012), the research we described and criticized in Section 1.6. We needed a realistic estimate of the extent to which veridicality actually fails, assuming that it does, in a more natural environment and with more appropriate stimuli than Foley used. Our calibrated experimental chamber provided an almost ideal environment for examining the human being's perception of binocular visual space. Our subject viewed three pieces of furniture (real objects, not lights in darkness) that were placed directly in front of him. He then instructed the experimenter to move them around until they formed what looked to the subject as a right isosceles triangle (a triangle with a 90° angle and two equal sides). An LED, mounted on each object, was used to locate its position exactly, and the subject was instructed to use the LEDs on these three objects as the vertices of the triangle. The positions of the LEDs were measured by the Phasespace System described earlier. The subject viewed the room with both eyes, and his head was supported on a chin rest to minimize head movements. The room, which was illuminated at normal indoor levels had clearly visible walls, ceiling, and floor. Three subjects were tested in this relatively natural environment. One was naïve with respect to the purpose of the experiment. They all arranged their triangles to be very close to right isosceles triangles. The average ratio of the lengths of the two sides of the triangle (width/depth) for the individual subjects was 0.83 (naïve subject), 0.87, and 0.91. These results indicate a systematic but quite small compression of depth, much less than the errors reported by Foley and others who had been studying binocular space under less natural conditions. When we repeated the experiment with the subject's head free to move, the errors were even smaller: the aspect ratios ranged between 0.89 and 0.99. The standard deviation of these judgments was also modest, between 4% and 6%. This level of variability can be ascribed to the variability in judging the direction of gravity or the orientation of the horizontal floor. The average angle at the vertex of our subjects' triangles was 92° (naïve subject), 90°, and 87°, all 3 values are very close to the right angle's 90°. So, we can conclude that the nearly veridical binocular perception of 3D space demonstrated by Čapek, when he located the furniture so well in Figure 6.4, was not superhuman. Both Čapek and our human subjects perceive 3D spatial relationships quite accurately at least when appropriate conditions are used and careful measurements are made.

The results were equally accurate when the triangle experiment was repeated with monocular, rather than binocular, viewing of a natural indoor scene (Kwon, 2012). This will surprise many because it had been *well established* by Luneburg, Foley, and Koenderink that binocular space is systematically distorted (see Section 1.6). So, how on Earth can monocular visual space be accurate when the most effective depth cue, binocular disparity, is not available? The answer here is the same as the answer we have provided up to now in this book, namely, that veridical perception relies on the operation of constraints not on visual cues. The position of each object on the ground is uniquely determined by the object's 2D retinal image if the orientation of the horizontal ground is perceived accurately by a monocular observer. Technically, the 3D position of the object can be computed as an intersection of the visual ray emanating from the 2D retinal image of the object with the plane representing the ground. The orientation of the horizontal ground-plane can, in turn, be estimated from the direction of gravity. Recall that gravity can be sensed by the vestibular system in the inner ear, but there is another way that a monocular observer can estimate the orientation of the ground, a way that does not require using any non-visual cues. It is known that a 3D mirror-symmetrical shape can be recovered accurately from a single 2D *perspective* image (Li et al., 2012), so if a 3D shape touches the ground at 3 or more points, as all objects do, the orientation of the ground can be computed from the 3D shape that was recovered. If there is more than one 3D shape in the scene, as there almost always is, the estimation of the *common* ground can be done with precision comparable to, or even exceeding, the very best visual cues, including stereoacuity. This is why subject TK, whose stereoacuity was much poorer than the acuity of other subjects (see Section 5.5), was able to perform in the triangle experiment as well as the other subjects could. Visual space perception (both binocular and monocular), under normal viewing conditions, is veridical because of the effective operation of the symmetry constraint. The perception of space, depth, and size may actually follow, rather than precede, the perception of 3D shape. A few more steps must be completed before a 3D shape can be recovered from a single 2D image. The next step, now that we have computed its top view representation, is finding the object in the 2D image.

6.4 Finding Objects in the 2D Image

This step is fairly simple. The 3D points, representing individual objects, are *projected* to the original 2D image in the camera and objects are identified by computing 2D convex hulls of the objects in the 2D image. These convex hulls represent solutions of the FGO problem in the 2D perspective image. We were successful in finding convex hulls in the 2D image that corresponded to each of the individual objects. Figure 6.4 shows contours of five such convex hulls, one for each piece of furniture. Note that these convex hulls partially overlap. This overlap is caused by the partial occlusion of some objects by others. These convex hulls are not always perfect in the sense that parts of the region representing a given object in some cases lie outside its convex hull. These small imperfections should not be allowed to obscure the fact that our solution of the 2D FGO problem is extremely good. You can appreciate what we mean by saying "extremely good" by examining Figure 6.6 where we drew the outlines of the convex hulls that represent our solution of the FGO problems contained within the very complex scene shown in Figure 6.3. There is no algorithm out there, other than ours, whose solution of these 2D FGO problems comes even close to what you see in Figure 6.6. We went even further and tested the algorithm developed for solving both the 3D and 2D FGO problems with wide variety of natural objects, including people wandering around a room with our software tracking their convex hulls as they moved about. When we started doing this, 2D FGO problem could be solved 5 to 10 times each second with software written in MatLab. These developments were demonstrated first at the Visual Science Society meeting in 2011, where they caused a lot of excitement. Several people stood in front of Čapek as it "watched" them standing still, or walking in front of it, or hiding behind furniture, or even hiding behind each other as both hid behind a piece of furniture. The participants, as well as dozens of spectators became quite festive, even boisterous, when they

FIGURE 6.6. Regions in a 2D image representing individual objects shown in Figure 6.3.

began to understand what was going on and what this demo meant. Čapek seemed to "see" what was going on as well as they did.

Now that you are familiar with the convex hulls that contain the objects, it is the time to switch to the analysis of contours within the 2D image. You will not be surprised to hear that the way the contours in the 2D image are detected and how these 2D contours are organized after detecting them is based on 3D *a priori* constraints. There is no other way this could be done. The 2D characteristics measured on the human retina or in a robot's camera's image are unlikely to represent *permanent* characteristics of 3D objects and 3D scenes, so applying 2D operations and 2D *a priori* constraints to 2D images is not likely to work very well. This is not to say that we will never use 2D operations. The important thing to understand here is that 3D operations and 3D constraints will often take the precedence over 2D operations and 2D constraints. Figure 6.7 provides an example to make this clear. In Figure 6.7, any conventional contour grouping algorithm is likely to merge the two edges near each other in the middle into one longer edge (the Gestalt Psychologists would have

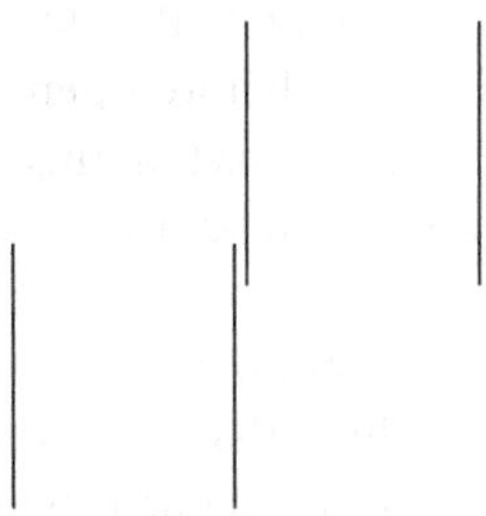

FIGURE 6.7. Can you see these four "sticks" form a 3D box?

expected just this because of the grouping principles they called "proximity" and "good continuation"). But, this kind of grouping could be inappropriate. You are as likely to see 4 equally-long sticks forming a 3D symmetrical configuration, an elongated box. If you do see this 3D configuration, one could say that your visual system used 3D symmetry to override the 2D contour grouping operations.

6.5 Extracting Relevant Edges, Grouping Them, and Establishing Symmetry Correspondence

Which 3D *a priori* constraints can be applied to the detection and analysis of contours in a 2D perspective image and what are they like? Look at Figure 6.8. The photo in (a) is a perspective image of several pieces of furniture. All these pieces have vertical legs or surfaces that define vertical edges. Perspective images of these edges are not vertical in this image. This is illustrated below the photo where they can be seen to intersect at a vanishing-point. The vanishing-point is shown below the photo to keep this figure simple. It allowed the furniture to be shown right side up. In a camera, as well as in the eye, the image would be upside down. This vanishing point is called the "*vertical vanishing point*" to distinguish it from other vanishing points. It may surprise you to discover that the position of this vanishing point can be determined without acquiring the 2D image and without analyzing any images of vertical edges in this 3D scene. How this can be done is explained in Figures 6.8b and c. The line drawing in (b) is the side view of how the image is acquired, and the picture in (c) illustrates all aspects of what is shown in (a) and (b) together.

Making this work requires that you start by assuming that a robot or a human observer can determine the direction of gravity relative to the camera or to the eye by using a mechanical sensor called an inclinometer attached to a robot or the biological sensor called the utricle located in the vestibular system within the human's inner ear. Then, imagine drawing a line from the center of the perspective projection of the camera or from the nodal point (optical center) of the eye that is parallel to the direction of gravity. This line will intersect the image-plane of the camera, or the human retina, at the vertical vanishing-point shown in Figure 6.8. It follows that the visual system can compute this vanishing point even before opening your eyes or before you turn your robot's camera on. This means that this vanishing point will provide valuable *a priori* information that can be used as a constraint when you need to find 2D images of line segments that are vertical in the environment. This vanishing point can serve as a constraint because the 2D images of any vertical lines out there will *always* lie on lines that emanate from the vertical vanishing point. No matter where in the room you put a chair and how you orient it relative to the camera, the 2D images of its vertical legs will project to lines that go

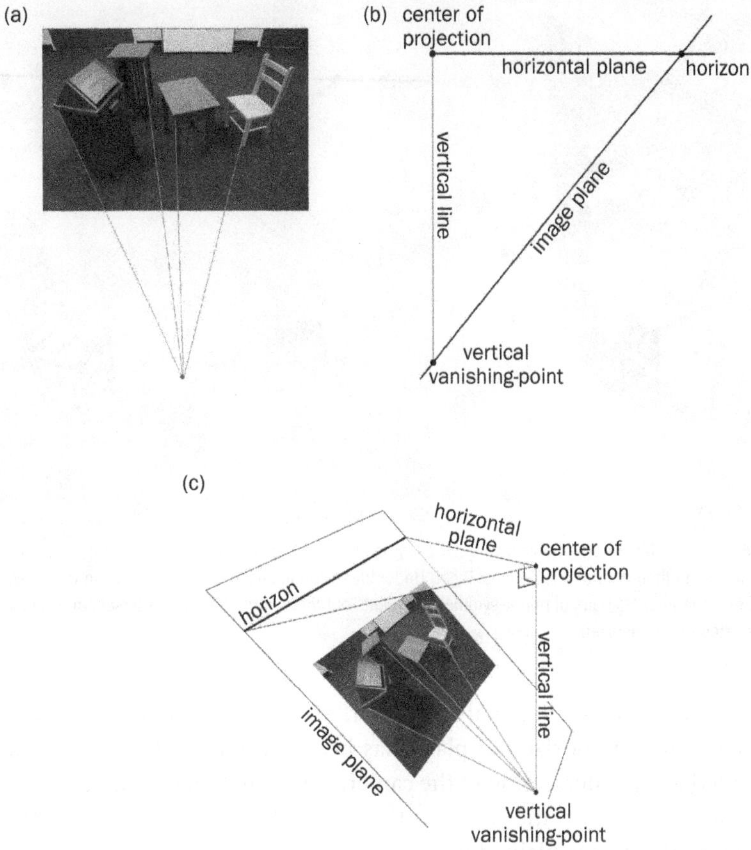

FIGURE 6.8. (a) The extrapolation of edges in a 2D camera image that represent the vertical edges in a 3D scene. They intersect at the vanishing point shown below the photo. Technically, this is called the "vertical vanishing point." (b) Illustrates how the horizon and the vertical vanishing point can be found in the 2D image. (c) If the camera were transparent, you could have seen the camera image. The horizon and the vertical vanishing point are shown. (From Li et al., 2012).

through the vertical vanishing point. In technical language, the vertical vanishing point is an invariant of the perspective transformation of natural objects in a natural environment. Also, if nonvisual information about the direction of gravity is not available or if it is unreliable, the observer will have to estimate the location (or position) of the surface of the ground, visually, and if this surface is horizontal, the direction of gravity required to compute the vertical vanishing point will be orthogonal (at 90°) to this surface.

But there is even more to this story. Information about the horizontal surface of the ground allows the observer to compute the *horizon*. The horizon is at least as important as the vertical vanishing point. Keep in mind that the orientation of the horizontal ground-plane can be obtained in two ways, either by sensing gravity directly with sensors that do not use visual information and

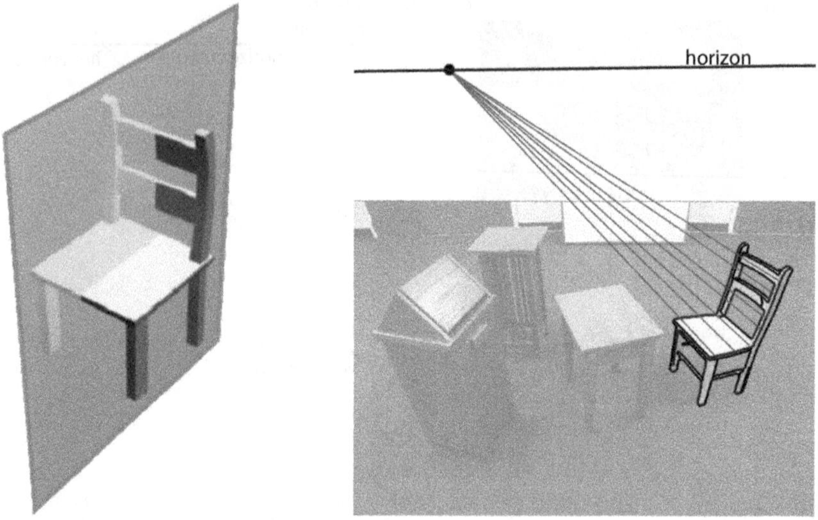

FIGURE 6.9. Left: Most natural objects are mirror-symmetrical and their symmetry plane is usually vertical when they are in their natural orientations. Right: Under these conditions, pairs of 2D points in the perspective image, which represents pairs of mirror-symmetrical points out there, form lines that intersect at a vanishing point located on the horizon.

then use the plane orthogonal (90°) to it, or by estimating the ground-plane visually. Once the horizontal plane has been estimated, the horizon can be computed as the intersection of the camera, or retinal image, and the horizontal plane that contains the center of the perspective projection of the camera, or the eye (this was explained in Figure 6.8).

The horizon is very important for the 3D recovery of mirror-symmetrical shapes. Recall from what you learned in Section 3.1 that pairs of mirror-symmetrical points of a 3D object form parallel line-segments called symmetry line segments. When a mirror-symmetrical object is in its natural orientation in our natural environment, its plane of symmetry is orthogonal (90°) to the horizontal ground and its symmetry line segments are horizontal. It follows that these lines project to lines in the 2D perspective image that intersect at a vanishing point on the horizon (see Figure 6.9). This vanishing point is essential for determining 3D symmetry correspondence in the 2D perspective image. But how can this vanishing point be found before correspondence is established? Our top view representation can provide this important information. Recall from Figure 6.4 that the projection of an object's points on the horizontal plane is approximated by a rectangle. One side of this rectangle represents the orientation of the symmetry plane of this object and the other side represents the direction of symmetry line segments. This information is sufficient to estimate the vanishing point that represents the symmetry of this object. As you already know, the 3D symmetry constraint in our model is applied to contours, not to surfaces. So, the vanishing point, which is based on information provided by surfaces, is used to recover 3D contours. It is at this stage that *the transition from the analysis of surfaces to the analysis of contours is done.* Could the model continue using surfaces and apply a 3D symmetry constraint to them rather than make this transition? Theoretically, it could, but practically, this will not work well because it is more difficult to solve the symmetry correspondence problem for surfaces. Symmetry cannot be applied to surfaces because 3D mirror symmetry is a spatially global characteristic, and when identical surface features are far away they are unlikely to be identical in the 2D perspective image. They are unlikely to be identical in the 2D image because of differences of illumination and because of perspective distortions. In fact, the problem is even more general and even more difficult. It is more difficult because the symmetry of a 3D shape does not imply symmetry of the texture on the surfaces of the 3D object. Imagine a painted human face, the kind of decoration sports fans sometimes apply. If you paint the American flag on your face, the 3D surface of your face, now *represented* by the colors of flag, is no longer symmetrical, despite the fact that your face's actual shape obviously remains symmetrical. Symmetry correspondence is not like binocular correspondence, which does not suffer when a face is painted with the flag because solving the binocular correspondence problem is based on finding points in the two retinas, or in a robot's camera, that are projections of the *same* physical point. Symmetry correspondence is different. It is based on *two different* physical points, and if you paint them differently, it will be hard to verify that one corresponds to the other. So *solving symmetry correspondence must be based on different characteristics than solving binocular correspondence.* Binocular correspondence works well with surface texture, which makes it useful for breaking camouflage and for solving the figure-ground organization problem. Symmetry correspondence works well with contours, which makes it useful for recovering 3D shapes. *If you are interested in both 3D shape and in 3D symmetry, you must work with contours, which are abstractions of the 3D geometry of the object, not with surface texture, which is merely a physical characteristic of the object.*

Now look at Figure 6.10, which shows several examples of how contours have been extracted from real camera images and how their symmetry correspondence was established. This was done by applying the method described in this section and with the method described in Section 4.4, where you saw an example of symmetry correspondence in Figure 4.8. We promised in Chapter 4 that you would be given more examples after we had explained how 3D and 2D FGO is established. Here they are. Figure 6.10 shows, side by side, the original gray-scale camera image (800 x 600 pixels) of an object and the contours that were extracted from this image. The edges, for which symmetry correspondence was established, are labeled.

Several important observations can be made. The chair shown on top has only one plane of symmetry. The other three objects in Figure 6.10 have two planes of symmetry and our algorithm detected both. In Figure 6.10, we show only the symmetry correspondence for one of the two planes of symmetry. Symmetry correspondence could not always be established perfectly. Symmetry could not be established for the edges shown in gray in these images. In other cases, symmetry correspondence could only be established for parts of edges. This symmetry, despite being only partial, was sufficient to recover the overall 3D structure of these objects. This is illustrated by four examples shown in DEMO 6.2.[9] The red cube in the demos represents the position and orientation of the camera. The green dot is the projection of the center of the cube onto the floor. The floor is represented by a regular grid, whose size is 20 x 20 centimeters.

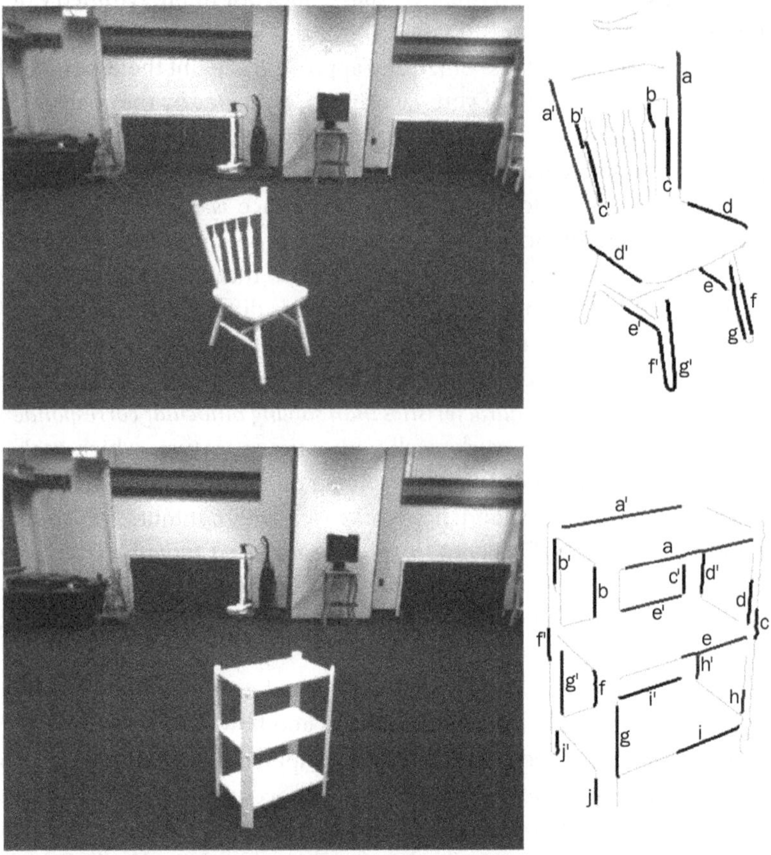

FIGURE 6.10. Original gray-scale camera images (800 x 600 pixels) shown side by side with the contours that were extracted from this image. The edges for which symmetry correspondence was established are shown in black and labeled. Edges where symmetry correspondence could not be established are shown in light gray.

[9] http://shapebook.psych.purdue.edu/6.2

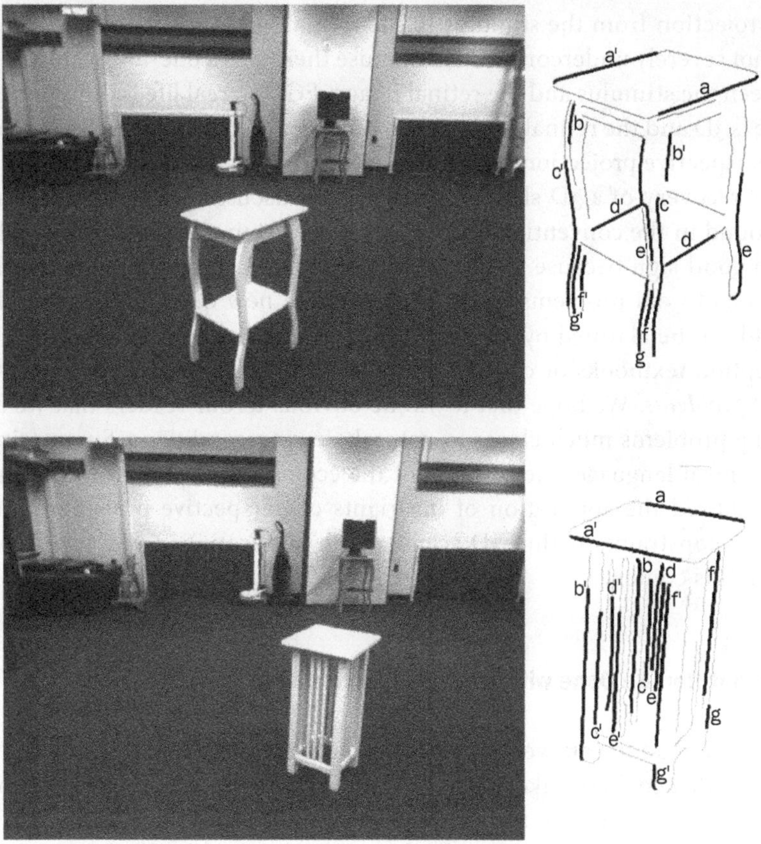

FIGURE 6.10. Continued

This grid was included to convey information about the sizes and distances that were recovered. Note that children's furniture was used in all of this work and its size, along horizontal directions, was 1 foot by 1 foot. When symmetry correspondence was actually established, the 3D recovery of the contours was perfect. One can go back to the 2D image and establish the symmetry correspondence of the remaining edges once a partial correspondence and 3D recovery has been accomplished.

To summarize, one of the most surprising aspects of our work on FGO was the importance of geometrical invariants and *a priori* constraints. We knew that constraints were likely to be important in 3D shape perception and we thought that the only question facing us was the nature of the constraints that would be needed. FGO seemed to be different, at least when viewed with respect to all prior conventional research. In all prior conventional research on FGO, the stimuli were 2D and the retinal image was a 2D copy of the stimulus. This meant that despite potential perceptual ambiguities, the projection from the stimulus to the retinal image was trivial and FGO was not severely underconstrained because there was a one-to-one mapping between the stimulus and the retinal image. FGO in real life is different: the scene is 3D and the retinal image is 2D. This meant that the 2D retinal image is a perspective projection of the 3D scene and FGO is as underconstrained as the recovery of a 3D shape. The problems discussed in this chapter are not found in the conventional FGO literature. From our point of view, this was a good sign because it meant that we would not only be able to offer solutions to old problems, we could also raise new questions. The reader should not be alarmed by how different this chapter is when compared to perception textbooks or contemporary journal articles. *We are solving different problems.* We hope that it will be obvious to our readers that we are solving problems much closer to natural viewing conditions. Summarized in technical language, the solution of the ecologically valid problems chosen required the application of invariants of perspective projections and *a priori* constraints within 3D scenes. Both applications were quite novel within this context.

6.6 What Can Be Done with a Spatially-global Map of a 3D Scene?

One of us[10] had the answer to this question long before work started on the machine that could see like us. He had been working on solving spatial problems in visual navigation for almost 20 years, so he knew much more about navigation than he knew about 3D shape recovery and FGO when work on this book began. This section provides another example of the benefits inherent in studying later mental processes to help one decide how earlier mental processes should be studied. When work started on FGO, we had already solved two problems for which FGO provides the input, namely, recovering the 3D shape of objects from 2D images and path planning. So far, you have only heard about 3D shape recovery. The time has come to tell you about path planning, including what it is like and how it is done. Whenever human beings are not meandering around their environment immersed in thought, they are making movements designed to get them to some kind of goal (recall our treatment of Tolman's approach to behavior in Section 1.4). Navigating in a real environment requires finding paths and tours needed to achieve one's goals. The simplest task is called the *shortest path problem* (SPP). If you are in a classroom, when the bell rings it tells you that it is time to go, and if you decide to leave, you will probably look for an exit sign or an appropriate door, and then proceed towards it, using a path that avoids

[10]Pizlo.

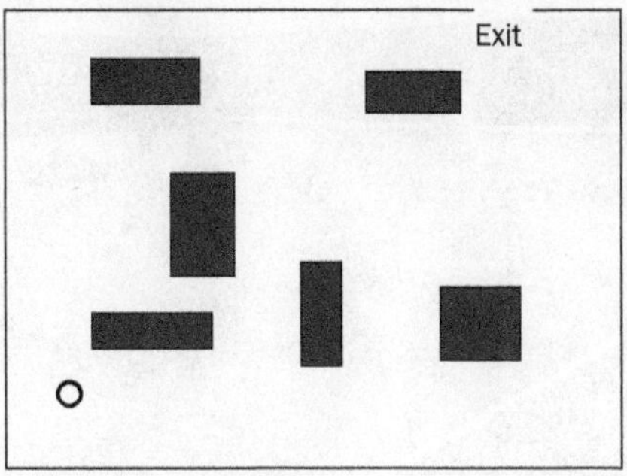

FIGURE 6.11. Plan the shortest (or best) path to the "exit," starting at the unfilled circle.

obstacles, such as chairs and any people in the path you chose. We know that human beings can choose such paths nearly optimally (Saalweachter & Pizlo, 2008). They can do it almost as well as it can be done. Is planning such paths difficult? It seems to be quite simple because it needs little special prior training and everyone tested so far has done it well. Look at the top view of the scene in Figure 6.11. Imagine that you (the unfilled circle) are standing on bottom left, planning to exit this room. The rectangles represent boxes. Having a top view makes path-planning easy. It is easy to see that two paths are shorter than the other paths.

Planning a *path* by using a map of the 3D scene, particularly when represented in a top view, is not particularly difficult from a computational point of view. Very efficient algorithms for finding such paths are available, and we already know that the human visual system makes use of one of them (Saalweachter & Pizlo, 2008). What do we know about planning *tours*, navigations that are more complex than finding shortest paths? More is known than you might suspect because methods for analyzing complex navigations have been available for quite a while. To illustrate, suppose you want to plan a vacation starting from home, or from some other place, and then return to it. This kind of tour is called the *traveling salesman problem* (TSP). A similar problem arises when you want to collect exams in a room with 30 chairs and 10 students scattered among them. You want to walk efficiently around the room to collect their exams as expeditiously as possible. Another example taken from everyday life is shown in Figure 6.12. Here, one of us is collecting 200 tennis balls that are scattered haphazardly all over a tennis court after 15 minutes of returning balls thrown at him by a ball-machine. He does this about once each week. He can rent a ball-machine for throwing balls in his direction, but he cannot rent a machine for collecting them efficiently because collecting them is computationally difficult. Throwing balls at him with variations of speed and of direction is not. For readers who prefer to do their scientific thinking in their offices rather than at the gym, this task is called a *200-City TSP*. In this tour, each ball represents a city that the salesman must visit once if he wants

FIGURE 6.12. One of us collecting tennis balls; see the text for an explanation.

to sell all of his wares. Success is measured by the length of the tour used to pick all of the balls up, or by the time it took to do it, or both. It was during one such weekly exercise that the idea of making a machine that sees like us was born. It came to mind because if you want to produce a short tour to pick up all the balls, the agent collecting them must be able to recover the spatial relationships among all of the tennis balls with virtually perfect veridicality. Technically, the ratios of distances among the balls must be recovered accurately. Any distortion of perceived depth would prevent any algorithm from producing an optimal tour. It was obvious right from the start that all theories and results suggesting that there were large distortions of the perception of visual space simply cannot be correct. Any person who can collect these tennis balls, almost optimally, must have a veridical representation of the top view of the tennis court, or something very similar to it. When we required human subjects to perform such tasks, they could perform them very well, and when you have finished this chapter, you will know that our machine can do it as well as our subjects.

Despite the superficial similarity between the SPP and the TSP, the salesman problem is much more difficult computationally. There are no efficient algorithms that guarantee finding an optimal tour. TSP is called *intractable* because finding the optimal (shortest) tour may require trying *all* possible tours. The complexity of this problem is even higher than the complexity of the partition problem discussed in Section 3.1, where we considered the question of training the visual system to detect patterns and objects from a large number of unorganized retinal receptors (recall Lotze's *local signs*). Using comparisons like those used in Chapter 3, the number of tours in a 60 city problem is equal to the number of atoms in the Universe and the number of tours in a 15 city problem is larger than the number of neurons in your brain.

Why are these combinatorial optimization problems so common? We seem to find them wherever we go in our studies in visual perception. They really are ubiquitous but *only* when vision is studied with real images of real scenes. This fact is not as widely-appreciated as it should be. All of our work suggests that visual perception is computationally very difficult (technically intractable), and most, perhaps even almost all, vision problems that deal with natural scenes require using very powerful optimization methods.

The human visual system solves the path- and tour-planning problems using its multiscale/multiresolution architecture, the pyramidal architecture explained in Section 3.1. We know that effective and fast solutions of spatially global optimization problems cannot be based on spatially global search. The best (perhaps the only) way to avoid global search is to use multiscale pyramids. This architecture leads to very fast algorithms (technically, linear complexity algorithms) that produce nearly optimal solutions. Furthermore, this pyramidal architecture allows implementation of one of the most basic and most critical aspects of perception and motor behavior that was called the "speed-accuracy tradeoff" earlier. It is one thing to be able to solve a problem, but it is quite another, actually a completely different ball-game, to be able to produce a whole family of solutions that are fast but less accurate, as well as more accurate if more time is allowed. It is at least interesting, perhaps almost shocking, that both the robotic and computer vision communities are largely unaware of the speed-accuracy tradeoff phenomenon, a phenomenon in print since Fitts published his law in 1954. As pointed out earlier, the speed-accuracy tradeoff reflects the operation of a scale/resolution symmetry in vision. It is essential to realize that the poor accuracy observed when response time is short, and the long response times observed when accuracy is high, do not represent *limitations* of biological systems that need not be replicated in machines. This trade-off is a virtue not a vice, and it should be incorporated in machines because it works so well in us.

DEMO 6.3[11] shows an example of how a 50-city TSP problem is solved by our pyramidal model. We tested our subjects with problems in which there were "only" 6 to 50 cities. Other investigators have used as many as 120 cities. Unless very special incentives are provided, solving the larger problems can be exceedingly boring. This may be why no one to our knowledge has tested subjects with problems much larger than 100 cities. The 50-city tours we used were hard enough to provide a demanding test for any human being, as well as for our model. The model not only captures the scale/resolution symmetry of visual operations, it also emulates the non-uniform distribution of receptors on the surface the retina and the spatially-localized attentional mechanisms and eye movements of a human subject. The model produces its

[11] http://shapebook.psych.purdue.edu/6.3

solution in the following way: it begins by producing multiple representations of the retinal image containing the cities. The representations closer to the top of the pyramid are coarser, so at the higher levels of the pyramid it can only see clusters of cities; it cannot see individual cities by themselves. The model first finds a tour of the largest clusters. This is not difficult to do. For example, there is only one way to tour 2 or 3 clusters and this way is optimal. Once such a tour of the largest clusters has been produced, it is "projected" down onto the higher resolution representation that has more but smaller clusters. The original, coarse tour is now modified to incorporate the new smaller clusters. This is not difficult to do because a given cluster will be included in the tour on the basis of which segment of the tour is closest to it. It follows that this is simple because it can be handled by a local search. Once the tour incorporates all of the clusters present on this level, the tour is projected one step further down in the pyramidal representation where more and still smaller clusters reside. The tour gets updated again and the entire process is repeated until all cities have been incorporated into the tour. In the demo, you can see that the model elaborates the tour sequentially, that is, after an initial analysis of a coarse representation, it chooses one of the cities near the bottom, proceeds in a counterclockwise direction, and ends at the city from which it started. A human subject solves the TSP this way, too. You can either watch the movie as programmed to run in the demo or you can control it manually. Controlling it manually will allow you to see what is going on at various stages as it proceeds towards solution. When you, as well as our model, look directly at one part of the problem, say the dots at the bottom, you can see individual nearby red dots easily, but it is hard to see the individual dots that are far away from the dots you can see clearly. Recall that the model was given the same kind of visual system and attentional mechanisms a human being has, so it should not be surprising that it "sees" and "attends to" the dots in the same way you do. After an initial tour among several clusters has been produced, the model focuses its attention on the bottom part of the problem and works its way all around the region containing all of the cities in a counterclockwise direction. The part of the tour that is shown in green is based on clusters incorporating several individual cities. The other parts of the tour, which are shown in various shades of gray, incorporate a diverse variety of clusters, the brighter the color, the coarser its resolution.

It should be obvious that the process of producing a tour is recursive and that it consists of identical steps applied at different scales and at different resolutions. This is why we call these visual operations "symmetrical (self-similar) in scale and resolution." But there is even more. It is known that human working memory can store and manipulate only a few pieces (chunks) of information at a time (Neath & Surprenant, 2003). This might seem to be in conflict with the pyramidal representation our model uses. If the task is to solve a 50-city TSP, the model will have to store the information about all of the cities and about all of the clusters of all of the cities. This amounts to at least hundred chunks, not to several chunks. Can our model be modified to have very small requirements for its working memory; a working memory as small as the memory measured for human beings? The answer is yes. The self-similarity of the pyramidal representation and the clustering operations allow the model to store information about only a few clusters at a time and these clusters can be removed from model's memory when the model completes their analysis. Furthermore, the model can "look" at any part of the problem and form a cluster or break it into smaller clusters as they are needed. We tested this idea by simulating a working memory, which stores at most 5 clusters at a time. This model worked as well as the model that kept the entire pyramidal representation in its memory (Pizlo & Stefanov, 2013).

To summarize and reflect briefly on it, the fact that our pyramidal model of the visual system can handle combinatorial optimization problems as difficult as TSP is encouraging. Finding paths and tours is important in two quite different tasks, namely, when we plan visual navigation and when the visual system detects contours in images. But even more important, if it is actually true, as we think it is, that most visual processes are equivalent to solving combinatorial optimization problems and solving them quickly, the pyramidal architecture of the visual system is likely to be the most critical, until now, under-appreciated characteristic of the visual system. In technical parlance, the main strength of the pyramidal architecture and of the pyramidal operations is its ability to produce near-optimal solutions to global optimization problems without ever performing a global search. Avoiding a global search allows answers to be produced very quickly.

7

What Made This Possible and What Comes Next?

We built a machine that sees like us within less than a decade when so many others have tried for much longer and did not succeed. What did the trick? The single, most important aspect of our work that was underappreciated, perhaps even missed entirely by everyone else, is the importance of a number of predilections, inherent in human nature, that we have called "*a priori* constraints" when technical references were made to them throughout this book.[1] Our visual perceptions, in general, and *perceptual constancies,* in particular, are determined primarily by these *a priori* constraints, rather than by visual data available in the retinal images, because it is these constraints, not data in the retinal images, that represent *permanent characteristics* of our natural world. The less emphasis a seeing machine puts on sensory data, the more veridical its perceptions will be. This claim is surely anathema to many, probably most, of our colleagues, but the machine does work. Surely, this is what counts in the end.

Our work to date has achieved its initial goal—making a machine that, without any help from us, can "see" a complex 3D scene and objects within it as we do but more remains to be done. What is left? There are three human visual functions (abilities) that need to be understood sufficiently to be solved by our preferred criterion, that is, to be implemented in our machine. The first is finding an object within a natural 3D scene entirely on the basis of the information contained in a *single* 2D retinal image. This ability does not seem to be important ecologically because it only comes into play when *still* pictures of 3D objects and 3D scenes are viewed, when such objects and scenes are far away, and when the observer remains still or only moves very slightly. Emulating these human abilities in our machine will improve its performance substantially by permitting it to perform under a wider range of viewing conditions than can be set up in any laboratory. Being able to deal effectively with far away scenes is more important than improving how the machine can handle nearby objects because keeping the head almost stationary is almost impossible to

[1]Our *a priori* constraints resemble Plato's "universals" and Reid's, as well as Kant's, "intuitions."

do. Vision like this is pretty much confined to laboratory research where biting-boards and chin-rests are usually needed and used in vision research. The second visual function still to be implemented is the ability to deal with *dynamical* environments in real time. To do this, the machine must be able to predict what the scene will look like in the near future. Technically, the visual interpretation of the scene as it was several seconds ago must be integrated with the scene as it is now and with the scene as it will be some fraction of a second in the future. A seeing machine that actually emulates us must be able to predict what is likely to be out there in the future to operate effectively in real time. We humans do this quite well as anyone who plays or watches tennis surely knows.[2] Simply put, *the machine must see its predictions to act in the present.* If it does not, the *current* percept will represent the *past* because of delays introduced by the time it takes to (1) convert the light energy into bioelectrical energy in the retinal receptors, (2) transmit the bioelectrical signals along the optic nerve, and (3) compute what is needed to produce the percept. Finally, a seeing machine must be able to recognize familiar objects and scenes because it is one thing to *see* objects and scenes veridically, and quite another to recognize the person in front of me, know that the room I am currently in is my office, or see that the novel object in front of me belongs to the category called "chairs." We will begin this chapter by highlighting a few of our accomplishments, both conceptual and technical. These highlights will allow us to point out some new and important implications of what we did. This discussion will set the stage for explaining what remains to be done intuitively and with some technical rigor.

7.1 Five Important Conceptual Contributions

(1) 3D Vision is an inverse problem.

Poggio et al. (1985) deserve a lot of credit for pointing out that vision *is* an inverse problem and that regularization theory and Bayesian inference are the right tools for modeling vision. Their insight was of fundamental importance and it should have been accepted universally overnight. But it was not. Psychologists did not, and still do not, like this idea because it requires changing the way they do visual science completely. Suddenly, the retinal image is not the only thing that

---

[2] We actually know quite a bit about how well people do this thanks to the large body of seminal research done by David ("Martin") Regan (2012). He did both monocular and binocular research on this topic in the context of cricket, baseball, flying high-performance real aircraft and highway driving. The bottom line is that experts know the instant to within about 0.005 second that an approaching object will arrive to within about 10 centimeters at a future location! We provided a reference for a recent review of this work in our References.

matters and one has to start thinking about invisible and intangible *a priori* constraints (priors). Furthermore, formulating theories of vision presents some intellectual challenges that cannot be remedied easily. The scientist's working vocabulary must now include such concepts as "optimization," "ill-posedness," "probability," "Bayes," "cost function," "numerical methods," and "computer algorithms." Mastering these concepts to the point where they can actually be put to good use requires changing the curriculum and the admission prerequisites of any graduate psychology program that wants to have an up-to-date program in vision. This cannot be done overnight, even if it can be done at all. The Theory of Inverse Problems and its application in vision has not received the status it deserved by vision scientists. We began by recognizing that the inverse problems approach can be, and should be, pushed much further than it had been up to then. Our decision to go in this direction can probably be attributed to many happy hours spent reading old books and taking historically significant old ideas and old "theories" seriously, particularly, such gems as Commonsense, Nativism, and Prägnanz, as well as the Gestalt and Cognitive Revolutions. Our field, once viewed from this perspective, can be seen to have been waiting for the formalism of inverse problems for at least a century. For us, *adopting the inverse problems approach was not the first cautious step in a new direction; it was the last and bold step in a direction that was well-established before we began.*

(2) Nature of *a priori* constraints (priors).
The Gestalt psychologists are well-known for placing emphasis on the role of a simplicity principle in visual perception (see Wertheimer's, 1923 and Koffka's, 1935, treatment of the *Law of Prägnanz).* This principle made a lot of sense, but it had very little predictive power. This limitation in time contributed to a decline in the influence of the Gestalt approach in visual perception. This decline in interest held back the study of vision for decades. The first breakthrough in providing a tool that could be used to put the simplicity principle on a firm mathematical and computational basis came shortly after World War II with Shannon's (1948) formulation of Information Theory. Now that 65 years have elapsed since Shannon published, what have we learned about the simplicity principle used by our visual system by developing a machine that sees as we do? We learned that the perception of 3D objects and 3D scenes is based on *a priori* constraints that do *not* represent *concrete* objects and scenes; they represent their *abstract* characteristics, such as the symmetry of the objects, their 3D compactness, the planarity of their contours, as well as the direction of gravity with its corresponding vanishing point, and the orientation of the horizontal ground with its

corresponding vanishing line called the *horizon*. These constraints, which refer to abstract and permanent characteristics of objects and scenes, become both *objective* and *informative* when they are described with technical terminology. They are *objective* in the sense that they can be derived and proved mathematically without relying on any reference to particular examples of objects and scenes. They are *informative* in the sense that they actually apply to natural objects and scenes. This creates a surprising, but fortunate, situation because it means that there is no reason to assume that the visual system has to rely on learning to establish these constraints (priors) or to improve (update) the constraints (priors) on the basis of experience (empirically). Learning constraints (priors) through experience has always been problematical in theories of vision because it requires repeated viewing of every object. This takes time, and it is not likely to be reliable, especially with objects that are "unlikely." If the probability of seeing a given object is, say, one in a million, the observer would have needed millions of experiences with the object before the prior could have been estimated reasonably well. But, a constraint (prior), such as mirror-symmetry, is a mathematical concept that can be defined and analyzed without knowing that objects out there are mirror-symmetrical. In this sense, the symmetry constraint (prior) resembles one of Plato's universals that *exists* independently from particular objects. In fact, no real object is ever *perfectly* symmetrical, which means that mirror-symmetry could not be learned from experience with objects in the first place.

(3) Veridicality as *the* central concept in vision.

You have already heard a lot about the importance, and the controversial nature of veridicality in perception. Some of our adversarial perception experts will surely tell us that they have "shown" that human perceptions, tested with unnatural laboratory conditions, are never veridical, not even nearly so. We will deal with this complaint here simply by reminding you that when we look around in our normal environment, we can be confident that "we see things veridically," that is, we see them "as they are out there" and we are sure you do, too. We, and you, never experience illusions in everyday life. Illusions exist only in textbooks devoted to perception and in specially prepared demos shown in undergraduate classes and at scientific conferences. The claim that perception is not veridical has been the biggest blunder in visual science to date, in a science with quite a few faults. Falling for such nonsense up to now can be understood in the absence of a formal Theory of Veridical Vision, but now that we understand how veridical vision is achieved, and now that it can be emulated by our machine, we believe that it is time to accept that we actually do see things veridically and that our machine sees them the same way, too. Accepting this claim means that it will be necessary to rewrite our perception textbooks. It will also force a major shift in vision research. Illusory perceptions produced with synthetic stimuli will *never* be taught in schools again *nor* shown at scientific conferences. Only veridical perceptions with *real* images of *real* objects and *real* scenes will be studied from here on. Needless to say, but said nonetheless, this utopian view of a real science of veridical visual perception is not likely to appear in the foreseeable future. A few small steps in this direction are the best hope for now.

(4) Computational and robotic modeling is the only good way to formulate theories in vision from here on.

Vision and other mental events are much *more* complex than events in physics, chemistry, or even in biology. Once it is accepted that perceptions actually are very complicated phenomena, it seems both natural and necessary to formulate theories of complex functions by using computational modeling because both visual and cognitive functions are based on processing information. This insight, which was obvious in 1943 to Kenneth Craik, an Experimental Psychologist in Great Britain, was lost for several dozen years. Most people interested in translating what we know about the human mind into theories of the mind, now realize that the only sensible way to go about doing this is to formulate computational models or, even better, build a machine that sees and thinks like us. Turing, the British mathematician/computer scientist who laid the foundations for British Artificial Intelligence during and after WWII, proposed a test based on the performance of a system when it was required to process input conveyed in ordinary language. We are proposing for vision something similar to what is now called the *Turing test* for assessing whether a machine can communicate with human beings as well as we humans do. We have, at this time, a quite good understanding of the nature of vision, much better than our understanding of the meanings conveyed by words, so our visual test may prove to be more effective than a verbal test. Turing developed and published his work on what is called *Artificial Intelligence* (AI) at the beginning of the Cognitive Revolution, when much less was known about human cognition and communication than we know today. Much remains to be worked out in this area even now. The situation is also far from settled in vision, where half of the vision community is convinced that vision is an impossible problem and the other half hopes that it is possible, but are not prepared to tell you when, if ever, this problem will be solved. From a mathematical and computational point of view, *there may be only a single way to solve the vision problem because it is so difficult.* We know there is at least one solution because the mammalian visual system solves it, so it follows that *if you succeed in building a machine that can see very well, as well as we do, the theory underlying this machine's success may provide a foundation for a new theory of human vision.*

(5) Our new analytical definition of shape is based on an object's symmetries.
Every theorist interested in shape knew that shape refers to those geometrical characteristics of an object that do not change after a 3D rigid transformation. Once you are prepared to talk about *shape perception*, you should be willing to talk about *shape constancy, as a phenomenon.* Such talk seems to be at least required—one might even say essential. Appreciating this encouraged us to adopt our *operational* definition of shape—you can only talk about shape if your shape shows constancy, that is, the percept of the shape remains the same when the object is viewed from different directions. You should not be surprised to discover that this definition, straightforward as it is, elicited a great deal of controversy when first proposed publicly in 2008. We told you about this in Section 2.4 when we described the European Conference on Visual Perception Meeting in Utrecht in 2008. It was still an issue at the Vision Sciences Society Meeting in 2011 when we tried, in vain, to convince one of our adversaries that a chair is perceived the same way regardless of its orientation relative to him. Suffice it to say, these complaints were only given the attention we thought they deserved, and we went on to propose the new, analytical definition of shape that was explained in Section 1.3. In this new analytical definition, a mere description of the object is not equivalent to a specification of its shape. Shape, by our new definition, must be extracted by specifying the object's symmetries (the similarities within the object). We think that this definition makes a lot of sense because it can explain why shape constancy is observed with natural objects in the natural world and why it fails with unnatural objects in the laboratory.

7.2 Three of Our Technical Contributions

(1) The role of symmetries in 3D shape perception.
We discovered that 3D symmetry plays the essential role in human 3D vision. Without symmetry, vision, as we know it, would not be possible. No one has been able to show how a machine vision system could, *without using* a priori *constraints*, reconstruct 3D objects and 3D scenes from one or more 2D views. We showed that human

beings cannot do this either. When human observers are tested with stimuli completely devoid of symmetry, their performance is very poor; there are always large systematic errors and large variability across the observers, across the stimuli, and across repetitions with the same observer and the same stimuli. They simply cannot recover shapes that have no symmetry. Technically, symmetry is essential in vision for two fundamental reasons. First, there are *invariants* of 3D to 2D perspective projections of symmetrical objects. Recall that the line-segments connecting pairs of 3D mirror-symmetrical points project to parallel line-segments in a 2D orthographic image and they intersect at a vanishing point in a 2D perspective image. When the object is a 3D generalized cone, the images of planar (flat) cross sections are all related to one another by 2D affine or 2D projective transformation. There are also approximate invariants that are at least as important as the exact invariants, but note that there are no invariants when an arbitrary 3D object is used. In plain English, invariants allow you to know that you are looking at a 3D symmetrical shape despite the fact that the 2D images in your eyes are not symmetrical. Invariants are critical. Second, symmetry plays the role of an *a priori* constraint when a 3D shape is recovered from 2D images. Again, in plain English, symmetry makes up for what was lost in the projection from the 3D scene to the 2D retinal image. This is essential for producing 3D representations of both objects and scenes. Recall that all permanent characteristics of the 3D natural world are 3D. Without an explicit 3D representation, it would be difficult, if possible at all, to have any meaningful interaction with the objects, scenes, and other agents out there.

(2) A new theory of binocular 3D shape recovery based on stereoacuity. Binocular shape perception is one of these rare but clear examples where it is fairly obvious that there is only one way that a vision problem can be solved. The binocular perception of 3D symmetrical shapes is *always* veridical. This seems to be as inevitable as the proverbial death and taxes. There was nothing, to our knowledge, in the psychophysical or computational literature that could give us even a hint of how this is done. It took us a few days, perhaps, as much as a week, to come up with a possible computational explanation. Only one; a second explanation did not, and has not, come to mind since then. There was obviously no need to engage in any kind of model selection analysis to find out how we should proceed. There was only one model and only one human performance known to us that could produce anything like this perfect binocular performance. This inescapable fact came as a surprise to everyone involved. Why were we

so surprised? We were surprised because we had clearly shown that binocular vision is actually *perfect* after a century of research that had claimed repeatedly, and contrary to everyone's common sense, that our binocular vision is always *very sloppy*. Why were our results so different from all those reported before? Once again, it was simply a matter of using natural stimuli under natural conditions and letting our subjects do what came naturally. This work produced a second surprise, one that was not anticipated because of what had always happened when we had presented unexpected results publicly before. Namely, there has been not even a hint of outrage and very few complaints. No member in even one of our audiences to date, in person or in print, have raised any concern, or have offered any criticism of either our results or our conclusion, perhaps because we were able to provide a straightforward computational explanation.

(3) Recovering the back parts of objects and the invisible spaces among them.

The best way to motivate this section is to begin with the hoary anecdote about a mathematician, a physicist, and an engineer driving through the countryside in Scotland. The engineer looks at a hill and seeing a black sheep among a number of white sheep states: "there *are* black sheep in Scotland!" The physicist corrects him stating: "there is *at least one* black sheep in Scotland." The mathematician goes on to improve the inference even further stating: "there is at least one sheep in Scotland that is *black at least on one side*." David Marr (1982) can assume the role of the mathematician in this anecdote because he insisted on using a *2.5D*, rather than a 3D, representation of the world out there. He did not want to go far beyond what you can actually observe. Marr assumed that human beings only have visual access to the front, visible surfaces of 3D opaque objects. His common sense must have told him that this was not true, but he, and many since, did not take this into account in computational theories of vision. Marr even gave this "visual deficiency" a special name. He called it the *2.5D sketch* because the back surface of the 3D object was invisible. Everyone laughs at least the first time they hear this anecdote because the mathematician is obviously being silly, but somehow few dared to laugh at David Marr when he said much the same thing. One of us[3] knows this all too well. This was no joke when he criticized Marr for his unwarranted emphasis on directly available visual data at the expense of *a priori* constraints in his book on shape. A number of people complained about what they called his neglect of Marr after they

[3]Pizlo.

read the book on 3D shape despite the fact that more than 30% of the book's content was organized around Marr's influence. We will segue back to the invisible surfaces of 3D objects now that you know more about the sociology that has been associated with our work.

Our computational model (machine) recovers the back invisible parts of a 3D shape as well as it recovers the visible parts in front. You saw this in our demos and we explained how this was done both technically and intuitively. Human beings recover invisible back parts, too. They can do this because it is simple as well as possible computationally. How else could a human achieve perfect shape constancy when a 3D object is rotated in depth through 90°? Think about it: You are never surprised by what you see when you walk around a 3D object. Its backside always looks exactly as you expect it to look. Cats viewed from their fronts do not look like mice from their backs. Furthermore, there is no reason to assume that this comes about because you learned what all six sides of a cat looked like as a child. You would also be very surprised, even shocked, if the back half of a 3D object was actually not there. Recovering the entire 3D shape of an object, knowing what it looks like from all viewing directions, including sides that currently cannot be seen, is one of the most remarkable examples of prediction in vision. This phenomenon is analogous but much more important and pervasive than filling-in the blind spot; a discovery that received a lot of attention since Mariotte found a way to make it visible four centuries ago. Filling-in the blind spot gets much more attention than it deserves but filling-in invisible parts of 3D objects gets much less. Neither phenomenon is normally noticed but the second is far more important in everyday life than the first. It is ubiquitous and it calls attention to the important role that prediction plays in normal vision. But this is by no means the whole story about the role of prediction in vision. We showed you in Section 6.3 how our model sees and represents the invisible spaces behind all of the objects in a 3D scene. This is another example of visual filling-in. This capacity is essential both for our veridical perception of 3D objects and 3D scenes and also for using vision to navigate within our 3D environment. In the next section we will describe another example of visual prediction, this time in the temporal (when) rather than in the spatial (where) domain. Here, it will become clear, once again, that there is nothing unusual about the visual system filling-in missing information. We will explain how humans can also see into the future. Why not, both are simple and possible computationally.

7.3 Making Our Machine Perceive and Predict in Dynamical Environments

We begin with phenomenology again because it has proven so useful before when we decided to study shape constancy instead of shape illusions, and when we made 3D symmetry a central concept in shape perception. You are surely convinced that you see what is going on around you in real time all the time. You also are surely convinced of this whenever you interact with another person, when you talk with them, when you collaborate on moving some furniture, or when you play games like table-tennis. There is much more going on here than you might think. We will explain why we brought this up by asking you to perform a simple experiment in which you pay careful attention to what you see when you watch yourself performing two similar tasks.[4] First, look at a mirror and talk to yourself or make some gestures with your hands. When you do this, you are perceiving the movements you are making in real time. You see each one as it actually occurs. Now use Skype to talk with a friend, but do not bother looking at the video of your friend. Look at your own video image, the image that is being sent to your friend. The image on your monitor looks like the image in your mirror, *but* this video image is *not* perceived in real time. It is actually delayed appreciably. What you see on your monitor is always delayed by the processing taking place in your camera and computer. In the video on your monitor, you see yourself doing something in the past, not as it actually being done as you watch. This video image is at least a fraction of a second behind. So what? What is surprising in this comparison? Once you realize that your brain introduces delays at least as large, actually probably larger, than those introduced by your computer, you should question why you did not *notice any delay* when you used a mirror and watched yourself in action. It was delayed a lot. It takes about six hundredths of a second for the light hitting your retina to produce and deliver a neural message about your action to the visual processing areas in your brain. The brain, itself, needs at least four hundredths of second to process this input before you can see a 3D object. So, the visual delay in your brain can be as much or more than a tenth of a second. A tenth of a second is not an eternity, but it is not negligible either. A tenth of a second made the difference between being a silver medalist in the Men's 100 meter dash in the 2012 Olympic Games and winning no medal by coming in fourth. There are similar delays when all motor actions are executed, so seeing something and doing anything about it, is always delayed by well over quarter of a second. Clearly, without the ability to predict, no

---

[4]You can perform this as a *Gedankenexperiment* (German for "thought experiment") but actually doing it with a mirror and SKYPE will be more convincing.

one would be able to play table-tennis or cricket because the delay in the visuo-motor loop would be much too long (Regan, 2012). The fact that the brain predicts is not news, but currently, conventional wisdom holds that prediction only takes place in the motor part of the visuo-motor system (Nijhawan, 2008). Most experts believe that prediction *only* takes place with actions; what you do, not with what you see. The importance of prediction in visual perception has rarely been considered. So, according to conventional wisdom, when you play table-tennis, the motor system is always anticipating what is going to happen. You initiate movements of your hand sooner than you would if you used the visual signal that was present when you moved. This allows your arm to arrive where it needs to be in real time. You see the past, and you use this out-of-date visual information to guide the movements of your hand so that your hand actually acts in the present. This simply cannot be a correct description of what is going on because visual-motor prediction is not just about moving your hand sooner. Prediction is also about figuring out how the ball is going to bounce before it does. Technically, predicting the shape of the trajectory after the bounce is not as simple as making a linear or spline extrapolation. It is, however, reasonable to propose that the visual system can compute the shape of the ball's complex trajectory because we know that the visual system can compute much more complex shapes, but, in plain English, claiming that the *motor* system performs this prediction boils down to claiming that the *motor* system is the system that actually does the seeing. If you accept this claim, you will not be the first to do so. The Bishop Berkeley proposed this 304 years ago. We think this is not a good idea and hope that you will be surprised to hear that it has been taken seriously by many since Berkeley's day. His explanation of the relationship between vision and motor acts, often called the "Motor Theory of Vision" has been revived and discredited many times since Berkeley proposed it. It still rears up from time to time, but no vision scientist today, who knows about the earlier failures, should try to explain 3D shape perception on the basis of motor action, rather than on vision.

We think that the time has come to develop a model of visual prediction that works realistically outside of the laboratory. The time is now because we have a fairly good idea about how the human visual system actually works out there. Developing a model of visual prediction should not be difficult because it can begin by making the predictions needed when an observer (human or machine) plans navigations in a *stationary* environment. In this environment, the observer can easily produce a 3D model of the scene in front of him when he views it from a single stationary vantage point—most of this book has been devoted to describing how this is done. As you know, this stationary model includes the back invisible parts of 3D objects and the invisible spaces behind the objects, as well as the visible parts and spaces among them. An observer can also manipulate a complete 3D model like this mentally in a manner analogous to the kinds of mental rotations that were described by Shepard and Metzler in Section 6.3. Specifically, the observer simply imagines how a particular 3D scene would look when viewed from a different vantage point. Once the observer can do this standing still, he can also do it while he walks around in the 3D scene. He will be able to see the 3D scene in real time, not some fraction of a second in the past, simply by synchronizing his walking with his mental manipulation of the 3D model of the scene. There is nothing either counter-intuitive or computationally difficult, much less impossible, in what is being proposed. Once our machine is able to make use of such visual predictions, it should be possible to convince everyone, even the most skeptical, that we humans predict *visually*, too. Prediction is surely not confined to motor actions.

It is easy to see that visual prediction can also be applied to moving objects because the inertia of objects prevents them from changing their direction of motion very rapidly. It also keeps them from getting started too rapidly. In effect, inertia assures that the 3D trajectory of an object's motion will be smooth. We know that the visual system handles the interpolation and extrapolation of 3D surfaces by using a surface smoothness constraint so it is reasonable to assume that this system could apply a smoothness constraint to extrapolate (predict) the movement of an object. Such predictions might be relatively easy with animate objects because the locomotion of animals is known to obey the constraint imposed by the animal's symmetry. A dog usually runs forward, that is, in the direction parallel to its body's plane of symmetry. A dog never runs sideways but some crabs almost always do. Birds fly in the direction parallel to their plane of symmetry, as airplanes do. Fish and marine mammals swim the same way. Human beings usually walk and run forward, that is, in the direction of their symmetry plane. The *pas de chat* (cat's step) in classical ballet is a striking and quite graceful exception. Human beings can move sideways and backwards, but their movements are never as fast or as natural as their forward motion. If you doubt this claim, ask any ballet student or ballerina whether it is easy to perform a *pas de chat* rapidly and artfully without a lot of training, and after she says "a lot," ask her about how much work at the barre is required to keep it up to par. Unnatural motions are hard to learn and their preservation requires continual practice. Musicians know this well. So, in those rare cases in which a human's locomotion defies the constraints imposed by his body's symmetry, the movement will be slower, and once it is slower, it will be easier to predict. Now you may wonder whether we predict all movements of all objects in our natural visual environments. Probably not. You may also wonder whether we can predict movement of more than one object at a time. Perhaps. It might be possible to learn how to do this very well, but it will surely be hard to do and to maintain without a lot of practice. Remember how difficult it was to learn how to pass a vehicle on a two-lane road, when another vehicle comes your way. Then remember how much your prediction changed when you discovered that it was a large fast-moving truck. Prediction surely contributes a lot to the effectiveness of our visual perceptions of objects and events in everyday life. We are looking forward to finding out how prediction works when we implement it in our machine.

7.4 Solving the Figure-ground Organization Problem with Only a Single 2D Image

We humans have no difficulty seeing 3D objects and 3D scenes in 2D photographs, so a machine that sees like us should be able to do this, too. Why should we be interested in 2D photographs and solving FGO with only a single 2D image, once we know that human observers can never be completely stationary and we know that they almost always look at things with two eyes? It is clear that two, not one 2D image, is the limiting case at least in our natural world. The easy, but less than satisfactory answer, is that we have this visual ability so it should be modeled simply *because it is there.* A more satisfactory answer is that mechanisms, which are effective with a single 2D image, *could be very useful.* They could complement the mechanisms we discovered that require two or more images. How might such a single-image mechanism work? Recall how much fuss we made in Section 6.5 about the importance of the transition from the binocular analysis of *regions* to a monocular analysis of *contours.* If there are FGO mechanisms, which are even partially effective when only a single 2D image is available, they might prove to be invaluable in facilitating a transition just like this. If nothing else, simply enhancing the speed of visual processing would fully justify using such a mechanism. We are not the only people concerned with how FGO is achieved when there is only a single 2D image. Recently, the computer vision community has devoted considerable effort to trying to solve this problem (see Dickinson & Pizlo, 2013, for a review).

The problem seeking a solution in FGO is finding individual objects in 2D images when these images contain a lot of details. Brute force approaches based on trying many subsets of pixels will not work because of combinatorial explosion (recall our discussion of the Bell number in Section 3.1). Human beings solve this problem effortlessly so there must be some still unknown additional *a priori* constraints. Color might prove useful here because not all objects in the scene are likely to have identical color. The same is true of texture. But, using color and texture will not be easy because even if they are uniform on the surface of the 3D object, they will not be uniform in the 2D image because of (1) variations in the way the light falling on the colored surface is reflected and (2) distortions caused by the perspective projection to the camera's image. We believe that some effort should be devoted to working this out because a lot is known about how light interacts with matte and shiny surfaces and because the rules of perspective projection are fully understood. Color and texture are not the only properties that might be used for establishing FGO with a single 2D image. Camera images also contain the shadows of the objects in the scene. Shadows of these objects are likely to be useful because shadows on flat surfaces, like floors, are like the camera's images of 3D objects. When shadows are used, the floor plays the role of the camera's image and it follows that the configuration formed by an object and its shadow is analogous to the configuration called "skewed-symmetry." Once this kind of symmetry is detected in the 2D image, FGO has been solved for the object that produced the shadow. You read a lot about skewed-symmetry, the kind of symmetry found in the 2D images of natural objects in Chapters 3 and 4, so you know that this kind of symmetry is important when working with real objects in natural environments. Furthermore, if there are two or more objects with the same or with a similar 3D shape, as there are when several people appear together in a photo, solving the correspondence problem among the 2D images of these objects provides a big step towards identifying the objects, themselves, and thereby solving their FGO problem. This technique will also work when an individual 3D object has multiple parts whose shapes are identical or similar; for example, the arms and legs of animals' bodies. But, there are even more interesting possibilities for solving FGO with a single image. The *a priori* constraints provided by gravity and by the horizontality of surfaces are also very likely to help solve the FGO problem in a single 2D image. You can get an idea about how important these constraints may prove to be simply by trying to count the number of people, or by trying to establish which region represents each individual, in the right-side up and upside-down versions of the famous painting reproduced in Figure 7.1.

If the analyses of 2D symmetries, similarities, and redundancies are not going to lead to a combinatorial explosion, they must be supplemented by an efficient method for finding closed contours within the 2D regions that represent entire objects or their parts. Such a method was described in Section 4.3 where we showed how solving a Shortest Path Problem in the cortical representation of the retinal image can provide a mechanism that uses a spatially global interpolation that could establish closed contours in a retinal or camera image. We believe that the visual system, because of its pyramidal architecture, may actually use this kind of mechanism to find closed contours in many parts of the retina simultaneously and independently. It should be easy to establish each contour computationally because this can be done with spatially local computations. Only some of these contours will "match" the symmetries represented by color and texture. These regions are likely to correspond to the "figures" associated with the 3D objects.

FIGURE 7.1. Jacopo Bassano: Last Supper 1542.

7.5 Recognizing Individual Objects by Using a Fast Search of Memory

Most of us operate most of the time in familiar environments that contain many familiar objects. This means, at least in principle, that once the 3D shape of an object is recovered, it could be compared to a shape stored in our memory, providing it was stored in way that made it accessible to on-line recognition. It is possible, also in principle, that our ability to recover familiar shapes could be speeded up, or even freed from the burden of recovering the 3D shape from one of its 2D images. Note that for this to work it must be done quickly if it is going to be used for shape recognition in real life in real time. The visual system must also be able to do this regardless of the number of shapes that must be stored. This idea, like so many discussed before, is hardly new. Human, as well as machine, memory has been characterized as *content addressable memory* (CAM) for quite a while (see Beis & Lowe, 1997; Dickinson, 1999, for some examples). CAM in this application simply means that a particular 2D image on the retina or a particular 3D recovered shape provides the address of an identical, or at least a similar 3D shape, in an observer's memory. Once this is done, the visual system does not have to perform any search of memory to be able to recognize the shape in front of the observer. This type of memory is plausible but is it realistic computationally? Theoretically, it is, but no one has made it work to date. Perhaps the best attempt so far was Biederman's (1987) Recognition-By-Components Theory mentioned in Section 1.3. It is based on the fact that all complex objects, such as animal bodies, cars, and furniture, are composed of a number of simple parts. It is also a fact that similar objects have similar parts and dissimilar objects have different parts. If the number of qualitatively different parts needed to encompass all of the objects we commonly see is small, as Biederman hoped they would be, the labels of the parts themselves could be used as the address of a complex object stored in an observer's memory. For example, if an object has four legs (LLLL), it must be an animal. If an object has four wheels (WWWW), it is probably a car. And so on. A modest, finite number of parts can be used to compose addresses for an almost an endless number of objects. Some readers have surely noticed what Biederman (1987) pointed out in his paper—that this scheme is analogous to the way only 26 letters in our alphabet can be used to form an endless number of sentences. Biederman's idea was great, but nobody to date has been able to make it work for shapes.

We think that we have a better idea, an idea that might actually work. It is based on our definition of shape, which makes use of an object's symmetries. "Symmetries" might work much better than "component parts" for modeling a content-addressable memory of shapes. Substituting the abstract, intangible concept called "symmetry" for Biederman's concrete, tangible shapes called "geons" should be at least as effective as substituting our symmetry *a priori* constraint for associative learning with concrete objects proved to be when symmetry was used to recover 3D shapes. Abstract universals like shape must be handled by symmetry tools that are equally abstract examples of perfection. Shape should not be blemished by using instantiations of concrete objects that must always be imperfect. Particular, imperfect concrete parts cannot be the appropriate way to address the universal, abstract *whole* called *shape*. Some readers may realize that the odd language we just used, our "philosophizing," implies that we view our work on making the machine that sees as fitting into what Whitehead (1929) called a "footnote to Plato."[5] We like to believe it does

[5]Whitehead claimed that "*the safest general characterization of the European philosophical tradition is that it consists of a series of footnotes to Plato.*"

because believing this instills confidence. We like to think that our work flows rather directly from Plato's ideas because we, like him, assume that "not everything that is in the mind had to be in the senses, first."[6] Using this assumption has paid off for us well so far. Now we must see how well these ideas work out when applied to the role of prediction in vision, how we model memories of 3D shapes and how figure-ground organization is accomplished with a single 2D image.

[6]This is a paraphrase of the peripatetic axiom: "*nihil est in intellectu quod non prius in sensu* (Latin for: "nothing is in the intellect (mind) that was not first in the senses"), attributed to Thomas Aquinas (1225–1274), which originated with Aristotle and the empiristic school of thought that he established. Plato's views on the role of sensory experience were completely opposite to those held by his pupil, Aristotle. The study of perception since Plato's day might have fared much better had he not accepted Aristotle as his student. Clearly, considerable thought must go into accepting one's students. Common sense can be as important as intelligence.

Note Added in Proofs

SYMMETRY, THE LEAST-ACTION PRINCIPLE, AND CONSERVATION LAWS IN PSYCHOLOGY[1]

Philosophers, psychologists, biologists, and physicists have wondered about the proper status of mental events in science for centuries. Initially, it was the private nature of mental events that raised the biggest concerns. This was reasonable because traditionally, science dealt with "public" events only, that is, events that can be observed by several observers at the same time. So, although I can be sure that I see and think, I do not have direct, experimental access to anybody else's perceptions and thoughts in the same way that you and I can measure the weight of a body and its acceleration. This criterion, requiring direct observation, is no longer considered to be essential in such fields as quantum physics, astrophysics, and molecular biology, but despite this, the status of mental events in natural science is still unclear. This concern was expressed forcefully by Richard Feynman (1974), the Nobel Prize winner in physics, who insisted that "psychology" is a "pseudo science." By this he meant that psychologists merely *imitate* the behavior of scientists. They collect data, present talks at conferences, put forth hypotheses, test them and publish papers, but they are not discovering any laws of nature and they do not understand the phenomena under study. We will take exception to Feynman's claim by arguing that an emerging specialty of psychology, a specialty we call "Computational Cognitive Science" (CCS), satisfies the criteria used today in such hard sciences as physics. In fact, CCS actually goes beyond physics because it includes the elements of control systems that are needed to be able to account for purposive behavior.

Purposive behavior is arguably the most fundamental characteristic of human mental life (Tolman, 1932).[2] *All* of our voluntary actions are directed

---

[1]Reflecting on material in this book during the year that elapsed between the submission of the manuscript and publication, it became clear that the story made it both possible and useful to reconsider the relationship between vision science, psychology, and physics. A new view of this relationship is explained in this section.

[2]"Purposive vision" as studied by Y. Aloimonos of CfAR at the University of Maryland in College Park bears a superficial resemblance to terms we use, but Aloimonos uses concepts called purpose, qualitative vision and action to change the computational difficulty of vision tasks, such as obstacle avoidance. He did this to make them easier and faster. Aloimonos' approach is completely different from ours in that it is done to minimize the role of *a priori* constraints.

toward some future goal. This is what makes our actions intelligent. Without purposive behavior, there would be no schools, no books, no language, no movies, no tools, no furniture, no houses, no factories, no cars, no ships or airplanes, no stock market, no retirement plans, and not even computer games. Once we believe that humans are smarter than other animals, it seems obvious that our purposive behavior is the main factor responsible for this critical difference. Note that all currently available robots and Artificial Intelligence (AI) systems are not very smart once purposive behavior serves as the criterion for smartness. A computer can play chess very well but it cannot have a conversation with its opponent, cannot learn linear algebra by participating in a traditional college class, or use tools to repair a piece of furniture. Robots cannot do these everyday human tasks because doing them is far from trivial. A typical contemporary robot is an elegant collection of hardware that can do many things in our physical world, but it does not posses the kind of intelligence that permits it to *predict the future;* the kind of intelligence that is essential for purposive behavior.

Superficially, purposive behavior seems to defy the laws of physics despite the fact that this kind of behavior may actually appear to be trivial. Now consider how Aristotle, who discussed this issue more than 2300 years ago, explained purposive behavior. His explanation was "teleological," which means that the "present" event is caused by the "future" outcome. Using one of Aristotle's examples, a piece of rock, when dropped, falls down toward the earth *because* the earth is its natural place. Next, consider a teleological explanation of a commonplace contemporary example taken from human behavior, rather than from the behavior of falling rocks. I turn on a coffee-maker to make coffee that I will drink when it is ready 5 minutes from now. So, drinking coffee 5 minutes in the future *caused* me to turn on the coffee-maker, now. We all know that this kind of explanation is wrong. Today, contrary to Aristotle's claim, it is universally accepted that the future event cannot be a cause of the present event. But, *a model, which can anticipate, predict, or expect a future event, can be the cause of the present event.* Today, this is how both control systems and purposive behavior are understood to work (Rosenblueth et al., 1943; Miller et al., 1960). In fact, there is no other way to produce purposive behavior. A person, who has a model of the environment in his mind, can use this model to decide what to do *now* in order to accomplish something in the *future*. But note that having purposive actions in our repertoire, not only allows us to produce *some* behavior that is directed toward *some* goals, it also allows us to produce *optimal* behavior that can be used to *outsmart our competitors in the food chain.* Surely, our ability to produce such behaviors was, at least in part, responsible for our achieving our dominant position in the animal kingdom. Note well that *producing optimal behavior in order to outsmart competitors would be impossible if we could not make mental models.* Purposive action is not guaranteed to be successful all of the time because a model of the future event cannot always be perfect. For example, the coffee-maker could be broken unbeknownst to the person who is turning it on. But if the model is good, the goal is likely to be achieved, providing only that the necessary machinery is in working order. This is how we do all of the things we do all of the time.

Note that when Wiener (1948) formulated his theory of control systems, he emphasized the feedback part of the system. In simple control systems such as homeostasis (Cannon, 1932), that is, controlling the level of sugar in the blood and body temperature, or in missile guidance, feedback is by far the most important feature. For example, will feedback be optimal or will it lead to oscillation, the activity underlying some motor dysfunctions in biological systems as well as in machines? In Wiener's theory, the model of the future was assigned a trivial status, called the "set point." If the set point of human body temperature is assumed to be 36.6 C, the current body temperature will be compared to this value and the error will be fed back to the input of the system with a negative sign to make any necessary correction. With human purposive behavior, the model of the future event is much more complex than a number representing body temperature or a pair of numbers representing the direction of a missile. Here, a model of the future is likely to be a dynamical 3D scene such as when one walks around at a poster session, drives a car on a busy street, or considers the state of the national economy a year from now when a decision about a retirement portfolio must be made. So, once purposive behavior is of interest to us we will continue to talk about control systems but the emphasis will shift from the effectiveness of feedback to the veridicality of the mental model of future events.

Now, where do these models come from? For the coffee-maker, either the salesman showed us how to operate it, we used the User Instruction Manual, or we figured out how to use it by using trial and error. The models used for visual navigation within our office, house, and around streets in our neighborhood are produced by our visual system, which recovers 3D scenes by using the kind of computations described in this book. We even use models for our social relations, where we adopt one or another norm of social behavior or simply try to understand what is going on by watching and listening to members of a particular social group. In all these cases, mental models are *inferred* on the basis of the available sensory data. In applied mathematics, this inferential process is called solving an "inverse problem" and it is known that most inverse problems are "underconstrained," which means that there is always more than one model that can account for the data (Poggio et al., 1985; Knill & Richards, 1996; Pizlo, 2001, 2008). This means that the mind must combine the available sensory data with *a priori* constraints about the external world and solve an optimization problem to produce a unique accurate model. The optimization problem can be solved by using either a Regularization or a Bayesian method. Note that finding a minimum or maximum of a cost function in order to solve an inverse problem is commonly referred to as applying a minimum principle and the application of this principle closely resembles the operation of a *least-action principle* in physics (Feynman et al., 1970). Furthermore, the fact that our mental models of the physical world, as well as our mental models of other people's minds, work well means that the minimum principle that was used to produce the model results in something resembling *conservation laws* in physics with an important difference, namely, in purposive behavior it is some abstract characteristic of the physical or the social world, rather than energy and momentum, that are mapped without change into the mental model. One of the best examples for such a mental conservation law is the veridicality of 3D shape perception. By veridical shape perception we mean that we see 3D shapes as they are out there in the physical world. Natural objects are characterized by symmetries and the human visual system uses symmetry as an *a priori* constraint to recover 3D shapes from 2D images. This recovery has recently been shown to be perfect and a computational model has been developed that allows a seeing machine to recover 3D shapes as well as the human recovers them (Li et al., 2011). This fact suggests that *shape remains unchanged in the transformation from the physical world to the mental world.* Once we have a computational model of how the human visual system recovers 3D shapes, it is not an overstatement to say that the shape conservation law applies to seeing machines as well as to human beings. This development opens up the interesting possibility of establishing relationships between the minds of humans and machines, the relationship that lies at the foundation of Artificial Intelligence.

The concept called *"symmetry,"* which played a central role in this book, needs to be emphasized here because it is the third building block of modern physics. Symmetry in mathematics means invariance under a transformation. If a physics experiment produces the same result when it is performed twice in different places or twice in the same place, we say that the underlying law of physics is invariant (symmetrical) under translation in space and time. There is a one-to-one mapping between symmetries and conservation laws and the latter are derived from the former through the application of the least-action principle (Noether, 1918). Our physical world is characterized by symmetries and we, humans, are well aware of them. When we walk across a room we perceive the room as the same despite the fact that our relation to this room changes. When we walk into the same room on the next day we recognize it as the same room. We can detect translations and rotations in space as well as the passage of time, but we can also easily detect that not everything has changed.

The bodies of animals are mirror-symmetrical and we see them as mirror symmetrical. Flowers are rotationally symmetrical and we perceive them as such. Man-made objects are characterized by one or another symmetry and we perceive them as such. Many objects are actually functional because of their symmetries. We made them symmetrical to make them useful.

To summarize, the purposive actions studied in cognitive psychology satisfy the three classical criteria now used in modern physics, as well as in modern science, in general. These criteria are symmetries (invariances), conservation laws (veridical mental representations), and a least-action principle (a minimum principle) that relates the other two. Now, we will quote a representative statement made by physicists about symmetry and conservation laws in physics to bridge the divide between physics and Computational Cognitive Science:

> *"The most important handle to the laws of nature that we have, as long as the laws of nature themselves are not fully known (if, indeed, they ever will be or could be), is their symmetries and conservations. [...] Symmetries and conservations of physics are one of the most intriguing areas of physics. They are certainly assigned a very fundamental status in physics; they serve as guides in the construction of theories and are the touchstones by which theories are initially screened, before any more detailed comparison with experiment is attempted. Nature can be persuaded to disclose her symmetries and conservations by our performing experiments, analyzing the data, and looking for regularities." (Rosen and Freundlich, 1978).*

This view of physics seems to fit very well with purposive behavior in CCS. Both the physical and biological worlds are replete with symmetries. In fact, our purposive behavior reflects symmetry on two levels: our actions and perceptions are characterized by invariants, which are symmetries, and our perceptions use symmetry of objects as an *a priori* constraint. It seems that CCS makes more use of symmetry than physics does. We humans form mental representations (models) of the outside world, including the minds and actions of other humans, on the basis of sensory data and by solving inverse problems. Our minds apply a minimum principle, which corresponds to the least-action principle in physics, to make sure that these models are veridical because these inverse problems are ill-posed. Here, again, our purposive behavior reflects the operation of a minimum principle on two levels. First, solving the inverse problem of producing veridical mental models is accomplished by finding a minimum of a cost function. Second, using these models to plan optimal behavior is, like every optimization task, equivalent to applying a minimum principle. Here we can say that CCS makes more use of a least-action principle than physics does. Finally, veridicality means that some important characteristics of the outside world remain unchanged in our mental representations. Veridicality in visual perception corresponds to the conservation laws in physics. But here again, as was the case with symmetry and the least-action principle, our purposive behavior reflects the operation of conservation laws on more than one level, namely, a person forms veridical mental models of physical reality based on his sensory data which is produced by his interaction with this reality. Then, a second person (collaborator or competitor) forms veridical mental models of the first person's thoughts based on sensory data produced by observing and talking to him. Once this is done, the first person forms mental models of the mental models of the second person, and so forth. So here again, CCS makes more use of the conservation laws than physics does. So, mental phenomena are governed by three principles, namely symmetry, least-action, and conservations that are identical, or at least analogous, to the principles of physics. But CCS is richer than physics for at least two reasons. First, each of the three principles is used recursively in cognition. It is not used recursively in physics. Second, CCS makes use of the concept called purposive behavior, which has no role in physics.[3] Fortunately, engineers are well aware of the concept of purpose or function, but state-of-the-art robots have not been able to do much with it, to date. It seems that the field of AI has underappreciated, or perhaps even overlooked altogether, the importance of forming mental models at the expense of collecting sensory data and optimizing the function of feedback.

In conclusion, *purposive behavior* in CCS and in AI satisfies the three modern criteria for being a "real hard science."It is not clear, at this point, what other mental events and behaviors can be included, but even if none can be added, it seems clear that the future of cognitive science is bright and we can hope that the common foundation based on (i) symmetries, (ii) the least-action principle, and (iii) the conservation laws will provide new stimulation and lead to new questions. It will surely open up new lines of interdisciplinary collaborations between cognitive psychologists and physicists because both of these groups share a common interest in the natural sciences. Once both of these communities try to understand natural phenomena using the same formalism, there will be almost unlimited opportunities to apply modern mathematics and physics to advancing our understanding of the complex system called the human mind and its relation to the physical and biological world. It goes without saying that this new view of "natural" phenomena will help re-establish the connection between cognitive psychology and Artificial Intelligence, a connection that was strong 60 years ago and disappeared shortly thereafter.

---

[3]But note that when the least-action principle was gaining widespread attention in 19th C physics, some physicists speculated that the operation of this principle represented a teleological relationship that resembled purposive actions. By way of providing an example, according to Fermat's principle, when a beam of light "chooses" a path that minimizes a total time of travel, it may seem that the light knew the total travel time required before it started.

We close by re-stating the essence of our argument, namely, veridicality is an essential characteristic of perception and cognition. It is absolutely essential. *Perception and cognition without veridicality would be like physics without the conservation laws.*

REFERENCES

Adelson, E.H., Anderson, C.H., Bergen, J.R., Burt, P.J., & Ogden, J.M. (1984). Pyramid methods in image processing. *RCA Engineer, 29*, 33–41.

Alhazen. (1083/1989). *The optics*. Books 1-3. (Translated by A.I. Sabra), London: The Warburg Institute.

Attneave, F. (1954). Some informational aspects of visual perception. *Psychological Review, 61*, 183–193.

Attneave, F. (1959). *Applications of information theory to psychology*. New York: Holt.

Attneave, F., & Frost, R. (1969). The determination of perceived tridimensional orientation by minimum criteria. *Perception & Psychophysics, 6*, 391–396.

Ballard, D.H., & Brown, C.M. (1982). *Computer vision*. Englewood Cliffs, NJ: Prentice Hall.

Barlow, H.B. (1962). A method of determining the overall quantum efficiency of visual discriminations. *Journal of Physiology (London), 160*, 155–168.

Beis, J.S., & Lowe, D.G. (1997). Shape indexing using approximate nearest-neighbour search in high-dimensional spaces. *IEEE Conference on Computer Vision and Pattern Recognition*, June 17–19.

Berkeley, G. (1709/1910). *A new theory of vision*. New York: Dutton.

Biederman, I. (1987). Recognition-by-components: a theory of human image understanding. *Psychological Review, 94*, 115–147.

Biederman, I., & Gerhardstein, P.C. (1993). Recognizing depth-rotated objects: Evidence and conditions from three-dimensional viewpoint invariance. *Journal of Experimental Psychology: Human Perception & Performance, 19*, 1162–1182.

Binford, T.O. (1971). Visual perception by computer. *IEEE Conference on Systems and Control*. Miami, FL (December).

Bishop, C.M. (2006). *Pattern recognition and machine learning*. New York: Springer.

Blum, H. (1967). A transformation for extracting new descriptors of shape. In W. Wathen-Dunn (Ed.), *Models for the perception of speech and visual form* (pp. 362–380). Cambridge, MA: MIT Press.

Blum, H. (1973). Biological shape and visual science. *Journal of Theoretical Biology, 38*, 205–287.

Blumenfeld, W. (1913). Untersuchungen über die scheinbare Grösse in Sehräume. *Zeitschrift für Psychologie, 65*, 241–404.

Brady, M., & Yuille, A. (1983). Inferring 3D orientation from 2D contour (an extremum principle). In W. Richards (Ed.), *Natural computation* (pp. 99–106). Cambridge, MA: MIT Press.

Brindley, G.S. (1960). *Physiology of the retina and visual pathway*. Baltimore: Williams & Wilkins.

Brunswik, E. (1956). *Perception and the representative design of psychological experiments*. Berkeley: University of California Press.

Campbell, F.W., & Robson, J.G. (1968). Application of Fourier analysis to the visibility of gratings. *Journal of Physiology, 197*, 551–566.

Cannon, W.B. (1932). *The wisdom of the body*. NY: Norton.

Chan, M.W., Stevenson, A.K., Li, Y., & Pizlo, Z. (2006). Binocular shape constancy from novel views: the role of a priori constraints. *Perception & Psychophysics, 68*, 1124–1139.

Chater, N. (1996). Reconciling simplicity and likelihood principles in perceptual organization. *Psychological Review, 103*, 566–581.

Clark, J.J., & Yuille, A.L. (1990). *Data fusion for sensory information processing systems*. Boston: Kluwer.

Cortes, C., & Vapnik, V. (1995). Support-vector networks. *Machine Learning, 20*, 273–297.

Craik, K.J.W. (1943). *The nature of explanation*. Cambridge: Cambridge University Press.

Curie, P. (1894/1982). On symmetry in physical phenomena, symmetry of an electric field and of a magnetic field. In J. Rosen (Ed.), *Symmetry in physics: selected reprints* (pp. 17–25). Stony Brook, NY: American Association of Physics Teachers.

Dewey, J. (1896). The reflex arc concept in psychology. *Psychological Review, 3*, 357–370.

Dickinson, S.J. (1999). Object representation and recognition. In E. Lepore and Z. Pylyshyn (Eds.), *Rutgers University Lectures on Cognitive Science* (pp. 172–207). Oxford, UK: Basil Blackwell Publishers.

Dickinson, S. (2009). The evolution of object categorization and the challenge of image abstraction. In S.J. Dickinson, A. Leonardis, B. Schiele, M.J. Tarr (Eds.), *Object categorization: computer and human vision perspectives* (pp. 1–58). New York: Cambridge University Press.

Dickinson, S.J., & Pizlo, Z. (2013). *Shape perception in human and computer vision*. London: Springer.

Duncker, K. (1945). On problem solving. *Psychological Monographs*. 58, No. 270.

Estrada, F.J., & Elder, J.H. (2006). Multi-scale contour extraction based on natural image statistics, *Proc. IEEE Workshop on Perceptual Organization in Computer Vision. Computer Vision and Pattern Recognition*, New York, NY.

Fechner, G. (1860/1966). *Elements of psychophysics*. New York: Holt, Rinehart & Winston.

Feldman, J., & Singh, M. (2005). Information along contours and object boundaries. *Psychological Review, 112*, 243–252.

Feldman, J., & Singh, M. (2006). Bayesian estimation of the shape skeleton. *Proceedings of the National Academy of Sciences, 103*, 18014–18019.

Feynman, R. P., Leighton, R. B., & Sands, M. (1970). *The Feynman Lectures on Physics*. Boston: Addison-Wesley.

Feynman, R.P. (1974). Caltech commencement address. http://neurotheory.columbia.edu/~ken/cargo_cult.html.

Fitts, P.M. (1954). The information capacity of the human motor system in controlling the amplitude of movement. *Journal of Experimental Psychology, 47*, 281–391.

Foley, J.M. (1972). The size-distance relation and intrinsic geometry of visual space: Implications for processing. *Vision Research, 12*, 323–332.

Geisler, W.S. (1989). Sequential ideal-observer analysis of visual discriminations. *Psychological Review, 96*, 267–314.

Geisler, W.S., & Perry, J.S. (2011). Statistics for optimal point prediction in natural images. *Journal of Vision, 11*(12):14, 1–17.

Gibson, J.J. (1950). *The perception of the visual world.* Boston: Houghton Mifflin.

Gibson, J.J. (1966). *The senses considered as perceptual systems.* Boston: Houghton Mifflin.

Gibson, J.J. (1979). *The ecological approach to visual perception.* Boston: Houghton Mifflin.

Green, D.M., & Swets, J.A. (1966). *Signal detection theory and psychophysics* (Vol. 1974). New York: Wiley.

Gupte, S., Li, Y., & Pizlo, Z. (2012). The shortest path as a spatially global interpolation of contours in images. *Annual Meeting of the Society for Mathematical Psychology*, Columbus, OH.

Guzman, A. (1968). Decomposition of a visual scene into three-dimensional bodies. *Proceedings of AFIPS Conference, 33*, 291–304. Washington, DC: Thompson.

Hawking, S. (2001). *The universe in a nutshell.* Random House Publishing Group.

Hebb, D.O. (1949). *The organization of behavior.* New York: Wiley.

Helmholtz, H. von (1867/2000). *Treatise on physiological optic.* (Translated from German, by J.P.C. Southall). Bristol: Thoemmes.

Hildreth, E.C. (1984). The computation of the velocity field. *Proceedings of the Royal Society of London, B221*, 189–220.

Hochberg, J. (1987). Machines should not see as people do, but must know how people see. *Computer Vision, Graphics, and Image Processing, 37*, 221–237.

Hochberg, J., & McAlister, E. (1953). A quantitative approach to figural "goodness." *Journal of Experimental Psychology, 46*, 361–364.

Hoffman, D. (2009). The interface theory of perception. In S. Dickinson, M. Tarr, A. Leonardis, B. Schiele (Eds.), *Object categorization: computer and human vision perspectives* (pp. 148–165). Cambridge, UK: Cambridge University Press.

James, W. (1890/1950). *The principles of psychology.* New York: Dover.

Julesz, B. (1960). Binocular depth perception of computer-generated patterns. *Bell System Technical Journal, 39*, 1125–1162.

Julesz, B. (1971). *Foundations of cyclopean perception.* Chicago: University of Chicago Press.

Kanade, T. (1981). Recovery of the three-dimensional shape of an object from a single view. *Artificial Intelligence, 17*, 409–460.

Kant, I. (1781/1990). *Critique of pure reason.* New York: Prometheus Books.

Kellman, P.J., & Shipley, T.F. (1991). A theory of visual interpolation in object perception. *Cognitive Psychology, 23*(2), 141–221.

Klein, F. (1939). *Elementary mathematics from an advanced standpoint: Geometry.* New York: Dover.

Knill, D.C. (1992). Perception of surface contours and surface shape: from computation to psychophysics. *Journal of the Optical Society of America, A9*, 1449–1464.

Knill, D.C. (2001). Contour into texture: information content of surface contours and texture flow. *Journal of the Optical Society of America, A18*, 12–35.

Knill, D.C., & Richards, W. (1996). *Perception as Bayesian inference.* Cambridge: Cambridge University Press.

Koenderink, J.J., van Doorn, A.J., & Kappers, A.M.L. (1992). Surface perception in pictures. *Perception & Psychophysics, 52*, 487–496.

Koenderink, J.J., van Doorn, A.J., & Kappers, A.M.L. (1995). Depth relief. *Perception, 24*, 115–126.

Koffka, K. (1935). *Principles of Gestalt psychology.* New York: Harcourt, Brace.

Kuhn, T. (1962). *The structure of scientific revolutions.* Chicago: University of Chicago Press.

Kwon, O.-S., Zelaznik, H.N., Chiu, G., & Pizlo, Z. (2011). Human motor transfer is determined by the scaling of size and accuracy of movement. *Journal of Motor Behavior, 43*, 15–26.

Kwon, T. (2012). *Human recovery of the shape and size of a 3D indoor scene* (master's Thesis). Department of Psychological Sciences, Purdue University.

Landy, M.S., Maloney, L.T., Johnston, E.B., & Young, M. (1995). Measurement and modeling of depth cue combination: in defense of weak fusion. *Vision Research, 35*, 389–412.

Lawler, E.L., Lenstra, J.K., Rinnooy Kan, A.H.G., & Shmoys, D.B. (1985). *The traveling salesman problem*. New York: Wiley.

Leeuwenberg, E.L.J. (1971). A perceptual coding language for visual and auditory patterns. *American Journal of Psychology, 84*, 307–349.

Leeuwenberg, E., & van der Helm, P. (2013). *Structural information theory: the simplicity of visual form*. New York: Cambridge University Press.

Leyton, M. (1992). *Symmetry, causality, mind*. Cambridge, MA: MIT Press.

Leyton, M. (2001). *A generative theory of shape*. New York: Springer.

Leyton, M. (2006). *Shape as memory*. Basel, Switzerland: Birkhäuser.

Li, Y. (2009). Perception of parallelepipeds: Perkins' law. *Perception, 38*, 1767–1781.

Li, Y., Pizlo, Z., & Steinman, R.M. (2009). A computational model that recovers the 3D shape of an object from a single 2D retinal representation. *Vision Research, 49*, 979–991.

Li, Y., & Pizlo, Z. (2011). Depth cues vs. simplicity principle in 3D shape perception. *Topics in Cognitive Science, 3*, 667–685.

Li, Y., Sawada, T., Shi, Y., Kwon, T., & Pizlo, Z. (2011). A Bayesian model of binocular perception of 3D mirror symmetric polyhedra. *Journal of Vision, 11*(4), 1–20.

Li, Y., Sawada, T., Latecki, L.J., Steinman, R.M., & Pizlo, Z. (2012). A tutorial explaining a machine vision model that emulates human performance when it recovers natural 3D scenes from 2D images. *Journal of Mathematical Psychology, 56*, 217–231.

Li, Y., Sawada, T., Shi, Y., Steinman, R.M., & Pizlo, Z. (2013). Symmetry is the sine qua non of shape. In S. Dickinson & Z. Pizlo (Eds.), *Shape perception in human and computer vision* (pp. 21–40). London: Springer.

Li, M., & Vitanyi, P. (1997). *An introduction to Kolmogorov complexity and its applications*. New York: Springer.

Longuet-Higgins, H.C. (1986). The reconstruction of a plane surface from two perspective projections. Proceedings of the Royal Society of London. Series B. *Biological Sciences, 227*, 399–410.

Lotze, H. (1852/1886). *Outlines of psychology*. Boston: Ginn.

Luneburg, R.K. (1947). *Mathematical analysis of binocular vision*. Princeton: Princeton University Press.

Mach, E. (1906/1959). *The Analysis of Sensations*. New York: Dover.

Mamassian, P., & Landy, M.S. (1998). Observer biases in the 3D interpretation of line drawings. *Vision Research, 38*, 2817–2832.

Mandelbrot, B.B. (1982). *The fractal geometry of nature*. New York: Holt.

Marr, D. (1982). *Vision*. New York: W.H. Freeman.

Miller, G.A., Galanter, E., & Pribram, K.H. (1960). *Plans and the structure of behavior*. New York: Holt.

Mishkin, M., Ungerleider, L.G., & Macko, K.A. (1983). Object vision and spatial vision: two cortical pathways. *Trends in Neurosciences, 6*, 414–417.

Neath, I., & Surprenant, A.M. (2003). *Human memory: An introduction to research, data, and theory* (2nd ed.). Belmont, CA: Wadsworth.

Newnham, R.E. (2005). *Properties of materials.* Oxford: Oxford University Press.

Nijhawan, R. (2008). Visual prediction: psychophysics and neurophysiology of compensation for time delays. *Behavioral and Brain Sciences, 31,* 179–239.

Noether, E. (1918). Invariante Variationsprobleme. *Nachr. D. König. Gesellsch. D. Wiss. Zu Göttingen, Math-phys. Klasse* 1918: 235–257.

Norman, J.F., Phillips, F., Holmin, J.S., Norman, H.F., Beers, A.M., Boswell, A.M., Cheeseman, J.R., Stethen, A.G., & Ronning, C. (2012). Solid shape discrimination from vision and haptics: Natural objects (Capsicum annuum) and Gibson's "feelies." *Experimental Brain Research, 222,* 321–332.

Paterson, J.R., Garcia-Bellido, D.C., Lee, M.S.Y., Brock, G.A., Jago, J.B., & Edgecombe, G.D. (2011). Acute vision in the giant Cambrian predator Anomalocaris and the origin of compound eyes. *Nature, 480,* 237–240.

Pizlo, Z. (1994). A theory of shape constancy based on perspective invariants. *Vision Research, 34,* 1637–1658.

Pizlo, Z. (2001). Perception viewed as an inverse problem. *Vision Research, 41,* 3145–3161.

Pizlo, Z. (2008). *3D shape: its unique place in visual perception.* Cambridge, MA: MIT Press.

Pizlo, Z., Li, Y., & Francis, G. (2005). A new look at binocular stereopsis. *Vision Research, 45,* 2244–2255.

Pizlo, Z., Li, Y., & Steinman, R.M. (2008). Binocular disparity only comes into play when everything else fails; a finding with broader implications than one might suppose. *Spatial Vision, 21,* 495–508.

Pizlo, Z., Rosenfeld, A., & Epelboim, J. (1995). An exponential pyramid model of the time course of size processing. *Vision Research, 35,* 1089–1107.

Pizlo, Z., Sawada, T., Li, Y., Kropatsch, W.G., & Steinman, R.M. (2010). New approach to the perception of 3D shape based on veridicality, complexity, symmetry and volume. Minireview. *Vision Research, 50,* 1–11.

Pizlo, Z., Stefanov, E., Saalweachter, J., Li, Z., Haxhimusa, Y., & Kropatsch, W.G. (2006). Traveling Salesman Problem: a Foveating Pyramid Model. *Journal of Problem Solving, 1,* 83–101.

Pizlo, Z., & Scheessele, M.R. (1998). Perception of 3-D scenes from pictures. *Proceedings of IS&T/SPIE Conference on Human Vision and Electronic Imaging,* vol. 3299, 410–423.

Pizlo, Z., & Stefanov, E. (2013). Solving large problems with a small working memory. *Journal of Problem Solving, 6,* 34–43.

Pizlo, Z., & Stevenson, A.K. (1999). Shape constancy from novel views. *Perception & Psychophysics, 61,* 1299–1307.

Pizlo, Z., Li, Y., & Steinman, R.M. (2012). *Reconstruction of shapes of objects from images.* US Patent No: 8,224,065.

Pizlo, Z., Sawada, T., & Li, Y. (2013). *Reconstruction of shapes of near symmetric and asymmetric objects.* US Patent No: 8,406,567.

Poggio, T., Torre, V., & Koch, C. (1985). Computational vision and regularization theory. *Nature, 317,* 314–319.

Pont, S.C., Nefs, H.T., van Doorn, A.J., Wijntjes, M.W., te Pas, S.F., de Ridder, H., & Koenderink, J.J. (2012). Depth in box spaces. *Seeing and Perceiving, 25,* 3–4.

Regan, D. (2012). Vision and cricket. *Ophthalmic and Physiological Optic, 32,* 257–270.

Reid, T. (1764/2000). *An inquiry into the human mind and the principles of the common sense.* University Park, PA: Penn State University Press.

Rissanen, J. (1978). A universal prior for integers and estimation by minimum description length. *Annals of Statistics, 11*, 416–431.

Roberts, L.G. (1965). Machine perception of three-dimensional solids. In J.T. Tippett, et al. (Eds.), *Optical and electro-optical information processing* (pp. 159–197). Cambridge, MA: MIT Press.

Rock, I. (1983). *The logic of perception*. Cambridge, MA: MIT Press.

Rock, I., & DiVita, J. (1987). A case of viewer-centered object perception. *Cognitive Psychology, 19*, 280–293.

Rosen, J. (1982). *Symmetry in physics: selected reprints.* Stony Brook, NY: American Association of Physics Teachers.

Rosen, J., & Freundlich, Y. (1978). Symmetry and conservation. *Am. J. Phys.* 46(10).

Rosenfeld, A., & Thurston, M. (1971). *Edge and curve detection for visual scene analysis.* IEEE Transactions on Computers C-20, 562–569.

Rosenblueth, A., Wiener, N., & Bigelow, J. (1943). Behavior, purpose and teleology. *Philosophy of Science*, 10, 18–24.

Saalweachter, J., & Pizlo, Z. (2008). Non-Euclidean Traveling Salesman Problem. In T. Kugler, J.C. Smith, Y-J. Sun, T. Connolly (Eds.), *Decision modeling and behavior in complex and uncertain environments* (pp. 339–358). New York: Springer.

Sawada, T. (2010). Visual detection of symmetry in 3D shapes. *Journal of Vision, 10*(6), 1–22.

Sawada, T., & Pizlo, Z. (2008). Detection of skewed symmetry. *Journal of Vision, 8*(5), No. 14.

Sawada, T., Li, Y., & Pizlo, Z. (2011). Any pair of 2D curves is consistent with a 3D symmetric interpretation. *Symmetry, 3*, 365–388.

Sawada, T., Li, Y., & Pizlo, Z. (2013). Organizing a 2D image for 3D shape recovery. In L. Maloney (Ed.), *Oxford handbook of computational perceptual organization.* Oxford: Oxford University Press (accepted).

Schwartz, E.L. (1980). Computational anatomy and functional architecture of striate cortex: A spatial approach to perceptual coding. *Vision Research, 20*, 645–669.

Shannon, C.E. (1948). A mathematical theory of communication. *The Bell System Technical Journal, 27*, 379–423, 623–656

Shepard, R.N., & Cooper, L.A. (1982), *Mental images and their transformations.* Cambridge, MA: MIT Press.

Shi, Y. (2012). *Recovering a 3D shape of a generalized cone from a single 2D image* (master's thesis). Department of Psychological Sciences, Purdue University, West Lafayette, IN.

Shubnikov, A.V., & Koptsik, V.A. (1974). *Symmetry in science and art.* New York: Plenum Press.

Solomonoff, R.J. (1964). A formal theory of inductive inference. Part I. *Information and Control, 7*(1), 1–22.

Steinman, R.M., Levinson, J.Z., Collewijn, H., & van der Steen, J. (1985). Vision in the presence of known natural retinal image motion. *Journal of the Optical Society of America, A2*, 226–233.

Stevens, K.A. (1981). The visual interpretation of surface contours. *Artificial Intelligence, 17*, 47–73.

Stevens, K. (1986). Inferring shape from contours across surfaces. In A.P. Pentland, (Ed.), *From pixels to predicates* (pp. 93–110). Norwood, NJ: Ablex Publishing Corporation.

Sugihara, K. (1986). *Machine interpretation of line drawings.* Cambridge, MA: MIT Press.

Thompson, D'Arcy W. (1942/1992). *On growth and form*. New York: Dover.

Thouless, R.H. (1931). Phenomenal regression to the real object. *British Journal of Psychology, 21*, 339–359; *22*, 1–30.

Tikhonov, A.N., & Arsenin, V.Y. (1977). *Solutions of ill-posed problems*. New York: John Wiley & Sons.

Tinker, M.A. (1932). Wundt's Doctorate students and their theses, *American Journal of Psychology, 44*, 630–637.

Tolman, E.C. (1932). *Purposive behavior in animals and men*. NY: Century.

Tsotsos, J.K. (2011). *A computational perspective on visual attention*. Cambridge, MA: MIT Press.

Vetter, T., & Poggio, T. (1994). Symmetric 3D objects are an easy case for 2D object recognition. *Spatial Vision, 8*(4), 443–453.

Wagemans, J., Elder, J.H., Kubovy, M., Palmer, S.E., Peterson, M.A., Singh, M., & von der Heydt, R. (2012a). A century of Gestalt psychology in visual perception: perceptual grouping and figure-ground organization. *Psychological Bulletin, 138*, 1172–1217.

Wagemans, J., Feldman, J., Gepshtein, S., Kimchi, R., Pomerantz, J.R., van der Helm, P.A., & van Leeuwen, C. (2012b). A century of Gestalt psychology in visual perception: conceptual and theoretical foundations. *Psychological Bulletin, 138*, 1218–1252.

Wallach, H., & O'Connell, D.N. (1953). The kinetic depth effect. *Journal of Experimental Psychology, 45*, 205–217.

Waltz, D. (1975). Understanding line drawings of scenes with shadows. In P.H. Winston (Ed.), *The psychology of computer vision* (pp. 19–91). New York: McGraw-Hill.

Wandell, B.A. (1995). *Foundations of vision*. Sunderland, MA: Sinauer Associates.

Wertheimer, M. (1923/1958). Principles of perceptual organization. In D.C. Beardslee & M. Wertheimer (Eds.), *Readings in perception* (pp. 115–135). New York: D. van Nostrand.

Wertheimer, M. (1945). *Productive Thinking*. New York: Harper & Brothers.

Wheatstone, C. (1838). Contributions to the physiology of vision—Part the first. On some remarkable and hitherto unobserved phenomena of binocular vision, Philos. *Transactions of the Royal Society of London, 128*, 371–394.

Whitehead, A.N. (1929). *Process and reality*. Free Press.

Wiener, N. (1948). *Cybernetics*. Cambridge: MIT Press.

Witkin, A.P. (1981). Recovering surface shape and orientation from texture. *Artificial Intelligence, 17*, 17–45.

INDEX

NOTE: Figures are indicated by f following the page number, and footnotes by n. Numbers in subheadings are alphabetized as spelled out, e.g., '3D' as 'three D.'

Numbers and Symbols
2.5D sketch (Marr), 211–212
2D images
  ambiguous, and figure-ground organization, 175–176, 177f
  finding objects in figure-ground organization and, 190–192, 191f
  mirror-symmetry perception from perspective images, 96–98
  single 2D image, figure-ground organization solution, 216–218
  symmetry constraints useless with unknown correspondence, 120
  3D symmetrical interpretations, 122–123
2D skeletons (Blum), 108–110, 108f
3D movies, 162–163, 171
3D objects. *See also* opaque 3D objects (occlusions); shape perception, 3D
  asymmetrical shapes perceived as symmetrical, 101
  depth cues in perception of, 19
  effects on binocular vision, 152
  fast search of memory and recognition of, 218–220
  geons and shape recognition, 12, 13f
  human perception of mirror-symmetry from perspective images, 99–105
  limitations of medial axis transform, 109
  mirror-symmetrical, characteristics, 99
  monocular 3D shape recovery, 73–82
  perceptual dimensionality of, 26
  Platonic solids, 15
  recovery of objects without volume from 2D image, 81–82
  space in, 30
  symmetries and shape measurement, 14
3D shape: its unique place in visual perception (Pizlo), 2, 72–73

Adelson, E.H., 93
adjustment, method of (psychophysics), 47
affine space, 34–35
a-hull, 172–173
albedo, 16
Alhazen, 17
alley experiment (Blumenfeld), 30–31, 32
allocentric frame of reference, 182
ambiguous shapes. *See* amorphous shapes
Ames's chair, 39–40
amorphous shapes
  about, 7–8
  bent wires, 52, 53, 55, 56f
  figure-ground organization and, 175–176, 177f
  lack of shape constancy, 19
  measurement of, 14–15
  non-rigid objects, 11, 12f
  secondary importance of, 13
AOC (attention operating characteristics), 47
appearance-based shape models, 20
appearances (color patches), 30
approximate computations, 85–96
  a priori constraints and, 91
  Bell number, 91n
  combinatorial explosions, 180, 216
  logic underlying, 90–93
  multi-scale pyramid, 201
  perspective projection and approximate knowledge, 90
  processing of visual information and, 93
  representations of visual stimuli, 92–94
a priori constraints. *See also* symmetry
  a priori knowledge, 37, 102
  compactness, 58–59, 64–65, 68, 104, 167–168
  as essential in vision, 62
  in figure-ground top view representation, 187, 216–217
  Gestalt psychology emphasizing, 54
  inverse problem solutions with, 40–42
  learning and, 104
  minimum surface, 69
  mirror-symmetry as, 66–68
  nature of, 206–207
  perception of 3D shape and, 101
  as permanent characteristic of natural world, 204
  planarity constraint, 58, 70, 96, 104
  recovery of generalized cones, 112–114
  regularization methods, 45
  representing abstract characteristics, 206–207

a priori constraints. (*Cont.*)
  surface, 104, 57
  veridical perception and, 3–4, 36
  viewing distance and 3D movies, 162–163
artificial intelligence, 208
associative learning, 176
Asymmetry Principle (Leyton), 114
attention operating characteristics (AOC), 47
Attneave, F., 69, 116, 126n
axis of symmetry, 88, 108–109, 108f

Bacon, Francis, 42
Barlow, Horace B., 54, 101–102
bas relief art, 34
Bayes, Thomas, 39
Bayesian inference (formalism)
  assigning *a priori* probabilities to interpretations, 44–45
  binocular shape perception, 164–169
  compactness and, 167–168
  compromise between likelihood and prior, 168–169
  likelihood function, 165, 166–167, 167f
  for modeling perception, 43–45, 205
  posterior, 168
  priors in, 43, 165
  probabilistic vs. deterministic, 164–165
  solving inverse problems, 42, 164
Bell number, 91n
bent wires, amorphous, 52, 53, 55, 56f
Berkeley, G. (Bishop), 36, 40, 97, 214
Biederman, I., 12, 52–53, 83, 176n2, 219
Binford, T.O., 109
binocular correspondence problem, 131–132, 147–148
binocular disparities
  horizontal disparity and relative depth (equation), 150
  measurement, 146, 146f
  size of, 131
  in 3D shape perception, 153, 161, 170–171
  types of, 149–150
binocular vision. *See also* binocular disparities
  Bayesian model of shape perception, 164–169
  breaking camouflage, 148, 173
  early research on, 145–149
  geometry, 145–146
  as late player in visual processing, 160
  orientation in shape recovery, 154
  random dot stereograms, 147–148, 148f
  "shape before disparity" phenomenon, 152–153, 153f
  stereoacuity and 3D shape recovery, 159–160, 210–211
  symmetrical 3D shapes, perception of, 158–160
  3D shapes affecting, 152
  veridical perception of 3D shapes, 146–147, 150, 154–156, 154f, 210–211
  visual space, 3D perception of, 188–189
biological forms, self-similarities of, 9–10
blind spot, 65, 65f, 69, 212
Blum, H., 108–110, 108f
Blumenfeld, W., 30–31, 32
Brady, M., 107–108
brain, as linear system, 176
Brindley, G.S., 46–48
Brown, Thomas, 38
Brunelleschi, 87, 145, 146
Brunswik, Egon, 36, 83, 137
Brunswik constancy ratio, 23

CAM (content addressable memory), 219
camera calibration, extrinsic, 183
camouflage, breaking, 148, 172–173
Campbell, F.W., 176
character recognition, 109–110, 110f
closure, 134
cognitive science, 50
color, 23–24, 216–217
color vision, 26
combinatorial explosions, 180, 216
combinatorial optimization problems, 135, 201, 203
combinatorial problem, spatially-global, 133, 201
compactness
  as *a priori* constraint, 58–59, 63–69, 104, 167–168
  in generalized cone recovery, 112
  maximizing for 3D shape recovery from 2D image, 68–69
complexity
  one-dimensional vs. 3D characteristics, 23
  of physical stimulus, 24–25
  uniqueness of shapes and, 23–28
computational models. *See also* seeing machine
  creation of, 2
  of machine vision, 2, 49, 50–51
  preliminary human intervention facilitating 3D recovery, 172
  solving ill-posed inverse problems, 48
  in vision theory formulation, 208–209
Comte, August, 30
cones, generalized. *See* generalized cones
cones, retinal, 26, 92
constancies
  in visual perception, 16, 22–23, 131, 204
constant stimuli (psychophysics), 47
content addressable memory (CAM), 219
context, stimulus judgment and, 28
contours
  in figure-ground organization, 191–192, 191f, 217, 218f
  as intangible abstractions, 181
  internal, as depth cue, 151
  interpolation, 132–135, 133f
  occluding, 172–173
  in shape perception, 16, 17f, 85–86, 95–96, 99, 99f, 100f
  3D, symmetry correspondence and recovery of, 195–197
convex hull, 81–82, 82f, 191

correspondence problems, 131–135. *See also* symmetry correspondence problem
- binocular, 131–132, 147–148
- contour interpolation, 132–135, 133f
- motion, 132
- object recognition, 132

Craik, Kenneth, 46, 208
Critique of Pure Reason (Kant), 38
crystallography, 114
cue combination, 170–171
Curie, Pierre, 114–115
curves. *See also* contours
- curvature vs. torsion in description, 127, 127n8
- recovery from degenerate 2D images, 125–128, 126f
- simplicity principle, 126–127, 126n

cyclopean image, 165, 166
cylinders, generalized. *See* generalized cones

da Vinci, Leonardo, 1, 145
degenerate views
- about, 83–84, 84f
- exclusion and spurious 3D symmetrical interpretations, 129–130, 129f
- planarity constraint excluding, 127–128, 128f
- rare occurrence in nature, 123, 130
- simplicity principle and, 124–125, 125f
- straight-line segments and, 124
- systematic errors in 3D shape perception, 161–162, 161f
- uselessness for 3D image recovery, 127

delay, visual, 213–214
depth constancy, 18
depth cues, 35, 151–152, 152f
depth-maps, 3D, 173
depth perception
- depth order of points, 165–166, 166f
- random dot stereograms vs. binocular vision, 147n
- in shape perception, 19

Descartes, René, 1, 16, 49
Dewey, J., 50
Direct Perception, theory of, 183
direct problems, 37, 39
DiVita, J., 52
Doctrine of Specific Nerve Energies, 168
dotted stimuli, 85–86, 95–96, 99, 99f

ecological validity of stimuli, 50, 83, 137
edges (line segments). *See also* symmetry line segments
- in mirror-symmetry, 76–77, 77f, 100–101
- straight-line, 91, 124–125

elements, periodic table of, 29
Elements of psychophysics (Fechner), 47
ellipses, 27, 34
energy spectrum of light, 24, 24f
environmental coordinate systems, 182
Euclidean space, 30
European Conference on Visual Perception (St. Petersburg, 2006), 2, 60–63
European Conference on Visual Perception (Utrecht, 2008), 71–73
evolutionary psychology, 21
experimental psychology, 29
experiments, psychophysical, 46–47
extrinsic camera calibration, 183

faces-vase illusion, 176, 176n2, 177f
Fechner, Gustav, 47
Feynman, Richard, 50
fiddler crab, 83
figure-ground organization (FGO)
- ambiguous stimuli and, 175–176, 177f
- *a priori* constraints, 187, 216–217
- contour analysis, 175, 191–192, 191f, 194–196, 217–218, 218f
- coarse analysis of positions and sizes of objects, 179–182, 180f
- estimating positions and orientations of objects, 174–175, 174f
- figure-figure organization, 184–185, 184f
- figure-ground segregation, 173
- finding objects in 2D image, 190–192, 191f
- gravity and ground-plane estimation, 177–179
- ground-plane orientation, 175–179
- ground truth, 185, 186
- horizon computation, 193–194
- occluding contours, 172–173
- problem of, 74–75, 136
- random dot stereograms and, 148
- relevant edges and symmetry correspondence, 192–198
- solution with single 2D image, 216–218
- space perception independent from shape perception, 185–186
- stereovision and breaking camouflage, 148
- surface and edges in, 181–182
- top view representation, production of, 182–190
- 2D stimuli and, 176n3
- veridical perception of 3D environment, 172–203, 188
- vertical orientation of objects, 173–174, 174f
- vertical vanishing point, 192–195, 193f

Fitts, P.M., 93, 201
Foley, John, 32–33, 32f, 33f, 188–189
forward problems, 41, 75, 183
frame of reference, allocentric, 182
Frost, R., 69

Galanter, E., 50
generalized cones
- *a priori* constraints in recovery of, 112–114
- examples of, 106f
- generation of, 105–106, 106f
- recover of 3D shape, human vs. computational model, 110–113, 111f, 112f
- redundant information in recovery, 112
- skeleton of, 109
- in 3D shape perception, 105–114
- translational symmetry producing, 8, 9f

geodesics, 7n
geometric spaces, 25
geometries, hierarchy of, 34
geons, 12, 13f, 52–53, 83, 219
Gerhardstein, P.C., 52
Gestalt psychology. *See also* simplicity principle
  percept different from elements, 101
  sensations vs. perception, 38
  simplicity in, 118, 206
  structural information theory violating assumptions of, 117–118
  Theory of Perceptual Organization, 134
Gibson, J.J., 50, 83, 106, 107f, 107, 142, 183
grassfire model (Blum), 108–110
gravity
  figure-ground organization with single 2D image, 217, 218f
  ground-plane estimation and, 177–179
ground-plane, estimating orientation of, 175–179
group theory, 34, 138
growth, self-similarity and, 9

Hawking, Stephen, 50
Hebb, D.O., 91
Helmholtz, Hermann von, 20, 91
hierarchy of geometries, 34
Hochberg, J., 3, 68, 116
Hoffman, D., 21
horizon, 193–195, 193f, 194f
human capacities, machines emulating, 1
human face, departures from symmetry, 78–79

ideal observer, 101–103
ideal performance, defined, 102
ill-posed problems, 39
illusions, 123, 146–147, 176, 176n2, 177f
inanimate objects, asymmetry of, 9–11
inattentional blindness, 92n
inclinometer, 177–178, 192
inferences, optimal, 102
infinitely dimensional spaces, 24
infinity, in perspective, 90
information theory, 15, 116–117, 206
interactive vision, 50
interface theory of mind, 21
intervening variables, 21
intractable problems, 134
invariants
  definition, 86
  geometrical, 197–198
  perspective projection of symmetrical objects, 88–90, 89f, 89n, 210
  shape as, under transformations, 6
  symmetry correspondence and, 138
inverse problems
  a priori constraints solving, 40–42
  Bayesian method for solving, 42
  computational models solving, 48
  defined, 37
  ill-posed, 39
  inferences in, 42
  perception as, 39–42
  regularization of, 41, 42
  theory of, 2, 37, 39, 57–59
  3D vision as, 183, 205–206
invisible back parts and spaces. *See* opaque 3D objects
isolated points, 85–86, 95–96, 99, 99f

James, William, 50, 74
Julesz, Bela, 54, 131, 147–148, 180

K2 (mountain), 10–11, 10f
Kanade, T., 85, 86f, 89f
Kant, Immanuel, 38
Kellman, P.J., 132, 133
Klein, Felix, 34–35
Knill, D.C., 57, 108, 140
knowledge
  approximate, 90
  a priori, 37, 102
Koenderink, J.J., 34, 35, 171, 189
Koffka, K., 68, 116
Kuhn, T., 169

Landy, Michael, 170–171
learning
  a priori constraints and, 104
  associative, 176
  3D perception and, 20–21
Leeuwenberg, E.L.J., 116–119
Leonardo da Vinci, 1, 145
Leyton, Michael, 114–116
light, 24f
light, perception of, 24–25
likelihood
  Bayesian formalism and, 165, 166–167, 167f
  compromise between prior and, 168–169
  simplicity and, 124–128
linear system, brain as, 176
line drawing, organized, 74–75
local signs, Lotze on, 91, 200
Locke, John, 38
Logical Positivism, 30
log polar transformation, 26n, 134
Lotze, H., 91, 200
Luneburg, Rudolf, 30, 31, 32, 189

Mach, Ernst, 106, 107f, 124–125
machine vision. *See* seeing machine
Mandelbrot, B.B., 93n
Marr, David, 57, 131, 147, 211–212
mathematics, applied, 42
maximal 3D compactness, 68–69
McAlister, E., 69, 116
medial axis transform, 108–109, 108f
memory, content addressable (CAM), 219
Mendeleev, Dmitri, 29
method of adjustment (psychophysics), 47
Mill, John Stuart, 29
Miller, G.A., 50
mind, interface theory of, 21
minimum description length, 15

minimum surface, 69
mirror-stereoscope, 146
mirror-symmetry
  animal bodies, 9
  as *a priori* constraint, 66–68, 66f, 67f, 139, 139f
  contours essential for detection, 95–96, 99, 99f, 100f
  definition, 8
  degenerate views and, 83–84, 84f, 123, 125, 125f
  horizon and recovery of 3D shapes, 194–195, 194f
  line-segments in, 76–77, 76f, 77f, 100–101
  orthogonal view and, 83–84, 84f
  orthographic projection invariants, 88–89
  perspective images and perception of, 99–105
  symmetry planes, characteristics, 183
  veridical perception and, 22–23
  verification in 2D image, 76–78, 76f, 77f
monocular 3D shape recovery, 73–82
motion correspondence problem, 132
motion parallax, 146, 177n
motor theory of vision, 214
mountains, shape of, 9–11, 10f
movies, 3D, 162–163, 171
Müller, Johannes, 168
multiple view theories of shape, 20

natural environment
  a priori constraints in, 204
  components for seeing machine model, 213–216
  machine perception of, 5f
  veridical perception of 3D objects, 4, 5f
nature–nurture problem, 42
navigation, visual, 198
non-Euclidean visual space, 30, 31–33
non-rigid objects, 11, 12f
Norman, J. F., 14, 15

object recognition, as correspondence problem, 132
Occam's razor, 42, 70
opaque 3D objects (occlusions)
  occluding contours, 172–173
  perspective images, 184, 184f
  prediction and filling-in missing information, 69–71, 68f
  recovery of invisible back parts and spaces, 18, 22, 113, 118, 211–213
  veridical space constancy, 18–19
optic disk, 65, 65f
optic flow, 183
The Optics (Alhazen), 17
orthographic images, 87–88, 89f, 159
orthographic projection
  described, 86–87, 89f
  invariants for planar mirror-symmetrical figures, 88–89
  perspective projection vs., 41
  skew-symmetry and, 141–142
  visual system treating retinal image as, 97
parallel line segments. *See* symmetry line segments
partitions, retinal image, 91, 91n
path planning, 198–203
perception. *See also* shape perception, 3D; veridical perception; visual perception
  Bayesian inference modeling, 43–45
  depth, 19, 147n, 165–166, 166f
  as inverse problem, 39–42
  light, 24–25
  perceptual constancies, 16, 22–23, 131, 204
  perceptual organization, 116, 117f
  space perception, 30, 31–33
periodic table of elements, 29
perspective images
  occlusion of objects, 184, 184f
  3D image recovery from 2D image, 159
  3D mirror-symmetry perception, 99–105
  3D translational-symmetry perception, 105–114
perspective projection
  approximate knowledge in 3D recovery from 2D image, 90
  invariant for planar mirror-symmetrical figures, 87–90, 89f
  orthographic projection vs., 41
  retinal image as, 97
  2D mirror-symmetry perception from perspective images, 96–98
  vanishing point, 90
phenomenology, 47
physical stimulus, complexity of, 24–25
piece-wise rigid objects, 11
Pizlo, Z., 2, 72–73, 90, 156
planarity constraint
  a priori, 96, 104
  excluding degenerate views, 127–128, 128f
  invisible parts of objects, 70–71
  as key to use of symmetry constraint, 123
  as predilection in visual system, 63–64, 63f
  simplicity principle and, 130
  skew-symmetrical figures, 85, 86f
  symmetry correspondence, 138
  3D image recovery from 2D image, 127
Plato, 4, 13, 104, 220, 219n, 220n
Platonic solids, 15, 16
Poggio, T., 38, 57, 59, 205
Pont, S.C., 21
Positivism, 30
Prägnanz Law. *See* simplicity principle
prediction, visual
  delay and, 212–213
  natural environment model components, 214–216
  in shape perception, 69–71, 68f, 214
Pribram, K.H., 50
probabilistic inferences, 165
projections. *See* orthographic projection; perspective projection
psychology. *See also* Gestalt psychology
  evolutionary, 21
  experimental, 29
  structural, 176

purposive behavior, 22
pyramidal representations. *See also* approximate computations
clustering operations, self-similarities and, 203
multi-scale, avoiding global search, 201
speed-accuracy tradeoff, 201
symmetry in, 91, 93–94, 94f

random dot stereograms (RDS), 147–148, 148f, 149
reality constraints (symmetry correspondence), 137–138, 138f
receiver operating characteristics (ROC), 47
receptors, visual, 26, 91–92
Recognition-by-components theory (Biederman), 219
redundancy, 112, 116
Regan, David "Martin," 153, 205n
regularization methods
a priori constraints, 45
inverse problems solutions, 41, 42
for vision modeling, 205
Reid, Thomas, 36–38, 42
relational structure, 175
relatability criterion, 132
Richards, W., 57
rigid motion, as transformation, 6
Robson, J.G., 176
ROC (receiver operating characteristics), 47
Rock, I., 52, 149
Rosenfeld, Azriel, 93
Rules of Perspective Projection, 146

sampling rate, 180–181
SAT (speed-accuracy tradeoff), 47, 93, 201
Sawada, Tadawasa, 99–100, 100f, 104–105
scale/resolution symmetry, 93, 94
seeing machine. *See also* computational models
approximate computation, 90–91
conceptual contributions to, 205–209
deemphasizing sensory data, 204
early experiments, 38–39
emulating human capacities, 1
fast memory search and object recognition, 218–220
figure-ground organization solution, 136, 216–218
perception of natural environment, 5f
prediction of near future, 205, 205n
recognizing familiar objects and scenes, 205
simplicity constraints, 113
technical contributions to, 209–213
3D perception, human vs. machine, 4, 5f
veridical perception, 204
visual perception in dynamic environments, 213–216
self-similarities. *See* symmetry
sensations, 29, 37–38
sensory coding, upper bound of, 102
sensory data, 204
shading, as depth cue, 151, 152
shadows, 217
Shannon, C.E., 206
shape. *See also* amorphous shapes; generalized cones; symmetry
as abstraction, 4
analytical definitions, 6–7, 7n, 14, 209
appearance based models, 20
complexity and uniqueness of, 23–28
as intrinsic characteristic of object, 9
memory and recognition of, 12
multiple view theories, 20
non-rigid vs. piece-wise rigid objects, 11–12, 12f
operational definition, 14, 54
physical stimulus and perception, 25–26, 25f
self-similarity defining, 6, 9
similarity transformation, 6–7, 7f
three points defining, 7
"shape before disparity" phenomenon, 152–153, 153f, 160
shape constancy
acceptance in vision science, 56
amorphous stimuli and failure of, 19
a priori constraints, 150–151
complexity, 27
controversy about, 52–59
depth constancy and, 18
depth cues and, 151–152, 152f
learning and perception, 20
opaque 3D objects, 18–19
operational shape definition and, 14, 54
as phenomenon, 15–23, 209
reliable achievement of, 56
symmetry and, 12
in 3D perception, 16, 17f
veridical perception and, 16–19
shape measurement
amorphous objects, 14–15
object-centered coordinate system, 19
shape vs. surfaces, 20
symmetries and, 14
volume and, 75, 81–82
shape perception, 3D. *See also* figure-ground organization (FGO); shape constancy
binocular, Bayesian model of, 164–169
as conflict between simplicity and 2D retinal image, 69
contours (*See under* contours)
human vs. machine, 4, 5f
independence from 3D space perception, 185–186
information theory, 116–117
learning and, 20–21
planarity constrain excluding degenerate views, 127–128, 128f
psychophysical measurements, 15
simplicity and likelihood of correct interpretation, 129–130, 129f
simplicity constraints and Gestalt assumptions, 118, 206

spurious symmetrical interpretation of arbitrary curves, 120–121, 121f
stereoacuity and, 144–145
symmetrical shapes from asymmetrical images, 85
symmetries role in, 209–210
visual prediction in, 69–71
Shepard, R.N., 215
Shipley, T.F., 132, 133
shortest path problem (SPP), 134, 198–199, 199f
signal detection (psychophysics), 47
signs, local, 91, 200
similarity transformation, 6–7, 7f
simplicity principle
Gestalt psychology and, 118, 206
likelihood of 3D interpretation derived from, 129–130
Mach and, 124
in perceptual organization, 134
Prägnanz Law, 96, 206
in recovery of curves, 126–127, 126n
relationship with likelihood, 124–128
visual system favoring simple interpretations, 130
SIT (Structural Information Theory), 116–119
skew-symmetrical images, 89f
approximate computations detecting, 94–95
characteristics, 85–86, 86f
skew-symmetry, translational, 107
SLAM (Simultaneous Localization and Mapping), 187
slant (geometry), 28n
smooth curves, 89f, 94–95
space perception, 30, 31–33
spatially-global combinatorial problem, 133, 201
spatial regularity, 8
spectral energy distribution, 24, 24f, 26
speed-accuracy tradeoff (SAT), 47, 93, 201
spiral symmetry, 8, 10f
SPP (shortest path problem), 134, 198–199, 199f
stereoacuity
depth-order of points, 144–145, 160
interaction with 3D symmetry, 160
as probabilistic, 165
3D shape perception, 144–145, 148
variation among observers, 169
stereo correspondence algorithm, 173, 178, 181–182
stereograms, 147, 147n
Stevens, K.A., 108, 140
stimuli
ambiguous, in figure-ground organization, 175–176, 176n3, 177f
dotted, 85–86, 95–96, 99, 99f
ecological validity of, 50, 83, 137
support vector machine, 103–104
symmetrical, neglect in perception research, 83
visual, approximate computations, 92–94, 92n
Structural Information Theory (SIT), 116–119
structural psychology, 176
support vector machine (SVM), 102–104
surfaces
a priori constraint, 57, 104
in figure-ground organization, 181–182
minimum, 69
shape vs., 20
3D, experimental methods for reconstructing, 107–108
visible, 19, 57
SVM (support vector machine), 102–104
symmetry. *See also* mirror-symmetry; translational symmetry
as *a priori* constraint, 59, 104–105, 136, 162, 210, 219
axis of, 88, 108–109, 108f
biological forms, 9–10
complications in using, 120–143
defining shape, 6, 8, 209
departures from, 78–79
discrimination tasks, 102–103, 103f
growth and, 9
neglect in visual perception studies, 29–30
planar symmetrical figure, 85, 86f
as predilection in visual system, 63
pyramidal representations, 91–94, 94f
as redundancy, 116
scale/resolution, 93, 94, 201
skew-symmetrical images, 85
spatial, 8–9, 10f
spiral, 8, 10f
spurious interpretation of arbitrary curves, 120–121, 121f
in 3D orientation of plane, 67n11
in veridical recovery of 3D shapes, 11, 209–211
symmetry correspondence problem
about, 135
characteristics of reality (constraints), 137–138, 138f
difficulties in solving, 131
figure-ground organization, 74–75, 136
geodesic constraints, 140
mirror-symmetry constraints, 139, 139f
orthographic vs. perspective projections and skew-symmetry, 141–142
planarity constraint, 138
recovery of 3D shape contours, 195–197, 196–197f
transformations producing 3D percept, 140–141, 140f
2D translational symmetry, 138–139, 139f
working solution, 136–143
symmetry line segments, 76–78
direction, 97–98
midpoints, 88, 95, 98–99
orthographic projection, 88–89, 89f, 90
polyhedral objects, 98–99
in 3D image recovery from 2D image, 100–101
Symmetry Principle (Curie), 114–115

texture
  as depth cue, 151, 152
  figure-ground organization and, 178, 216–217
  gradient, 107
  segregation, 54
  stereo correspondence and, 173
Theory of General Relativity (Einstein), 30
Theory of Inverse Problems. *See also* inverse problems
  acceptance by vision scientists, 57–58
  formulation of, 37, 39
  human and machine vision, 2
  shape model formulation using, 58–59
Theory of Spatial Frequency Channels, 176
Theory of Veridical 3D Shape Perception, 41
Thouless, R.H., 34
Thouless constancy ratio, 23
thresholds, measurement of, 47
Tolman, Edward C., 21, 22
torsion, 127
tours, planning, 199–203, 200f
transformations
  geodesics, 7n
  geometrical, defining symmetry, 44
  log polar, 26n, 134
  medial axis transform, 108–109
  physical stimulus to psychological percept, 24–25
  producing 3D percept, 140–141, 140f
  retinal image formation and, 86
  rigid motion, 6
  shape as invariant, 6
  similarity, 6–7, 7f
translational symmetry, 8, 9f, 83. *See also* generalized cones
  definition, 105–106
  of discrete elements, 108
  as self-similarity of shape, 110
  skew-symmetry, 107
  2D, Mach on, 106, 107f
  3D, human perception from perspective images, 105–114
traveling salesman problem (TSP), 134, 199–203, 200f
triangle experiments (Foley), 32–33, 32f, 33f, 188–189
triangles, simplicity of, 27–28
truck-like stimulus, 54–55, 55f, 58
Tsotsos, J.K., 93
Turing, Alan, 2, 208
Turing test, 208

Van der Helm, P., 117
vanishing point, 90, 192–195, 193f, 194
veridical perception
  a priori constraints and, 3–4, 36
  asymmetrical shape recovery errors, 121–122
  binocular vision and, 146–147
  as central concept in vision, 207–208
  common sense and, 36
  constraints vs. visual cues, 189–190
  as expectation for 3D shape perception experiments, 155–156
  mirror-symmetry, 21–22
  purposive behavior and, 22, 50
  as rule in everyday life, 176n2
  shape constancy and, 16–17
  simplicity/likelihood relationship in, 124
  simplification and, 86
  symmetry and recovery of 3D objects from 2D image, 11
Vetter, T., 59
viewer-oriented coordinate system, 19
viewing distance, binocular disparities and, 150
visible surfaces, 19, 57
vision, interactive, 50
vision models. *See also* computational models
  Bayesian, of binocular shape perception, 164–169
  definitions, 46
  Theory of Inverse Problems and shape models, 58–59
visual perception
  a priori constraints and, 204
  by computers, 2
  constancies in, 16, 22–23, 131, 204
  denying reality of, 21
  as forward problem, 75
  goal of visual task, 74
  innate ideas in, 38
  neglect of symmetry in studies of, 29–30
  prediction and delay in, 213–214
  simplicity constraints central to, 113–114
  spatial problems in navigation, 198
  theories of, 50–51
  3D vision as inverse problem, 183, 205–206
  veridical 3D shape interpretation, 40
  visual space, 31–33, 31f
visual prediction. *See* prediction, visual
visual system, human
  a priori constraints, 3, 36
  binocularity and visual processing, 160
  elementary building blocks, 117
  pyramidal architecture, 93, 201
  receptors, 26, 64, 91–92

Wallach, Hans, 146
Wandell, B.A., 93
well-posed problems, 39
Wertheimer, M., 116, 117f
Wheatstone, C., 145, 146
Whitehead, A.N., 219
Witkin, A.P., 107
working memory, 202–203
Wundt, Wilhelm, 29

Yuille, A., 107–108